The reduction of drug-related harm

'The War on Drugs' has traditionally had total abstinence as its target. The contributors to this book take a new and challenging approach to problem drug use, arguing that abstinence is not the only solution. They believe that existing methods of treatment and control have been inadequate in controlling or improving drug problems and they propose a radical alternative: reducing the harm associated with the use of illicit drugs.

International in scope, the book covers a broad range of drugs, and of social and individual problems. The spread of HIV infection, which has been described as a greater threat to individual and public health than drug misuse, is also considered and the contributors give an overview of the current theories and practices that have helped to minimize the harmful effects of drugs and describe national and city-level strategies towards drug problems. They also cover the drug policies of several agencies and organizations worldwide, including police, doctors, community groups and local authorities.

The first book to concentrate on reducing drug-related harm, this is an important contribution to the debate on the future shape of drug control systems. It questions the role and function of existing drug laws and discusses how harm reduction will shape day-to-day work with drug users. Provocative and persuasive, it should be read by all policy makers and practitioners faced with drug problems, and will do much to help establish new strategies for dealing with drug use, strategies that minimize rather than exacerbate drug-related harm.

P.A. O'Hare is Director of the Mersey Drug Training and Information Centre. **R. Newcombe** works at the Drugs and HIV Monitoring Unit of the Mersey Regional Health Authority. **A. Matthews** is Editor of the International Journal on Drug Policy. **Ernst C. Buning** is staff psychologist, Municipal Health Service, Amsterdam. **Ernest Drucker** is Professor of Epidemiology and Social Medicine at the Montefiore Medical Center, New York.

The reduction of drug-related harm

Edited by P. A. O'Hare,
R. Newcombe, A. Matthews
E. C. Buning and E. Drucker

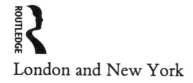

London and New York

First published in 1992
by Routledge
11 New Fetter Lane, London EC4P 4EE

Simultaneously published in the USA and Canada
by Routledge
a division of Routledge, Chapman and Hall Inc.
29 West 35th Street, New York, NY 10001

Typeset by Gilcom Ltd., Mitcham, Surrey
Printed and bound in Great Britain by
Mackays of Chatham PLC, Chatham, Kent

British Library Cataloguing in Publication Data
The reduction of drug-related harm.
  1. Drug abuse. Control
  I. O'Hare, Patrick Anthony
  363.45

Library of Congress Cataloging in Publication Data
The reduction of drug-related harm/edited by P.A. O'Hare [et al.].
  p. cm.
  Includes bibliographical references and index.
  1. Drug abuse. 2. Drug abuse–Social aspects. 3. Drug abuse–Complications
  and sequelae–Prevention. 4. Drug abuse–Government policy. I. O'Hare, P.
  A. (Patrick Anthony), 1947–
  [DNLM: 1. Public Policy. 2. Substance Abuse–prevention & control. 3.
  Substance Abuse–therapy. WM 270 R321]
  RC564.R43 1991
  362.29–dc20
  DNLM/DLC
  for Library of Congress
  91-15436
  CIP

ISBN 0–415–06692–1
       0–415–06693–X (pbk)

Contents

Figures and tables

FIGURES

TABLES

Contributors

Nico F.P. Adriaans is a community fieldworker at the EUR Addiction Research Inst. (IVO), Medical and Health Sciences Faculty, Erasmus University, Rotterdam, the Netherlands.

Cas Barendregt is a health educator and outreach worker at the HADON/Odyssee Foundation Rotterdam, Rotterdam, the Netherlands.

Peter Blanken is a researcher at the EUR Addiction Inst. (IVO), Medical and Health Sciences Faculty, Erasmus University, Rotterdam, the Netherlands.

Ernst Buning is a psychologist at the Drug Department, Municipal Health Dept., Amsterdam, the Netherlands.

Simon Davies is a journalist for the Australian Foundation on Drug Policy, NSW, Australia.

Nicholas Dorn is a criminologist and Development Director of the Institute for the Study of Drug Dependence, London, England.

Ernest Drucker is a Professor of Epidemiology and Social Medicine and Director of the Division of Community Health, Montefiore Medical Center, New York, USA.

P.G. Erickson is a criminologist at the Drug Policy Research Program, Addiction Research Foundation, Toronto, Canada.

C.S.J. Fazey is a criminologist and the Director of Demand Reduction, Division of Narcotic Drugs, United Nations Office at Vienna, Austria.

A. Fraser is Director of the Drug Advice and Information Service, Brighton, England.

Erik Fromberg is a neuro-physiologist at the Dutch Institute for Alcohol and Drugs, Utrecht, the Netherlands.

M. George is a psychologist at OPTIONS Project, Worthing, West Sussex, England.

Mark Gilman is Prevention Development Officer of the Institute for the Study of Drug Dependence, London, England.

Jean-Paul Grund is a researcher at the Addiction Research Institute, Erasmus University, Rotterdam, the Netherlands.

Robert Haemmig is a psychiatrist at Oberazt Ambulanter Drogendienst, Sozialpsychiatrische Klinik, Bern, Switzerland.

Sheila Henderson is HIV Development Officer of the Institute for the Study of Drug Dependence, London, England.

Charles D. Kaplan is Rotterdam Volksbond Foundation Chair for the Addictive Diseases at the EUR Addiction Research Inst. (IVO), Medical and Health Sciences Faculty, Erasmus University, Rotterdam, the Netherlands.

A. Matthews is Editor of The International Journal on Drug Policy, Liverpool, England.

Peter McDermott is a freelance writer in Liverpool, England.

Mart Meeuwsen is Services Coordinator of the HADON/Odyssee Foundation Rotterdam, Rotterdam, the Netherlands.

Russell Newcombe is Director of the Drugs & HIV Monitoring Unit, Mersey Regional Health Authority, Liverpool, England.

Pat O'Hare is Director of the Mersey Drug Training & Information Centre, Liverpool, England.

Geoffrey Pearson is Wates Professor of Sociology, Social Work Dept., Goldsmiths College, London, England.

Klaus Schuller works at the Deutsche AIDS Hilfe, Berlin, Germany.

Loren Siegel works at the American Civil Liberties Union, New York, USA.

L. Synn Stern is an outreach worker at the Montefiore Medical Center, Department of Epidemiology and Social Medicine, New York, USA.

Gerry Stimson is a medical sociologist and Director of The Centre for Research on Drugs & Health Behaviour, London, England.

Heino Stover works for Deutsche AIDS Hilfe, Berlin, Germany.

Griel van Brussel works at the Drug Department, GG & GD Amsterdam, Amsterdam, the Netherlands.

Gerit van Santen works at the Drug Department, GG & GD Amsterdam, Amsterdam, the Netherlands.

V. Watson is a researcher on the Drug Policy Research Program, Prevention Studies Department, Addiction Research Foundation, Toronto, Canada.

T. Weber is a researcher on the Drug Policy Research Program, Prevention Studies Department, Addiction Research Foundation, Toronto, Canada.

Alex Wodak is Director of the Drug and Alcohol Services, St Vincents Hospital, Darlinghurst, NSW, Australia.

Leo Zaal is the Chief Narcotics Officer, Municipal Police, Amsterdam, the Netherlands.

ERRATUM

On page xiii, chapter subheading, *for* reducton *read* reduction

Preface
A note on the concept of harm reducton

P. A. O'Hare

The concept of harm reduction became common currency in the late 1980s in response to two particular pressures. The first was the problem of HIV infection among injecting drug users. The second was a growing suspicion that the strategies we had adopted to deal with drug use exacerbated the problem, rather than ameliorating it.

Merseyside, along with many other British provinces, witnessed an epidemic spread of drug use, particularly heroin, in the early 1980s. Today, it has the highest ratio of notified addicts in England, 1,718 per million population. The national average is 288. About half of these are estimated to be injecting drug users. Despite having this large number of injecting drug users, the region has the second lowest number of notified HIV positive injecting drug users, six per million population. Furthermore, despite high unemployment in the area, in 1990 the Merseyside police were the only force who had a drop in reported crime. Though there is little conclusive research available to test these issues, people who know the area well feel that low prevalence of crime and HIV infection can only be related to the various policies for dealing with drug use in the area. The existence of these policies has resulted in the construction of a conceptual model of drug service provision aimed primarily at reducing drug-related harms that has achieved an international reputation as the 'Mersey model of harm reduction'.

There were three important factors that led to the establishment of this model. The first was the policy of the local Drug Dependency Clinic. Merseyside's major city, Liverpool, did not have its own Drug Dependency Clinic until the mid-1980s. Prior to this, out-patient drug treatment was limited to a few general psychiatrists who, in contrast with most other parts of the country, did not completely abandon all vestiges of the old British System. Injectable opiates continued to be prescribed on a take-home basis, a consequence of which was that supplies of sterile injecting equipment may have been more widely available than elsewhere. When Liverpool's specialist Drug Dependency Clinic was finally opened in 1985, this policy of prescribing injectable drugs continued.

Second, in 1986, the Mersey Regional Drug Training and Information Centre began one of the first syringe exchange schemes in the UK, with the aim of increasing the availability of sterile injecting equipment to drug users in the area. The model for syringe exchange schemes, now a central part of many strategies for reducing the transmission of HIV, was devised not by doctors or sociologists or psychologists, but by drug users. The first syringe exchange was devised by the Amsterdam Junkiebond, a drug-users' self-help organization, and was aimed at reducing the transmission of the hepatitis B virus. Unlike many of other early schemes, the Liverpool scheme was based upon the principle of providing an accessible, user-friendly service. It was recognized that if we are to persuade drug users to make contact, services must be relevant to the needs of those for whom the service is designed. The days when policy makers and treatment services could ignore their criticisms were now over.

The third factor in the emergence of the Merseyside model arose from the cooperation of the local police. They gave an undertaking not to place drug services under observation and began to refer to services those drug users who had been arrested. By no means soft on drugs, the Drug Squad of the Merseyside police force arrest and charge a greater number of people for drug offences than all other provincial forces. However, they now effectively operate a harm reduction policy of their own. A cautioning policy for first offenders found in possession of any drug is aimed at avoiding the amplification of a drug-using career that may stem from a first conviction.

Gerry Stimson has written elsewhere that drug use does not fit neatly into any of the existing paradigms that we use to understand the world. While this is undoubtedly correct, in the past, two models drawn from particular professions have dominated public discourse on drugs and drug use – law enforcement and medicine. Medicine views the phenomenon of illicit drug use primarily through the use of a disease model of addiction. Law enforcement perceives drug use as a problem of criminality. However, drug use covers a wide spectrum of behaviour which ranges from the pleasant to the problematic. The current distinctions between legal and illegal drugs are based not on the inherent dangers of the drug itself, but on many other factors such as racism, moral entrepreneurism and professional closure, the ability of professional élites to determine social policy agenda. Despite the recent attempts of the 'zero tolerance' model to shift the blame for the violence and corruption of the illicit drug trade to the consumer, unless all those who drink are prepared to accept responsibility for each case of foetal alcohol syndrome or cirrhosis of the liver, personal drug use must still essentially be viewed as a victimless crime. The philosophy of harm reduction seeks to reduce the reliance upon strategies that are based on an arbitrary moralism, in the hope of replacing them with more pragmatic interventions.

There has been an increasing willingness by many to recognize that existing models of treatment and control have been inadequate to the task of ameliorating drug problems, and the old models, the old certainties, have increasingly come under attack. Perhaps this is reflected in the way in which the British Advisory Council on the Misuse of Drugs recently set new priorities for those working with drug users. It recognized the spread of HIV infection as 'a greater threat to individual and public health than drug misuse'. However, it is important to recognize that HIV is not the only harm that drug users face, and although the need to prevent the spread of AIDS is widely accepted, there is still debate over whether we are prepared to reduce the other harms associated with drug use and the nature of the interventions that will best achieve that.

As a consequence, drug services are to prioritize the need to make and maintain contact with injecting drug users in order that they might work upon changing behaviour. In order to maximize contact, services can no longer afford to work only with those who seek to stop using drugs. It has been estimated that only between 5 and 10 per cent of the drug-using population are prepared to consider entering an abstinence-orientated programme at any time. One strand in this debate is to discover ways in which drug services, whose goal once was to promote the cessation of use, are to work with the other 90 per cent.

For example, one of the factors that prevent drug users presenting to services is likely to be the social stigma associated with drug use. Employment discrimination occurs as a consequence of this stigma, therefore to present to a service may incur the further drug-related harm of unemployment, which is not inherently a function of drug consumption, but is a product of the societal reaction to it. This raises the question of whether the task of changing attitudes towards drug use and drug users is a reasonable role for those who work with this group. The growth of self-help organizations for drug users seeking to shift popular perceptions and exert political pressure is a recent phenomenon in many countries. In order to secure this representation, organizations that work with drug users need to lend such groups support.

The prescribing of injectable drugs means that injectors can collect sterile injecting equipment at the same time as their drugs, avoiding the need for entering social situations where the potential risk of HIV transmission is high. As Fazey suggests in Chapter 16, it may also have an impact upon the propensity of drug users to commit acquisitive crime. However, other evidence suggests that prescribing injectable drugs might well prolong the habit of injecting. How are we to determine which course of action is most desirable? The First International Conference on the Reduction of Drug-Related Harm was established in order that people could share their experience of working with these new priorities, and to debate the various issues that arose as a consequence of this new perspective.

In the past, the determination of drug policy was the task of a small élite. Policy makers took the advice of the medical profession when considering treatment policy, and law enforcement officers when determining legal policies. Harm reduction is not merely a debate over treatment, despite attempts by certain professional interests to restrict it in this way. The principle has implications for the future shape of drug control systems. It has already led to increased questioning of the role and function of our existing drug laws. As the most obvious harm that results from the use of certain drugs is the risk of prosecution for possession due to their legal status, a harm reduction perspective raises the question of whether the laws exist to reduce the harm that drug use causes, or whether they are a statement of dominant societal values. These questions cannot be decided solely by the medical profession, or by other experts, but must be determined through the widest possible consultation.

This book arose out of a conference held in Liverpool, because of the preparedness of many working in and around this city to contemplate and implement radical initiatives, and because their success in broadening the debate gained the city a reputation as the home of harm reduction. This concept has since gained common currency in drugs work, yet many of the implications remain under-theorized. There is a pressing need to consider how such concepts will effectively shape our day-to-day work with drug users. The book is a means of widening that debate, and of involving the many workers unable to attend the conference. The world has changed drastically over the last year. Theories of how we deal with the problem of drug use differ widely around the globe. The future shape of drug work and drug control is, as yet, still undetermined. It is our hope that this book can sow seeds leading to strategies for dealing with drug use that minimize, rather than exacerbate, the harms that might ensue.

Evaluating the effectiveness of interventions designed to reduce the harmful effects of drug use is a difficult task, requiring the selection of a set of criteria for evaluating outcomes, and recognition of the hierarchical nature of harm reduction goals. A distinction is made between risks and consequences, the former concept referring to the behaviour patterns associated with particular outcomes, and the latter concept referring to the negative and positive consequences (harms and benefits) of drug-taking. Measurement of the risks and consequences of drug use requires the deployment of conceptual schemes to organize the numerous varieties.

Harms and benefits are classified according to a two-dimensional scheme: type of consequence (health, social and economic) and level of consequence (individual, community and societal). Risks are classified according to quantitative dimensions (dosage, potency and frequency) and qualitative dimensions (access, preparation, route and style of administration, poly-use patterns, after-care, set and setting). This conceptual analysis provides a framework within which specific harm reduction interventions can be planned, implemented, evaluated and, if necessary, modified.

However, defining and measuring risks and harms can be complex, and interpreting and responding to the outcomes of harm reduction interventions can also be fraught with difficulties. Three hypotheticals are presented in Chapter 1 which highlight the problems of deciding whether or not a given intervention is successful or unsuccessful at reducing drug-related harm. The main problems concern conflicts between prevalence and harm reduction measurements, and conflicts between different outcomes on separate harm reduction measures (e.g. crime, health). It is concluded that resolutions of these problems will only be found by practising harm reduction.

Acknowledgements

The Editors would like to thank the following people for their invaluable assistance in the preparation of this book: Anne Barnes, Andrew Bennett, Sonia Berridge, Lisa Curphey and Michelle Durkin at the Mersey Drug Training and Information Centre; Maureen O'Hare for proof-reading and copy-editing; Sharon Lockett at the Montefiore Medical Center, New York; John Witton at ISDD for supplying references at short notice; Talia Rogers and Katy Wimhurst at Routledge for their patience; Craig Reinarman for help with some editorial matters; all of the authors for their patience and understanding when we couldn't give them the extra thousand words they wanted and everyone who submitted papers to the First International Conference on the Reduction of Drug-Related Harm.

Chapter 1

The reduction of drug-related harm
A conceptual framework for theory, practice and research

Russell Newcombe

INTRODUCTION

Harm reduction – also called damage limitation, risk reduction, and harm minimization – is a social policy which prioritizes the aim of decreasing the negative effects of drug use. Harm reduction is becoming the major alternative drug policy to abstentionism, which prioritizes the aim of decreasing the prevalence or incidence of drug use. Harm reduction has its main roots in the scientific public health model, with deeper roots in humanitarianism and libertarianism. It therefore contrasts with abstentionism, which is rooted more in the punitive law enforcement model, and in medical and religious paternalism.

Health care, criminal justice and educational services can specialize in either strategy (e.g. syringe exchange compared with rehabilitation) or can combine elements of both approaches (e.g. flexible prescribing clinics which offer detoxification and maintenance). However, in some fields (e.g. school drug education), abstentionism has an almost total monopoly. Rather than use either strategy out of faith, policy makers and service providers should monitor and evaluate how effective they are at achieving their aims and objectives. However, whereas abstentionist interventions are relatively easy to evaluate (i.e. how many people are prevented from starting or continuing to use drugs), harm reduction interventions require the selection of a subset of desired goals from a matrix of potential harm reduction options.

Harm reduction goals are also hierarchical – that is, they vary in their propensity for decreasing negative effects of drug use. The most well-known goal sequence is that endorsed by the British Government's Advisory Council on the Misuse of Drugs (1988, 1989) as a strategy for reducing the transmission of HIV infection among and from injecting drug users. Namely: the cessation of sharing of injection equipment; a

move from injectable to oral drug use; a reduction in the quantity of drugs consumed; and, finally, abstinence. Other sub-goals can also be added at various points in the hierarchy: for example, cleaning injection equipment before sharing it, reducing the number of people with whom equipment is shared, and switching from illicit to prescribed injectable drugs. An analogy can be made with an acrobat's safety-net system: if one net fails, there is another net underneath.

However, before we can rank harm reduction goals and measure the effectiveness of interventions at achieving them, it is necessary to decide which harms we want to reduce – a process which inevitably will be based on a complex mixture of organizational goals, moral beliefs, and rational analysis. This chapter attempts to develop an initial conceptual model for professionals theorizing about, practising, or evaluating harm reduction interventions with drug users. Although this model may turn out to be somewhat limited in its validity or usefulness, it should hopefully provide a springboard for others to develop more sophisticated conceptual frameworks (for earlier developments, see Newcombe, 1987a, b, c; 1988, 1989; Parker et al.,1988).

To unpack the concept of harm reduction, we first need to distinguish between the causes and effects of drug use, or, more precisely, the classes of drug-taking behaviour which are known or are suspected to produce particular classes of consequence (outcomes). Risk is a term used to describe the likelihood of a drug-taking behaviour resulting in any of a number of consequences. Harm and benefit are complementary terms used to describe whether a particular consequence is viewed as negative (undesirable) or positive (desirable). The next section will consider the concepts of harmful and beneficial effects of drug use and related interventions. The following section will examine the components of riskiness in drug-taking behaviour and the final section will go beyond measurement issues to consider how we can interpret and respond to the outcomes of harm reduction interventions.

HARMS AND BENEFITS

Drug-taking behaviours known or believed to be risky (e.g. mixing alcohol with heroin) are more likely to have harmful effects (e.g. overdose), whereas less risky behaviours (e.g. moderate consumption of alcohol alone) are more likely to be associated with neutral or even beneficial effects (e.g. increased longevity). More often, drug-taking behaviours may be said, from most perspectives, to result in a complex pattern of negative, positive and neutral effects (e.g. smoking tobacco aids concentration but decreases lung efficiency). Furthermore, deciding whether particular consequences of drug use are harms, benefits, or of neutral value, depends on the morals and values of the decision maker(s). Broadly speaking, a change (e.g. increase) in the level of a harm can be reconstrued as the same as the opposite change (e.g. decrease) in the level of benefit, suggesting that it may be more accurate to speak of optimizing consequences, which incorporates both reducing harm and increasing benefits. Though a consensus could probably be reached on the desirability of most consequences for most people, there are also several outcomes which would divide people of different political and ideological persuasions – for example: prescribed opiate use pacifying unemployed youths in cities; use of psychedelic drugs contributing to new art forms; decriminalized cannabis use leading to a reduction in youthful alcohol use or glue-sniffing. More generally, the very notion of beneficial effects of illicit psychoactive drug use appears to be universally rejected by drug policy makers, with surprisingly few having yet even made the conceptual leap from reducing the prevalence of drug use to reducing the prevalence of drug-related harm.

Figure 1.1 Classification of the consequences of drug use

TYPE

LEVEL	Health	Social	Economic
Individual			
Community			
Societal			

The present moral starting-point can be assumed to be that consensually held by most social/health professionals and authorities in the Western world, though space/time constraints preclude a more detailed analysis of this perspective here. Developing precise concepts is important because it allows us to measure the effectiveness of harm reduction interventions, and measurement is the basis of evaluation. Harms and benefits can be organized according to many schemes, depending on the objectives of the classifier and tolerance for complexity. Figure 1.1 shows one useful two-dimensional scheme, which produces nine categories of drug-taking consequences from the three-valued dimensions of type and level (the origins of this conceptual scheme can be found in Newcombe, 1987a, b, c, 1989; Working Party on Harm Minimization, 1989).

On the type dimension: health harm/benefit includes the extent and quality of disease, fitness, injury, medical conditions, psychological health and psychiatric problems; social harm/benefit includes the extent and quality of aggression/affiliation, public order/disorder, group conflict/cohesion and integration/marginalization; economic harm/benefit refers to the extent and quality of financial variables, including debt, acquisitive crime and the national economy.

On the level dimension: individual harm/benefit refers to outcomes for the drug user; community harm/benefit refers to consequences for the drug user's family, friends, neighbours and/or colleagues; societal harm/benefit refers to the effects on the structures and organizations of society (e.g. health services, criminal justice system, civil liberties, culture, the economy).

For instance, a case of cirrhosis of the liver from excessive alcohol use can be classified as an individual health harm; stigmatization of the relatives of drug users can be classified as a community social harm; and the cost of drug law enforcement can be classified as a societal economic harm. Similarly, a reduced level of social anxiety engendered by drinking alcohol can be classified as an individual social benefit; a lower prevalence of HIV infection produced by reduced equipment-sharing among drug injectors can be classified as a community health benefit; and the substantial boost to the economy provided by taxes on permitted drugs is a societal economic benefit. Clearly, the drug-taking behaviour of a single person can and usually does have consequences of each type at each level, so why bother to separate them? The main function of the harms/benefits model is to help policy makers and service providers decide which harms they are attempting to reduce, so that scientific evaluation is possible.

A more accurate classification of harms and benefits could be achieved by a multi-dimensional scheme, incorporating, for instance, a time dimension (e.g. short-, medium- and long-term effects), a duration dimension (e.g. temporary, permanent) and/or a scale dimension (e.g. minor, moderate, major). Furthermore, quantification of the various kinds of harms and benefits would also increase the scientific validity of evaluations of harm reduction interventions, though this is an extremely difficult task. Indeed, unless policy makers and service deliverers have enough resources for a comprehensive research programme extending over several years, it will not be possible to evaluate the positive and negative consequences of particular harm-reduction strategies within a multi-dimensional, quantifiable model – particularly those consequences which take a long time to show up (e.g. organ diseases, increased longevity) or which are difficult to define and measure (e.g. distress to relatives, social cohesion).

Thus, an organization attempting to implement a harm reduction strategy with its client group must decide both which types of outcome it would like to influence, and which outcomes it has the resources to measure. For instance, a syringe exchange scheme prioritizes reducing the spread of HIV infection, and a scheme with limited resources might evaluate this harm reduction goal by assessing the results of voluntary HIV tests every quarter year. Similarly, the evaluators of a local anti-drink/driving campaign could examine road accident statistics before, immediately after and three months after the intervention.

RISKS

Perhaps the easiest (most practical and inexpensive) way of evaluating many harm reduction interventions is to focus on risks rather than consequences (harms/benefits), because riskiness of drug-taking behaviour is usually easier to assess by observational, interview and questionnaire methods. For instance, it is easier to ask drug injectors if they are sharing injecting equipment (risk) than it is to discover how many are HIV-positive (harm). Similarly, it is easier to measure the effects of an anti-smoking intervention on the community prevalence or individual frequency of tobacco smoking, than it is to monitor the target group to see what individual health harms (e.g. lung cancer, heart disease) they eventually incur. However, the reliability and validity of risk measurements is typically lower than that for outcome measurements (particularly when we compare self-report data with physiological data). Therefore, ideally, evaluation of both risks and outcomes should be undertaken, though the context of evaluation is usually far from ideal.

One scheme for understanding drug-taking risks is based on factoring out the conceptual components of drug-taking behaviour into quantitative dimensions (dosage, potency and frequency) and qualitative dimensions (access, preparation, route and style of administration, poly-use pattern, after-care, set and setting), which can also be expressed as How? and Why? questions. Harm reduction interventions should be based on procedures which aim to change the behaviour of drug users towards the optimum point on the chosen dimensions (which raises another major issue for research). This analysis draws heavily on the work of Weil (1972), Weil and Rosen (1983) and Zinberg (1984, 1987), and some of its origins can be found in Newcombe (1987a, b, c, 1989).

Dosage

This refers to the quantity (how much?) of drug taken at one time (i.e. as a single *hit* or within a specific time period). It can be measured as quantity of pure drug taken (e.g. gram of cocaine), quantity of drug product taken (e.g. a pint of beer) or cost of drug taken (e.g. a £5 wrap). The risk here relates to exceeding the dose level at which negative effects start to outweigh positive effects, and thus risking (for example) overdose and significant poisoning.

Potency/toxicity

This refers to the scale of the mental and physical effects caused by a size/weight unit of a drug. For example, high nicotine cigarettes are more potent than low nicotine cigarettes, heroin is more potent than opium, and cocaine is more potent than coca leaf. The less potent and more natural forms of a drug are usually less likely to have harmful effects (Weil and Rosen, 1983). This argument could also be extended to different types of drug (e.g. caffeine is less potent than amphetamine, LSD is less potent than DOM).

Frequency

This refers to the number of times a person uses a drug in a given time period, and thus to the number and duration of periods of abstinence. A common distinction is between daily users, weekly users and occasional users. Though riskiness generally increases with frequency, occasional users (especially novices) also face higher risks because of their lack of knowledge of safer drug use techniques (Dorn, 1987).

There are also several qualitative dimensions of riskiness, where levels of risk are more easily attached to nominal categories rather than being measurable on a numerical scale. Seven qualitative categories of risk are examined here.

Access

This refers to the method by which a person gains possession of a drug – for instance, by stealing money or selling sex to get it, buying it on the black market, getting it on prescription, etc. One obvious consideration is that illegal drugs are more likely to contain adulterants than prescribed drugs, and are thus more likely to cause harm to the user.

Preparation

This refers to the relevant actions carried out before and during the administration of a drug, such as filtering adulterants out of injectable drugs, cleaning injection equipment, eating a meal before drinking alcohol, using a small plastic bag to inhale solvents, adding a filter to self-rolled cigarettes and chopping powdered drugs before sniffing them.

Route and style of use

These refer to the method of administration of a drug and the way in which a particular method is implemented. They are major determinants of the riskiness of drug use.

There are four main *routes* of drug use, involving the digestive, respiratory, membranal and circulatory systems of the body. The digestive route (swallowing) is arguably the safest route, both because it produces the slowest onset of intoxication (making effects more easy to handle) and because it has the advantage of ejecting remnants of the drug from the body if poisoning or over-intoxication occurs (though some argue that it is practically easier to swallow an overdose of a drug than it is to overdose by smoking or sniffing).

The second most popular route of drug use is respiratory, which can involve (a) inhaling the gaseous forms of chemicals which vaporize at room temperature (e.g. solvents) or when heated (e.g. heroin), or (b) sucking in the smoke of combusting substances from pipes, cigarettes or other devices (e.g. tobacco, cannabis). The long-term harmful effects of smoking, especially the smoking of products containing carcinogens, are well documented.

The third route of drug use is membranal, which typically involves either (a) chewing plants (e.g. tobacco, coca, khat) so that the active ingredients seep out and pass through the membranes of the mouth and throat, or (b) vigorously sniffing (snorting) powdered drugs onto the nasal membranes through the nostrils (other usable membranes include the anus and the genitals). Chewing some drugs can cause damage to the lining of the mouth and throat, and sniffing some drugs (e.g. cocaine) can damage the septum.

The fourth and least common route of drug use involves using a syringe and needle to inject drugs directly into the circulatory system, via a vein or muscle, or under the skin. Under ideal conditions, this method is potentially less harmful than respiratory or membranal methods. However, injectors of illegal drugs face several harmful effects, including overdose, physical damage and diseases such as hepatitis B and HIV/AIDS.

The *style* of drug administration also influences the riskiness of drug-taking. For instance, drinking alcohol spirits slowly may be less risky than gulping them down; inhaling tobacco smoke deep into the lungs may be more risky than drawing it into the mouth only; injecting drugs with the proper technique (e.g. angle and depth of penetration) is less risky than injecting drugs with no knowledge of injecting technique.

Poly-use patterns

Another major determinant of riskiness is poly-drug use, since combinations of two or more drugs produce, in physiological terms, a new drug, often far more potent than the sum of its parts. Combining depressant drugs such as opiates and alcohol is known to be particularly dangerous, though less is known about the possible effects of many other popular drug combinations (e.g. amphetamine and cannabis, cocaine and heroin).

After-care

This refers to individual risk-reducing activities taken after drugs have been administered, such as drinking plenty of water after heavy alcohol consumption (to avoid a dehydration-related hangover), washing out the nose with water after a session of drug-snorting, cleaning up skin penetration sites after injecting drugs, and disposing of used paraphernalia safely (e.g. needles, matches).

Set

This refers to the reasons why people take drugs, and their personality, knowledge, attitudes and mood at that time. For instance, if a neurotic person or someone in a bad mood took LSD, that person would face higher risk of a *bad trip* than a stable person or someone in a good mood. Similarly, if a person drinks several units of alcohol, unaware that this will cause a deterioration in driving performance, then he or she may be at more risk of an accident.

Setting

This can be expressed as the questions: where, when, who with, and what if...? In brief, this means that the riskiness of drug-taking can be affected by the situation in which the drug is taken (e.g. glue-sniffing is safer in a park than on a building site), the time of day the drug is taken (e.g. alcohol consumption may have more negative effects if drunk earlier in the day), the people in whose company the drug is taken (e.g. being stoned on cannabis among strangers can cause paranoia) and the occurrence of unexpected events (e.g. a necessity to drive arising when drunk, visitors arriving when *tripping* on LSD). Set and setting risks can be substantially reduced with foresight and planning.

Conclusion

In conclusion, it is possible to factor out the risk components of drug-taking behaviour, and measure them with observation, interview and questionnaire methods. Some harms and benefits can also be measured in this way, though the measurement of many positive and negative consequences of drug use requires an extensive range of multi-disciplinary research methods; hence the recommendation to harm reduction evaluators to focus on the measurement of the risk components of drug-taking behaviour. Once it has been decided which risk behaviours the intervention is designed to change, evaluation of effectiveness can begin with one or both of two options: comparisons of risk behaviour across time within the target group, and/or comparisons of risk behaviour in the target group compared with a control group (similar people who did not receive the intervention).

INTERPRETING AND RESPONDING TO THE OUTCOMES OF HARM REDUCTION INTERVENTIONS: SOME HYPOTHETICAL SCENARIOS

By employing conceptual schemes like those described in the previous section, it becomes possible to measure the outcomes of harm reduction interventions. But how do we then interpret these outcomes, and how do we respond to their implications? A thorough analysis of these issues is outside the scope of this chapter, but examination of some hypothetical outcomes of harm reduction interventions should highlight several problems inherent in these tasks.

First, consider a national mass media campaign aimed at reducing the harm associated with the use of solvents by 11–15-year-olds. For a six-month period, the target group is informed through television, magazines, hoardings and leaflets that inhaling solvents can cause death or serious health problems, but that if they are going to inhale solvents, some of the risks can be reduced through particular procedures (e.g. using a small plastic bag, so that accidental suffocation can be avoided). Before the campaign, a representative sample of 1,000 youths is surveyed, and it is found that 10 per cent have experimented with solvents in the previous year. Official statistics also reveal that 100 youths died from using solvents in the previous year, and that a further 500 suffered serious injuries/health problems related to solvent use. Now, consider two possible outcomes of the intervention when a follow-up is conducted a year after the campaign ended (Table 1.1).

Table 1.1 Results of follow-up one year after the campaign

Annual rates	Trying	Deaths	Health-harms
Before	10%	100	500
Outcome 1	20%	50	250
Outcome 2	60%	50	250

In the first outcome scenario, 20 per cent of a representative sample stated that they had experimented with solvents in the previous year, though the annual number of deaths is down to fifty and the annual number of solvents-related health problems is down to 250. Harm reductionists would accept that a higher prevalence of experimentation should be tolerated if deaths and health problems are being significantly reduced, whereas abstentionists would find an increased prevalence of use conflicting with their priorities.

In the second outcome scenario, 60 per cent of a representative sample of youths stated that they had experimented with solvents in the previous year, though the annual number of deaths and solvents-related health problems are down to the same levels as in the first scenario (i.e. 50 and 250). Many harm reduction practitioners might have difficulty accepting this outcome as a success, either because the much higher prevalence of use could lead to unforeseen negative consequences in the long term, or because this scenario activates deep-rooted abstentionist fears and desires.

The second example concerns the introduction of a syringe exchange scheme for injecting drug users (IDUs) in an inner city area, the primary objective of which is to reduce the spread of HIV infection among and from IDUs. Annual surveys in the three years before the intervention have revealed three reasonably stable rates: about 5 per cent of the adult community injects drugs, 60 per cent of IDUs are sharing injecting equipment, and the annual HIV incidence rate among IDUs is 10 per cent. Table 1.2 shows three possible outcome scenarios one year after the intervention:

Table 1.2 Three possible scenarios one year after intervention

	% Who are injecting	% Who are sharing	Annual HIV incidence rate
Before	5	60	10
Outcome 1	10	40	6
Outcome 2	10	20	2
Outcome 3	20	1	0

In the first hypothetical outcome, prevalence of injecting has doubled, though prevalence of equipment sharing dropped from 60 to 40 per cent and the annual HIV/IDU rate has dropped from 10 to 6 per cent. Do these moderate reductions in risk and harm justify the increase in prevalence of injecting? Given the primary goal of the intervention, the answer is positive only if the numerical incidence of syringe-sharing (risk behaviour) and/or HIV-seroconversion (harmful effect) are reduced.

To illustrate this, assume that the population of IDUs numbered 1,000 before the intervention: this means that 600 were sharing syringes and 100 had become HIV-positive in a year. One year later 2,000 people are injecting drugs: this means that 800 are sharing injecting equipment and the number of IDUs to become HIV-positive totals 120. In short, the problem with Outcome 1 is that although the proportions of IDUs engaging in syringe-sharing and becoming HIV-positive are reduced, the increased prevalence of injecting means that the numbers of people engaging in syringe-sharing and becoming HIV-positive are increased.

By contrast, Outcome 2 is more acceptable in terms of the criteria of effectiveness, because, although community prevalence of injecting has still doubled, syringe-sharing is down to 20 per cent and the HIV rate is down to 2 per cent, resulting in reduced numbers of people sharing syringes (400) or becoming HIV-positive (40). Lastly, Outcome 3 exhibits a quadrupling of prevalence to 20 per cent (4,000), though syringe-sharing is reduced to 1 per cent (40) and the monthly HIV rate to zero. This outcome is clearly the most effective in terms of HIV prevention, yet the correlate is 3,000 more people injecting. Even if these IDUs were receiving prescribed drugs and full medical care, would all people charged with responding to this outcome be able to accept a fourfold increase in drug injecting as the price for preventing the spread of HIV? What other harms might be invoked or increased by this higher level of prevalence? Clearly, acceptable targets on prevalence, risk and harm variables need to be decided before an intervention if policy makers and service providers are serious about evaluating the level of efficacy.

The final example involves the random allocation of 300 new opiate-injecting clients to one of three methadone conditions at a drug clinic: methadone detoxification, oral methadone maintenance, or injectable methadone maintenance. Putting the primary harm of HIV to one side for the purpose of this example, assume that the dual goals of treatment are reducing acquisitive crime (i.e. stealing money or property to buy drugs) and improving the health of the client (e.g. weight, white blood cell count). Ninety per cent are in poor health and involved in drug-related acquisitive crime on arrival at the clinic. Consider the two possible outcomes given in Table 1.3.

Table 1.3 Possible outcomes of three methadone conditions

	Detoxification	Oral maintenance	Injectable maintenance
Before			
Stealing to buy drugs	90	90	90
In poor health	90	90	90
Outcome 1			
Stealing to buy drugs	70	50	20
In poor health	20	40	60
Outcome 2			
Stealing to buy drugs	30	40	60
In poor health	80	20	10

Without going into a detailed analysis of this example, a few minutes' consideration should reveal the difficulties of interpreting and responding to both hypothetical outcomes. The main conflict is that each treatment option is effective at reducing one type of harm, but relatively ineffective at reducing the other. Resolution could be found in prioritizing either harm from the outset, or breaking each down into component harms (e.g. types of acquisitive crime, types of ill-health) and quantifying or ranking them.

CONCLUSION

Defining and measuring drug-related risks and harms is a complex and difficult task, as is interpreting and responding to the outcomes of harm reduction interventions. The main problems are likely to be conflicts between changes in prevalence and level of harm, and conflicts between changes in different categories of harm. However, evaluation of the effectiveness of harm reduction interventions is possible, if the aims of policy makers and the objectives of practitioners are clearly stated at the outset, using a conceptual framework like the one described here. Ideally, this means going beyond general goals such as a reduction in the levels of particular risks and harms, to a specification of quantifiable reduction targets on these levels, and a specified top limit for acceptable community prevalence of the relevant drug-taking behaviours.

Finally, it should be noted that the three hypothetical cases described above were simplified versions of real-world situations, and assumed that high-quality information was available to evaluate clearly defined criteria of effectiveness – which is rarely the case in practice. As in all new areas of endeavour, these problems will only be resolved by applying harm reduction through a combination of practice, theory and research. Though many of the risks and harms associated with drug use can undoubtedly be reduced by appropriate strategies, our incomplete understanding of drug use and the complexities of human nature should also forewarn us that many interventions will inexplicably fail, while others will succeed in ways that could not have been foreseen.

REFERENCES

Advisory Council on the Misuse of Drugs (1988) *AIDS and Drug Misuse, Part 1*, London: HMSO.
—— (1989) *AIDS and Drug Misuse, Part 2*, London: HMSO.
Dorn, N. (1987) 'Minimization of harm: a U-curve theory', *Druglink* 2 (2), 14–15.

Newcombe, R. (1987a) 'High time for harm reduction', *Druglink* 2 (1), 10–11.

—— (1987b) 'Willy Whizz: Harm reduction through drug education', Liverpool: Drug Education Project, South Sefton DHA (see also *Mersey Drugs Journal* 1 (2), 11).

—— (1987c) 'A framework for designing and evaluating drug education based on harm reduction', Report of the Drug Education Project to South Sefton DHA, Liverpool.

—— (1988) 'Serious fun: Drug education through popular culture', *Druglink* 3 (6),10–13.

—— (1989) 'Harm reduction research: Measuring harm and interpreting outcomes', Paper presented at the Harm Reduction Conference, Stirling University, Scotland (July 1989).

Parker, H., Bakx, K. and Newcombe, R. (1988) *Living with Heroin: The impact of a drugs 'epidemic' on an English community*, Milton Keynes: Open University Books (Chapters 8 and 9).

Weil, A. (1972) *The Natural Mind: A new way of looking at drugs and the higher consciousness*, London: Jonathan Cape (rev. edn, 1986).

—— and Rosen, W. (1983) *From Chocolate to Morphine: Understanding mind-active drugs*, Boston: Houghton-Mifflin.

Working Party on Harm Minimization (1989) Evaluating Drugs and AIDS Prevention Policies, London: Institute for the Study of Drug Dependence.

Zinberg, N. (1984) *Drug, Set and Setting: The basis for controlled intoxicant use*, New Haven, USA: Yale University Press.

—— (1987) *The Use and Misuse of Intoxicants: Factors in the development of controlled use*, Lexington, Mass.: Lexington Books.

Chapter 2

Drugs and criminal justice
A harm reduction perspective

Geoffrey Pearson

INTRODUCTION

The concept of 'harm reduction', and the practices which are associated with it, have been developed primarily in the contexts of health education and health care. There is a pressing need that the concept should be expanded to include drug enforcement, criminal justice and the penal system. When this is done, the principles of harm reduction can then be shown to have a surprisingly wide range of applications. The central aim of this chapter is to sketch in the implications of such an approach to illicit drug misuse.

I have said that the range of applications of the principles of harm reduction to drug enforcement is surprisingly large. It is a matter for some surprise because, as things stand, drug enforcement is often thought to be hostile to harm reduction strategies. Harm reduction, as usually conceived, is there to help individuals who use and misuse drugs. Enforcement measures, by the same logic, are there to control the supply of drugs by arresting, convicting and punishing drug users. Harm reduction and drug enforcement therefore stand opposed to each other. I shall argue that this is not necessarily so. Nevertheless, along the way I shall score a few 'own goals' because some of the ways in which drug enforcement is conceived are directly hostile to both the individual and collective interest.

 I am aware, of course, of that powerful tradition which suggests that in large measure the harms resulting from drug use are precisely a consequence of their illegality. On this view, one harm reduction stance might be to do away entirely with enforcement, through one form or another of legalization or decriminalization. I do not see it this way. Arguments in favour of legalization, which have been quite fashionable in recent years, are merely symptomatic of frustration with the failure of current drug control policies (Pearson, 1989a). It is certainly true that one could envisage a more rational system of regulation of the production, distribution and consumption of drugs – such as the position advanced by Francis Caballero in his *Droit de la Drogue* which promotes the idea of a 'passive commerce' involving a system of national monopolies and licensing arrangements which fall short of legalization (Caballero, 1989; Le Gendre, 1990).

However, so much of this debate is mere idle talk. Legalization is not going to happen, in any foreseeable future, without a sea-change in international systems of treaties. One can therefore waste a great deal of brainpower and breath in arguments about legalization. There is undoubtedly a strong case for the decriminalization of cannabis, which has been tried successfully in the Netherlands and which would also release a large amount of police resources in the British context where more than 80 per cent of convictions and cautions for drug offences are concerned with cannabis (Pearson, 1991). Where drugs such as heroin and cocaine are concerned, however, it is not self-evident that legalization would be desirable. It would certainly not solve the problems of Third World producer nations, and it would risk unleashing even greater problems of drug misuse in the metropolitan nations.

As a final word of introduction, it is perhaps as well to say where I am coming from in these arguments. What I have to say should be situated within the context of the heroin epidemic which has ripped through many British towns and cities during the 1980s. It is a problem which has been experienced in its most intense form in regions and localities already experiencing multiple social difficulties – high levels of unemployment, housing decay, and other forms of social deprivation (Pearson, *et al.*, 1985, 1986; Pearson, 1987a, b; Parker *et al.*, 1988). This is not to advance a simple-minded and mechanical argument – 'unemployment causes heroin misuse' – but to acknowledge the legacy of the interlocking problems which the heroin epidemic imposed on these already embattled and poverty-stricken neighbourhoods.

Those who work in drugs agencies, necessarily and understandably focus their attention on the needs and interests of the individual drug user. When the needs and interests of this wider community are weighed in the balance, however, then they must surely carry considerable weight and the emphasis of a fully rounded and competent drug control strategy must shift accordingly. These communities need systems of social defence against problems of drug misuse. One line of defence is provided through effective low-level law enforcement. It offers a means by which to restrain the recruitment of 'not-yet-users' into the system, while also providing a means to encourage existing users to take up treatment options at an earlier stage than they might otherwise have done. If employed within the spirit and practice of 'harm reduction', effective law enforcement need not be the enemy of the drug user; it can be a progressive and humane instrument.

HARM REDUCTION AND THE AIMS OF DRUG ENFORCEMENT

The aims of harm reduction in the criminal justice field can be organized under four broad principles:

- The containment of the numbers of new users recruited into the system through effective and focused low-level policing in conjunction with other prevention strategies.
- The encouragement of existing users to take 'early retirement' from drug-using careers, and to enter treatment programmes which include maintenance prescribing as an intermediate objective.
- The minimization of counter-productive aspects of enforcement strategies through arrest-referral schemes, diversion programmes and other community-based activities which avoid the excessive use of custodial measures and enhance the prospects of rehabilitation.
- The minimization of harm to the wider community, by a reduction of crime committed by users in order to sustain their habits.

These principles – directed towards the user, the not-yet-user and the wider community – involve an extension of vision by those who work in drug agencies. I have already noted the way in which their preoccupations and sympathies are understandably and necessarily directed towards individual drug users. What must also be admitted within drug discourses, however, are those wider community interests which cannot be met by services delivered to drug users. This is where focused enforcement efforts can assist in responding to the needs and interests of the wider community, and also to those of the individual drug users.

How might the four organizing principles which I have outlined be translated into a more specific set of aims and objectives, involving targeted sites of intervention and achievable outcomes?

MINIMIZING THE RECRUITMENT OF THE NOT-YET-USER

Where the 'not-yet-user' is concerned, this requires a shift of attention for law enforcement to include not only major trafficking organizations but also lower-level dealing operations and user-dealers (Pearson, 1989a, b). It is far too easy to slip into a comfortable moral rhetoric whereby the major traffickers are identified as the 'villains' of the piece who are legitimate targets for enforcement, as against user-dealers who are seen as the 'victims' of the drug business. This form of rhetoric not only ignores what we know about the active lifestyles of drug users and user-dealers which are difficult to reconcile with victim status (Preble and Casey, 1969; Johnson et al., 1985; Gilman and Pearson, 1991); it is also blind to the fact that it is through these low-level distribution systems that dangerous drugs are made available in vulnerable neighbourhoods, rather than through the so-called 'Barons' and 'Mr Bigs' of the international drug trade.

Effective performance indicators for police work in the sphere of drug enforcement are extremely difficult to formulate (Pearson, 1989b, 1990). Perhaps the best available formulation of an enforcement strategy which aims to limit the recruitment of new users into the system is that provided by Mark Moore (1977) in his book *Buy and Bust*. Moore admits that he does not know how to eliminate heroin distribution in New York — thus making him out as a sensible pragmatist amidst bizarre North American fantasies of 'zero tolerance' — but that an achievable aim would be to increase the amount of time a novice user takes to score heroin from five minutes to two hours. Moore's approach is one of 'inconvenience policing', which simply means that forms of local policing should be adopted whereby it becomes more difficult to cross the threshold from the not-yet-user to the user. Moore suggests that young police officers might be deployed in drug-dealing areas, for example, posing as novice users and then arresting dealers with whom they made contact. The objective is not to eliminate dealing in such a neighbourhood, but to make dealers wary of strangers: in other words, it is a focused enforcement strategy which merely aims to encourage the local drug market to draw in its horns.

Other aspects of Moore's strategy are more questionable in terms of harm reduction. For example, he suggests that an aim of enforcement should be to keep 'copping areas' on the move in order to further inconvenience novice buyers. However, by keeping dealers on the move this might simply result in widening the local availability of drugs. We know of the 'displacement effects' which can result from police drives in particular neighbourhoods against crimes such as burglary, and which are generally regarded as non-problematic in that they simply shift the problem from one area to another without exacerbating it.

However, in the field of drug enforcement 'displacement effects' are far from benign in that they increase the knowledge and availability of potentially dangerous drugs. It is one of the advantages of focused low-level enforcement strategies, however, that they do make it easier both to specify achievable objectives while also identifying undesirable outcomes of a local tactic (Pearson, 1989b).

ENCOURAGING EXISTING USERS TO TAKE 'EARLY RETIREMENT'

As applied to drug users themselves, harm reduction principles require that a central aim of a focused enforcement strategy is to encourage existing users to take up treatment options. This involves a number of related objectives and areas of activity. It also engages with arguments in the realm of moral philosophy about compulsion, civil liberties and voluntarism.

The central requirement must be to encourage users to take up treatment options at an earlier stage in their drug-using careers. Drug services currently operate on a quasi-medical model which assumes the willing compliance of an individual drug user who admits that he or she is in some way sick and in need of help and treatment. Once more, however, this fails to conform to what we know about the active lifestyles of drug users and the high status which they can enjoy within their local community (Gilman and Pearson, 1991). It seems likely, moreover, that drug users make choices to enter into contact with services under one form or another of subtle compulsion – from family, friends, social workers, etc. Targeted low-level enforcement strategies, when allied to rational and non-discriminatory cautioning and sentencing procedures, can offer a means by which the law formalizes these already-existing compulsions and focuses the attention of drug users on the rational choices which can be made available to them in the form of treatment, counselling and other systems of care and support.

Drug enforcement must be conceived of not simply as a constraint on individual liberties, which I take to be the position of conventional liberal moral philosophy in the drugs field, but also as a potentially humane and positive force. My own is a crude jurisprudence, no doubt, which aims to constrain people to be free. Medical approaches to drug problems rest on the myth of voluntarism – the motivated, self-acting and willing participant who admits to being sick. But drug users are not like this. They only become like this when they reach what appears to them to be a cul-de-sac in their drug use and their lives. It is often only when they have arrived at this dead-end point that drug users seek help, thus helping to confirm and reproduce the voluntarist philosophy of the medical model, as individuals willingly giving themselves into treatment.

But why should we wait until drug users reach the state of ill-health and low self-esteem that they sometimes do before they seek help? Two ideal-type cases can make the point. First, a man in his mid-thirties who has been an opiate user for twelve years, whose health is extremely poor with ulcerated legs and numerous abscesses. He is very thin and in considerable pain, funds his addiction by property crime and has been imprisoned in the past. Next, a woman aged thirty who is again in very poor health and is a regular groin injector with several open sores and abscesses. She has been using heroin for nine years and has had several detoxification treatments in the past. She is a hepatitis B carrier and funds her addiction by prostitution.

When one takes fully into account the awfulness of the human suffering endured by people in circumstances such as these, it must shift the moral ground in those arguments which are customarily paraded around drug questions concerning civil liberties, the freedom of the individual, and the voluntaristic emphasis of the medical model. What defence of civil liberties is it which allows people to get themselves into such states of wretched ill-health and multiple legal and financial problems?

One final consideration, of course, is that, not uncommonly, drug users are allowed to get into conditions such as these because doctors in their immediate locality are unsympathetic to the idea of maintenance prescribing as a treatment option. While agreeing that maintenance is only one option among many, there should nevertheless be a further legal requirement which is enforced on doctors themselves, requiring them to make available a full range of services and for these to be managed and offered in a balanced programme of activities. The law can muscle people into treatment options, but the full range of options for sometimes difficult and damaged people must be locally available.

MINIMIZING THE COUNTER-PRODUCTIVE EFFECTS OF ENFORCEMENT

The next objective is to minimize the counter-productive harms resulting from some enforcement strategies and sentencing trends. British government policy, as indicated by recent statements from the

Home Office (1988, 1990), is currently advocating the expansion of non-custodial community-based programmes for 'less serious' offenders. Specific attention has been given within these proposals to the needs of offenders with drug and alcohol-related problems (Gilman and Pearson, 1991; SCODA, 1990).

These proposals are in fundamental agreement, moreover, with the recommendations of the twin reports of the Advisory Council on the Misuse of Drugs (1988, 1989) on the question of AIDS and drug misuse. There is mounting evidence within Britain's decaying Victorian prison system not only of the widespread availability of illicit drugs, but also of the risks of HIV infection through the sharing of injection equipment and unsafe sex practices (Rahman et al., 1989; Prison Reform Trust, 1988; Carvell and Hart, 1990; Kennedy et al., 1990). It is going to be increasingly difficult to ignore this evidence, giving added encouragement to the development of non-custodial programmes for offenders with drug-related difficulties, including necessary adjustments to sentencing guidelines. In terms of street-level policing, the lesson would already seem to have been learned from the devastating experience of Edinburgh, where known levels of HIV seropositivity among intravenous drug users was already in excess of 50 per cent by the mid-1980s, that where police use the possession of injecting equipment as a pretext for arrest, this simply increases the likelihood that the drug users will share 'works' and that 'shooting galleries' will be established (Scottish Home and Health Department, 1986: 7; ACMD, 1988: 43).

The emergence of HIV and AIDS has had a paradoxical influence on public attitudes and policy debates towards drug misuse. On the one hand, it has led to the further stigmatization of marginal groups such as homosexuals and drug users. On the other hand, in Britain at least, it has blown gusts of fresh air through the public debate on drug misuse. There is now a growing awareness of the associated risks of not only drug misuse itself, but also thoughtless sentencing policies. While there are still pockets of doubt and uncertainty in some professional circles about viewing drug problems only through the prism of HIV and AIDS, which are entirely understandable, there is nevertheless a new fluidity within policy-thinking which must be grasped and turned in the most progressive and effective direction. It is a rare moment when humane considerations coincide with those likely to be most effective.

The expansion of community-based programmes to combat the excessive use of imprisonment will require new ways of working in the drugs field, involving multi-agency strategies which bring together the work of drug services, the police, the probation service and the courts.

Multi-agency work in the criminal justice sphere is never easy, and there are abundant sites of potential and actual conflict between agencies which must be recognized and overcome if effective inter-agency and inter-professional cooperation is to be secured (Blagg *et al.*, 1988; Sampson *et al.*, 1988, 1991; Pearson *et al.*, 1989, 1991).

There is, nevertheless, evidence of considerable success in the field of juvenile justice where in the course of the 1980s the use of custody has been halved by the development of credible and effective community-based alternatives (Children's Society, 1988). The challenge is to extend this success so as to reduce the excessive and counter-productive imprisonment of young adult offenders, including those with drug-related problems. For these purposes, drug enforcement and sentencing strategies need to be aligned with innovative projects such as syringe-exchange schemes, attempts to gain a more sensitive understanding of the reasons why people share injecting equipment, the exploitation of novel forms of communication in health education such as comics, the development of effective and 'user-friendly' services for women drug users and for black and other minority ethnic groups, and outreach work with high-risk groups such as drug-using prostitutes (Monitoring Research Group, 1988; McKeganey, 1989; Gilman, 1988; Awiah *et al.*, 1990; Plant, 1990).

The British system of drug control policy, with all its inadequacies, remains a highly flexible instrument which has traditionally combined enforcement efforts with systems of education and health care provision (Pearson, 1991). There is little point at the moment arguing about the most effective forms of community-based intervention, whether in terms of arrest-referral schemes, pre-trial diversion programmes, drug advisory services to courts, bail assistance schemes, custody-exit initiatives, etc. We simply do not have the experience to know, as yet, the most effective point at which to intervene in the decision-making processes of the criminal justice system. In all likelihood, different forms of intervention will have to be tailored to suit the needs of different categories of drug users. However, the combined approach of the Home Office non-custodial strategy and the Advisory Council's recommendations offers a real window of opportunity for the development of harm reduction strategies. Careful evaluation of different approaches will be necessary at some point, but for the present our aim should be to let a hundred flowers bloom.

REDUCING HARM TO THE WIDER COMMUNITY

If existing users can be encouraged to make contact with services through a strengthened and focused law enforcement effort, this will bring benefits to the wider community. It will reduce the amount of crime committed by drug users in order to support their habits. It will help to contain the spread of HIV infection. It will minimize the fiscal implications of the excessive use of imprisonment which otherwise incurs financial penalties against taxpayers and the welfare state.

In addition, drug enforcement at a local level needs to engage in a clear assessment of its aims and objectives, while also identifying the possible unintended consequences of different forms of enforcement. I have already suggested that some forms of policing operation can result in the increased likelihood that drug users will share injecting equipment. Other forms of policing simply move local drug-dealing networks from one neighbourhood to another, thus risking an even wider availability of dangerous drugs such as heroin and cocaine.

In order to deepen our understanding of how to design the most effective drug enforcement strategies, we need to build up case studies of the consequences – both direct and indirect – of different forms of local effort. I will offer three examples of the kinds of necessary consideration.

In one city in the north of England which experienced a sharp increase in heroin misuse during the 1980s, the low-level distribution system consisted largely of user-dealers who operated from their own houses and flats. These were easily identifiable and thus vulnerable to raids by the police. As a consequence, substantial numbers of user-dealers were convicted, while others decided to retire from dealing while the going was good. The outcome in this city is that drug-dealing has moved onto a different basis. What has emerged is a street-dealing scene, and it is not immediately obvious that this is an improvement on what went before. The earlier system had required dealers to maintain a certain level of security, so that it was only possible to buy drugs if you were already known and trusted. It was therefore more difficult for novice users and experimenters to cross the threshold from not-yet-user to user. The new street-dealing scene, on the other hand, involves no formalities of this kind. It is wide open and anonymous, thus lowering the threshold of entry into the system. The question needs to be asked: would policing have taken the form that it did, if forward-planning could have foreseen the actual outcome?

The second example has an international dimension, and involves a set of issues which are likely to grow in importance with the integration of the European community. The phenomenon known as 'drugs tourism' is a consequence of an imbalance in enforcement policies between neighbouring states or regions. There has been a particularly sharp expression of this kind of difficulty in the Dutch town of Arnhem which lies close to the border with West Germany, involving bitter conflicts within the local community as German drug users are 'sucked in' along the steep gradients of control and enforcement which exist between Germany and the Netherlands (Ephimenco, 1989). In this context, the Swiss Federal Commission (1989) recently published a report which advocates the de-penalization of all drug offences for simple possession. However, perhaps mindful of the Dutch experience, the report also recognized that if such a change in enforcement policy were implemented unilaterally, it would 'bring about drug tourism in Switzerland with all the undesirable effects which this implies' (ibid.: 78). In other words, here it was a liberalization of enforcement strategy which, although it had been considered to have great merit in terms of domestic policy, had unintended consequences for the wider community.

The question of 'drugs tourism' indicates something of the complexity of integrated drug policy formulation. There are many local and regional circumstances which involve similar considerations. The existence of a specific form of treatment facility in a given locality, for example, can produce an effect not dissimilar from 'drugs tourism' by attracting drug users from other regions and localities. Drug issues involve all manner of forms of local and regional diversity, requiring specific attention in the formulation of local policies which can otherwise backfire. Recently, for example, an attempt in the north-west of England to prohibit the sale of travel sickness preparations which contain cyclizine (a constituent of the opioid Diconal which was a preference drug for many opiate users) has led to an illicit market in cyclizine in the immediate locality (Pearson, et al., 1990). Again, one must ask, was this the intended outcome of the local enforcement attempt at prohibition?

My third example involves a further consideration, which is that the success of local drug enforcement efforts should not be judged simply in terms of the supply and demand of drugs. In this case, a local park had become the focus for low-level dealing. Quite apart from genuine dealing operations, the park had also attracted opportunists who aimed to 'rip-off' prospective buyers, armed with cocoa powder in one pocket and a knife in the other. Assaults and 'muggings' had also become common, so that the park was quite unusable as a public facility. As a result of a series of police sweeps, the park had subsequently been cleared of drug dealers. However, the police were unhappy about the outcome and judged the operation to have been a failure since they knew that many of the same people were still dealing drugs, although they were now operating from private households. Here we are simply giving the police the wrong message. As a narrowly defined drug enforcement operation, perhaps it is correct to say that it had failed. However, if a different focus were to be adopted, then the operation had been a major success. The park was once again a place where people could stroll, read a newspaper, push a pram. The operation might only have dented the drug-dealing system, but it had returned an important community resource to public utility.

The underlying principle in these three case studies is that we need a more highly nuanced set of aims and objectives for drug enforcement strategies. On any reading of the situation, the aim of eliminating domestic drug markets is not an achievable goal (Wagstaff and Maynard, 1988). The question for drug enforcement, as posed by Dorn and South (1990, 186) with a harm reduction model in mind, then becomes: 'What sort of markets do we least dislike, and how can we adjust the control mix so as to push markets in the least undesired direction?'

A HARM REDUCTION SPECTRUM: FROM THE PERSON TO THE PLANET

Throughout this chapter I have tried to illustrate how the principles of harm reduction have a much wider application than has been usually assumed. It is first necessary to recognize that different kinds of harm can result from drug misuse (Dorn, 1990). There are not only potential risks to health – which are the site upon which harm reduction strategies have been developed – but there are also different forms of social and emotional harm, financial harm, and legal harms such as arrest and imprisonment.

A second requirement is to recognize that harm can result not only to the individual drug user, but also to his or her immediate family and friends, and finally to the wider community. For example, through drug misuse the individual might put his or her health at risk. But he or she might also put the health of other members of the family at risk, which is commonly the focus for intervention by social workers in the field of child care and child protection. Then, there is harm to the wider community in the shape of burglaries and other forms of property crime to support drug habits. The accelerated transmission of HIV and AIDS through high risk practices such as sharing injecting equipment and not heeding safer sex advice also positions drug misuse within a public health discourse, rather than one solely devoted to the needs and interests of the individual.

The third and final requirement is to recognize that harm results not only from drug misuse itself, but also potentially from measures taken to combat it. I wish to distinguish here between two different approaches in the field of drug enforcement. On one side there are heavy-handed, scatter-gun approaches to law enforcement which fill the courts and prisons with people who really should be helped, which can result not only in harm to the individual – in the form of unhelpful and irrelevant punishment, or by exposing the individual to unsafe injection practices in prison – but also to the wider community in the form of fiscal penalties against tax-payers to build and maintain unnecessarily large prison systems. Opposed to this, one can begin to define a more realistic and focused strategy by which the police direct their efforts against heavy end-users and user-dealers in order to push them into community-based programmes offering alternative lifestyles.

The principles of harm reduction can even be extended to the global sphere. At this level of consideration there is harm in the form of agricultural resources diverted towards the production of illicit cash-crops which prove more lucrative in the global economy, at the expense of food production for a hungry world. International enforcement efforts sometimes compound the difficulty through crop eradication programmes which, while perhaps intended to destroy cannabis crops, also upset the delicate balance of other plant and animal life forms – resulting, for example, in the destruction of bees which are necessary to pollinate licit fruit-crops, thus deepening the problems of farmers and peasants; or unleashing ruinous ecological imbalances which lead to devastating invasions of insect pests. When we hear that international enforcement agencies have recently dreamt up schemes to introduce plagues of monster caterpillars in the Andes in order to check coca plantations, we are faced with a form of biological warfare against the plant itself in the name of the war on drugs.

I shall not, however, waste too many words criticizing current drug policies at international level. They write their own failure, by their incapacity to keep abreast of the changing and increasing drug problems in the cities of most metropolitan countries and in many Third World nations. The war on drugs has been lost, and with heavy casualties on both sides. Indeed, it was lost before it was started. It is a post-colonial debacle in which the central problem is those Third World nations whose economies have become massively distorted by the international drugs trade. If the problem is taken seriously in its global economic scale, it is not a question of sending a few helicopters to Bolivia, but of the restructuring of the economies of maybe two dozen Third World countries. It is a World Bank problem, not a Drug Squad problem.

In conclusion, when we take on board the wider implications of harm reduction, it becomes a vital necessity not only in the sphere of drug control policies, but also in our more global concerns as inhabitants of this planet. It would be totally unrealistic to aim for the elimination of drug problems as an achievable objective. It would be akin to asking meteorologists to stop the wind. While the wind continues to blow, we need more local forms of defence and shelter against the real harms which can result from drug misuse. These must be provided in the shape of effective domestic social policies, within which drug enforcement can assume a more focused and relevant form.

REFERENCES

Advisory Council on the Misuse of Drugs (1988) *AIDS and Drug Misuse, Part 1*, London: HMSO.
—— (1989) *AIDS and Drug Misuse, Part 2*, London: HMSO.
Awiah, J., Butt, S. and Dorn, N. (1990) 'The last place I would go. Black people and drug services in Britain', *Druglink*, Sept/Oct 1990.
Blagg, H., Pearson, G., Sampson, A., Smith, D. and Stubbs, P. (1988) 'Inter-agency co-operation; rhetoric and reality', in T. Hope and M. Shaw (eds) *Communities and Crime Reduction*, London: HMSO.
Caballero, F. (1989) *Droit de la Drogue*, Paris: Dalloz.
Carvell, A. L. M. and Hart, G. J. (1990) 'Risk behaviours for HIV infection among drug users in prison', *British Medical Journal* 300 (26 May): 1383–4.
Children's Society (1988) *Penal Custody for Juveniles: The least line of resistance*, Report of the Children's Society Advisory Committee on Penal Custody and its Alternatives for Juveniles, London: The Children's Society.
Dorn, N. (1990) 'Drug prevention for health and welfare professionals', in H. Ghodse and D. Maxwell (eds) *Substance Abuse and Dependence*, London: Macmillan.
—— and South, N. (1990) 'Drug markets and law enforcement', *British Journal of Criminology* 30 (2): 171–88.
Ephimenco, S. (1989) 'Arnhem livré aux croisés antidrogue', *Libération* (27 September): 23.
Gilman, M. (1988) 'Comics as a strategy in reducing drug related harm', in N. Dorn, L. Lucas and N. South (eds) *Drug Questions: An annual research register*, issue 4, London: ISDD.
—— and Pearson, G. (1991) 'Lifestyle and law enforcement: Using criminal justice to help drug users', in P. Bean and D. K. Whynes (eds) *Policing and*

Prescribing: The British system of drug control, London: Macmillan (in press).

Home Office (1988) *Punishment, Custody and the Community*, Cm. 424, London: HMSO.

—— (1990) *Crime, Justice and Protecting the Public: The government's proposals for legislation*, Cm. 965, London: HMSO.

Johnson, B.D., Goldstein, P.J., Preble, E., Schmeidler, J., Lipton, D.S., Spunt, B. and Miller, T. (1985) *Taking Care of Business: The economics of crime by heroin abusers*, Lexington, Mass: Lexington Books.

Kennedy, D., Mair, G., Elliot, L. and Ditton, J. (1990) *Illicit Drug Use Injecting and Syringe Sharing in Scottish Prisons in the 1990's*, Glasgow: START (Substance Treatment Agency Reporting Team), University of Glasgow.

Le Gendre, B. (1990) 'La drogue dans tous ses états', translated with an introduction by G. Pearson, *The International Journal on Drug Policy* 1 (4): 24–5.

McKeganey, N. (1989) 'Drug abuse in the community: needle-sharing and the risks of HIV infection', in S. Cunningham-Birley and N. McKeganey (eds), *Readings in Medical Sociology*, London: Routledge.

Monitoring Research Group (1988) *Injecting Equipment Exchange Schemes: Final Report*, London: Goldsmiths' College, University of London.

Moore, M. H. (1977) *Buy and Bust: The effective regulation of an illicit market in heroin*, Lexington, Mass.: Lexington Books.

Parker, H., Bakx, K. and Newcombe, R. (1988) *Living with Heroin: The impact of a drugs 'epidemic' on an English community*, Milton Keynes: Open University Press.

Pearson, G. (1987a) *The New Heroin Users*, Oxford: Basil Blackwell.

—— (1987b) 'Social deprivation, unemployment and patterns of heroin use', in N. Dorn and N. South (eds), *A Land Fit for Heroin? Drug Policies, Prevention and Practice*, London: Macmillan.

—— (1989a) 'The street connection', *New Statesman and Society* (15 September): 10-11.

—— (1989b) 'Low-level drug enforcement: A multi-agency perspective from Britain', paper presented to the conference *What Works: An International Perspective on Drug Abuse Treatment and Prevention Research*, New York (October).

—— (1990) 'Drugs, law enforcement and criminology', in V. Berridge (ed.) *Drugs Research and Policy in Britain*, Aldershot: Avebury.

—— (1991) 'Drug control policies in Britain', in M. Tonry and N. Morris (eds) *Crime and Justice*, vol. 14, Chicago: University of Chicago Press.

——, Gilman, M. and McIver, S. (1985) 'Heroin use in the north of England', *Health Education Journal* 45 (3): 186–9.

——, —— and —— (1986) *Young People and Heroin: An examination of heroin use in the north of England*, London: Health Education Council (2nd edn, 1987, Aldershot: Gower).

——, Sampson, A., Blagg, H., Stubbs, P. and Smith, D. (1989) 'Policing racism', in R. Morgan and D.J. Smith (eds) *Coming to Terms with Policing*, London: Routledge.

——, Gilman, M. and Traynor, P. (1990) 'Cyclizine misuse: The limits of intervention', *Druglink* 5 (3): 12–13.

——, Blagg, H., Smith, D., Sampson, A. and Stubbs, P. (1991) 'Crime, community and conflict: The multi-agency approach', in D. Downes (ed.) *Unravelling Criminal Justice*, London: Macmillan.

Plant, M. A.(ed.) (1990) *Aids, Drugs and Prostitution*, London: Routledge.

Preble, E. and Casey, J. J. (1969) 'Taking care of business: The heroin user's life in the street', *International Journal of the Addictions* 4 (1): 1-24.

Prison Reform Trust (1988) *HIV AIDS and Prisons*, London: Prison Reform Trust.

Rahman, M. Z., Ditton, J. & Forsyth, A. J. (1989) 'Variations in needle sharing practices among intravenous drug users in Possil (Glasgow)', *British Journal of Addiction* 84: 923–7.

Sampson, A., Stubbs, P., Smith, D., Pearson, G. and Blagg, H. (1988) 'Crime, localities and the multi-agency approach', *British Journal of Criminology* 28 (4): 478–93.

——, Smith, D., Pearson, G., Blagg, H. and Stubbs, P. (1991) 'Gender issues in inter-agency relations: police, probation and social services', in P. Abbott and C. Walace (eds) *Gender, Sexuality and Power*, London: Macmillan.

Scottish Home and Health Department (1986) *HIV Infection Scotland: Report of the Scottish Committee on HIV Infection and Intravenous Drug Misuse*, Edinburgh: HMSO.

Standing Conference on Drug Abuse (1990) *SCODA's Comments on the White Paper 'Crime, Justice and Protecting the Public'*, London: SCODA.

Swiss Federal Commission (1989) *Aspects de la Situation et de la Politique en Matière de Drogue en Suisse*, Rapport de la Sous-Commission 'Drogue' de la Commission Fédérale des Stupéfiants, Berne: Office Fédéral de la Santé.

Wagstaff, A. and Maynard, A. (1988) *Economic Aspects of the Illicit Drug Market and Drug Enforcement Policies in the United Kingdom*, Home Office Research Study No. 95, London: HMSO.

Chapter 3

The impact of harm reduction drug policy on AIDS prevention in Amsterdam

Ernst Buning, Giel van Brussel and Gerrit van Santen

INTRODUCTION

By 31 December 1989, 1,074 AIDS cases were reported in the Netherlands. Eighty-nine persons were drug injectors of whom seventy-five were heterosexual and fourteen were homosexual (Table 3.1).

Table 3.1 Number of AIDS cases among drug injectors in the Netherlands

	Heterosexual injectors	Homosexual injectors	Total cumulative	Increase
Jul.–Dec. 1985	1	1	2	
Jan.–Jun. 1986	3	1	4	+2
Jul.–Dec. 1986	8	1	9	+5
Jan.–Jun. 1987	14	2	16	+7
Jul.–Dec. 1987	24	6	30	+14
Jan.–Jun. 1988	35	10	45	+15
Jul.–Dec. 1988	45	11	56	+11
Jan.–Jun. 1989	61	13	74	+18
Jul.–Dec. 1989	75	14	89	+15

Source: Hoofd Inspektie van de Volksgezondheid.

In Amsterdam, a large epidemiological study has been underway among drug injectors since 1986 (van den Hoek *et al.*, 1988). Over 700 drug injectors have been tested for HIV and about 30 per cent found to be seropositive. This percentage has remained rather stable in the last couple of years. The number of hard drug users (mainly heroin in combination with cocaine) in Amsterdam is estimated at 5,500 to 7,000. About 60 per cent do not inject, but 'chase the dragon'. The remaining 40 per cent inject (about 3,000 people). So, in total, the number of seropositive drug users in Amsterdam is estimated at about 1,000 (30 per cent of 3,000).

Before discussing the AIDS prevention programme among drug users, the Amsterdam drug policy will be briefly described. The key words in the Amsterdam drug policy are 'pragmatic' and 'nonjudgmental'. Basically, this means that those interventions that turn out to be successful are adopted, while other less effective approaches are done away with. Some people who are not in favour of our policy rather call it *laissez faire*, but our policy is well thought out, is coherent, and there is a broad agreement and consensus among politicians, policy makers, the police and the drug helping system about our approach.

The Amsterdam approach led to a pluriform helping system which is built up along a continuum from 'harm reduction' to 'drug free therapy'. Harm reduction refers to all those activities which are *not* directly aimed at getting drug users entirely off drugs, but emphasize the need to reduce the harm that drug users cause to themselves and their environment. Needle exchange schemes and low-threshold methadone programmes are good examples of this harm reduction philosophy.

The system of drug free therapy in the Netherlands is very much the same as in most other western countries.

AIDS PREVENTION AMONG DRUG USERS

In Amsterdam, AIDS prevention among drug users is carried out along a simple model (see Figure 3.1). First, contact is made with as many drug users as possible. Second, information is given about safe sex and safer drug use. By doing so, it is hoped that drug users will change their attitude towards safe sex and safer drug use. Behaviour changes are facilitated through the provision of certain conditions, such as:

Figure 3.1 The Amsterdam AIDS prevention model

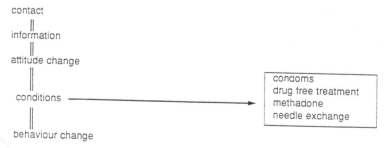

contact
||
information
||
attitude change
||
conditions ——————————————→ condoms
|| drug free treatment
|| methadone
behaviour change   needle exchange

- the availability of condoms;
- accessible drug free treatment (without long waiting lists) for those drug users who want to stop the habit;
- the provision of methadone to those drug users who want to reduce or stop injecting, but are not yet able to give up their opiate addiction;
- the provision of clean injecting material through needle exchange schemes.

This model will be elucidated later in this chapter.

CONTACT

An estimated 50–70 per cent of the drug users have contact with one or more of the drug helping agencies. This creates ample opportunities to give information about safe sex and safer drug use.

Streetwork

Streetworkers make frequent visits to places where concentrations of users can be found. They observe what is going on, provide verbal and/or written information (including information about AIDS) and serve as a 'bridge' to helping institutions, such as methadone programmes and the needle exchange scheme. The two foundations responsible for this streetwork employ about thirty streetworkers. One foundation has specialized female workers, who do outreach work among addicted prostitutes. The current involvement of streetworkers in AIDS prevention is not yet optimal, workers differ from one another and a single systematic approach has not yet been agreed.

Police stations

Since 1977, Municipal Health Service doctors visit local police stations twice a day to see arrested drug users. Medical first aid is given (including methadone) and the doctors give information about treatment facilities, the needle exchange schemes and AIDS-related issues. This project has turned out to be most effective for all those involved. The arrested drug user is relieved from withdrawal symptoms, the work of the police officers is done without interruption by agitated suspects, and the doctors gain a lot of information about developments in the drug scene. Every year about 2,000 drug users are seen in the police stations.

Contacting drug users through methadone

In the low threshold 'methadone by bus' programme many drug users are contacted. This project started with one bus in 1979 and with the addition of a second bus in 1982. Today, the specially built buses make a distinct route through Amsterdam, stopping at six different places in or near the 'drug scene'. In these buses liquid methadone is dispensed to drug users who have been referred to the buses by one of the Municipal Health doctors. Pre-conditions for participation in the project are:

- regular contact with a medical doctor (minimal once every three months);
- introduction into the central methadone registration;
- no take-home dosages.

No other demands are made on clients: (i.e. no urine check, no mandatory contact with a counsellor, etc.). Approximately 600 drug users visit these buses daily. Besides the methadone, information about AIDS is given, needles can be exchanged and condoms are available.

INFORMATION

The best way to get the 'safer sex' and 'safer drug use' message across is through personal counselling, where the user and the counsellor can discuss what safer sex and safer drug use mean and what social skills are needed to change behaviour. The recent availability of audiovisual material for showing in waiting areas of the various institutions has added an extra supporting dimension to the personal counselling. This material is composed of television documentaries and productions of the Amsterdam working group on AIDS and drugs. The latter part of the material makes use of interviews with (seropositive) drug users and consists of short spots to hold the attention of the drug users.

CONDOM DISTRIBUTION

A major concern is that HIV will spread from the drug-injecting population to the general population. If this occurs, the prevailing form of transmission will be through sexual contact. Accordingly, condoms are available in all out-patient clinics and distributed freely after an interview with a social worker, doctor or nurse, to reinforce safe-sex practices that have been discussed. Condoms are also available in a special VD clinic for addicted prostitutes. In 1989, about 45,000 condoms were distributed to prostitutes.

Data from a study on 'AIDS related-knowledge, attitude and behaviour among clients of methadone programmes' (Elorche and Korf, 1989; Buning, 1990) indicate that a relatively large proportion of the clients are sexually inactive: 44 per cent of 110 clients interviewed in the summer of 1989 reported no sexual contact in the month preceding the interview; 52 per cent of the interviewed clients had a regular partner, and in this group 23 per cent used condoms (five 'sometimes' and eight 'always'). Ten clients knew that they were seropositive. This group reported that they 'always' used condoms in sexual contacts with irregular partners. Although the knowledge about the risks for sexual transmission of HIV among this group was sufficient, more action is needed to persuade them towards safer sex practices.

THERAPEUTIC TREATMENT

Another issue in preventing the further spread of HIV among drug users, is to give therapeutic treatment to drug users who want to kick the habit. The fear of AIDS may be one of the reasons why they are motivated to do so. And if the treatment is successful, the risks in 'needle-sharing' will no longer occur.

Drug-free treatment is mainly done by the Amsterdam Jellinek Centrum and includes in-patient as well as out-patient facilities. Individual, group or family therapy is available. The aim is to realize substantial changes, among which is total abstinence. The in-patient treatment (about seventy beds) covers detoxification (three weeks) as well as long-term therapeutic treatment (five to nine months). The goals and means of these activities are similar to drug-free facilities in other European countries and North America.

Resocialization is done through two government-funded foundations. It is believed that the process of resocialization should start as early as possible in someone's 'drug career'. This implies that active drug users as well as ex-users are being involved in resocialization activities. Ex-users have an opportunity to work for one year as a civil servant. In a special experiment, the city of Amsterdam created forty jobs for ex-users, trying to set an example for other employers to follow.

METHADONE

In terms of AIDS prevention, it is also important to assist injecting drug users who want to stop injecting. In so doing, clients can be referred from the methadone buses to one of the three out-patient methadone clinics (*wijkposten*). These clinics provide services which are aimed at helping drug users to give up their illegal drug use. Urine samples are taken twice a week and medical and psycho-social help is provided. Clients are assisted if they are faced with problems concerning housing, financial and legal matters. Medical help is given in the form of a regular medical examination, providing contraception and referral to hospitals. Methadone can be prescribed on a maintenance basis. In this way an injecting opiate addiction can be reduced to an oral opiate addiction and a first step is made towards stabilizing the addiction. The risk of contracting HIV through needle sharing is avoided as long as the client doesn't relapse into injecting drug use. As soon as a rather stable condition is reached, the client's general practitioner is requested to take over the methadone prescription. In Amsterdam, about 200 of the 400 general practitioners prescribe methadone. They can be assisted by one of the doctors from the 'consultation project'. Yearly, about 3,000 drug users receive methadone in Municipal Health Service programmes (buses or out-patient clinics).

NEEDLE EXCHANGE

The Amsterdam needle and syringe exchange scheme began in the summer of 1984 and was initiated by the Junky Union (MDHG). The Junky Union is a league of drug users who take care of the interests of the drug-taking community. Fearing an outbreak of hepatitis B, they began to advocate better availability of clean injecting material. A small-scale experiment was initiated in 1984 and to date (1990), needle exchange is possible at eleven locations in Amsterdam (820,000 needles in 1989) and forty Municipalities in the Netherlands. The implementation of these exchange schemes was made possible on account of three factors:

First, the Ministry of Welfare and Health secured funds in support of local initiatives. Second, the outcome of the evaluation of the Amsterdam exchange schemes (Hartgers et al., 1988, 1989) allowed for positive expectations concerning the preventive value of needle exchange schemes. Third, the various groups of neighbourhoods did not actively oppose the initiatives in 1984. However, one needle exchange location is now threatened. This location is open seven days a week until midnight, and the large number of drug users visiting this scheme create problems for those who live in this particular area.

Does the needle exchange work?

First, the question was asked whether a needle exchange would lead to an increase in drug use. With the 'capture–recapture' method, the number of drug users in Amsterdam is estimated. From these data, it can be concluded that the estimated number of drug users has been rather stable since 1983 (Buning, 1990). Throughout the seven years of needle exchange and the other programmes in Amsterdam, the population of drug users has not increased.

In the evaluation study of the needle exchange in Amsterdam (Hartgers *et al.*, 1988) 148 injecting drug users were interviewed. Drug users who exchanged regularly were compared with drug users who never exchanged or who did so irregularly. Based on self-reports, only 29 per cent of the 'exchangers' indicated an increase in drug use in the six months preceding the interview, while 38 per cent reported a reduction of their drug use. In a follow-up study (Hartgers *et al*, 1989), where sixty drug users were interviewed for a second time, again no evidence was found of an increase in drug use.

Second, the research programme looked at the issue of whether the needle exchange scheme would help drug users to use drugs more safely. Needle-sharing hardly occurred within the group of 'exchangers'; only 9 per cent indicated that they had been involved in needle-sharing in the month preceding the interview. The 'non-exchangers' reported a higher percentage, namely 22 per cent. In the follow-up study, these findings were further supported. About half of the 'needle-sharers' indicated that they did this exclusively with their sexual partner. For the remaining half, needle-sharing was rare (one to five times in the month preceding the interview).

Third, an issue was addressed which is very important to the community at large, namely: 'Will the needle and syringe exchange protect the general public from needle-stick accidents with contaminated needles?'

People who have needle-stick accidents are requested to report this to the Municipal Health Service. In the period 1984–8 there has been no significant increase in the low number of reported needle-stick accidents. However, in 1987 complaints were reported about needles in parks and gutters in the inner city. It turned out that the return rate of the needle exchange was only 70 per cent. The Director of the Municipal Health Service stipulated that all the exchange schemes had to operate on a 'one for one' basis, and further emphasized that the continuation of the exchange schemes could be jeopardized if there was no improvement. This announcement, combined with the installation of better exchange equipment, led to an increase in the exchange rate. In 1989, the exchange rate was 87 per cent.

Based on the above-mentioned developments, it can be stated that the needle exchange did not lead to a decrease in the number of needle-stick accidents by the general public. Since this number was already low, it is questionable whether a reduction to zero could ever be attained. Action by Public Health Authorities to reduce the number of needles left in the environment were successful.

Finally, we looked at the development of the further spread of HIV and hepatitis B within the drug-using population. In Amsterdam drug users have been tested for HIV since December 1985. After corrections for risk behaviour, the HIV-prevalence among new intakes in the study has remained stable at around 30 per cent. Cases of acute hepatitis B are notified to the Municipal Health Service. Among drug users the number of notified cases of acute hepatitis B has decreased from twenty-six in 1984 to five in 1988.

CONCLUSIONS

Sometimes the war on drugs seems to be more a war on drug *users*. This is really jeopardizing AIDS prevention efforts. Drug users will go underground and will no longer be reached by prevention workers. Also, 'soldiers' in this war on drugs may only emphasize drug free treatment. Of course, drug free treatment is an important option. But we have to be realistic: most of the drug users are not willing to give up, or are not capable of giving up, their addiction (yet) and go from 'good' periods, where they stop or reduce their drug use, to 'bad' periods, where they relapse into heavy and high-risk drug use. We think that drug users who are not motivated to give up their drug use are entitled to professional and accessible care, which is geared to their specific needs. In this respect, harm reduction interventions play an essential role. In the light of the AIDS epidemic, this is becoming increasingly important.

A second issue we would like to discuss is the relationship between 'responsible behaviour' and 'marginalization'. The more society marginalizes drug users, the less can the drug user be expected to behave in a responsible way, i.e. not lending his or her needle to others, not throwing used needles in parks and gutters, always using condoms and refraining from becoming pregnant when seropositive.

Only the reinforcement of this form of responsible behaviour by drug users will save the community from the disaster of having to face a major AIDS epidemic in their midst. Epidemiological data from various Western countries indicate that HIV is spread from heterosexual drug injectors to non-injecting members of the community. Babies who get infected through seropositive drug-injecting mothers are, of course, the most tragic form of contamination. In cases where HIV is spread through sexual contact, one may rightly argue that it is the responsibility of both partners. So why blame the drug injector? Nevertheless, minimizing the further spread of HIV in the drug-injecting population may not only be beneficial for drug injectors, but will also have a major impact on the containment of AIDS in the heterosexual community at large.

REFERENCES

Bardoux, C., Buning, E. C., Leentvaar-Kuijpers, A., Verster A. and Coutinho, R. A. (1989) 'Declining incidence of acute hepatitis B among drug users may indicate a change in risk behaviour', Presentation at Vth International Aids Conference, Montreal.

Buning, E. C. (1990) *De GG&GD en het drug probleem in cijfers deel 4*, Publication GG&GD: Amsterdam.

Elorche, M. and Korf, D. J. (1989) *Druggebruikers en Aids, voorlopige resultaten van een onderzoek bij 110 clienten uit de methadonverstrekking van de GG&GD*, Interne Publikatie UvA.

Hartgers, C., Buning, E. C., Van Santen, G. E., Verster, A. D. and Coutinho R. A. (1988) 'Intravenues druggebruik en het spuitenomruilprogramma in Amsterdam', in *Tijdschrift Sociale Gezondheidszorg* 66: 207-10.

——, ——, ——, —— and —— (1989) 'The impact of the needle and syringe-exchange programme in Amsterdam on injecting risk behaviour', *AIDS* 3: 571–6.

van den Hoek, J. A. R., Coutinho, R. A., Van Haastrecht, H. J. A., Van Zadelhoff, A. W. and Goudsmit, J. (1988) 'Prevalence and risk factors of HIV infections among drug users and drug-using prostitutes in Amsterdam', *AIDS* 2: 55-60.

——, Van Haastrecht, H. J. A. and Coutinho R. A. (1989) 'Risk reduction among intravenous drug users in Amsterdam under the influence of Aids', *American Journal of Public Health* 79 (10).

——, ——, Van Zadelhoff, A.W., Goudsmit J. and Coutinho R. A., (1988) 'HIV-infectie onder druggebruikers in Amsterdam; prevalentie en risicofactoren', *Ned. Tijdschrijft Geneeskunde* 132, nr 16.

Chapter 4

Public health and health behaviour in the prevention of HIV infection

Gerry V. Stimson

INTRODUCTION

We are in the midst of a major transformation in the way we think about and respond to drug problems. Issues that had been pushed to the background, concerned very broadly with our options for the social control of drug problems, are suddenly part of a new and vibrant debate, and underpin whole new ways of working with drug problems. Ideas about risk reduction for HIV prevention, and of minimizing broader health risks for drug users and promoting healthy behaviour, have spilled over into a larger debate about reducing drug-related harm, and in particular a debate about changes in the legal controls over drug use and possession. Many of the issues could not have been discussed even two or three years ago. This debate examines some of the most difficult philosophical, political and practical issues concerning drug use.

Minimizing harm with respect to health can be difficult when there are strong legal controls and penalties for drug use. In the case of the use of some drugs, major personal hazards may come from the legal and penal system itself, rather than from health hazards of the drugs or the way in which they are used. However, it is my view that the issue is not about whether we want to have, or want to abolish, controls over drug use. The evidence is that all societies control drug use in one way or another, ranging from informal controls based in the social etiquette of daily drug use, through to the full panoply of legal and penal deterrence. The issue is rather a matter of choosing what sort of social controls we want.

Social controls both constrain and enable behaviour, both limit and create what is possible, and operate in social interaction and discourse, as well as in institutional sites and material circumstances. For example, at the level of everyday drug use, the social etiquette surrounding drug use (whether of alcohol, tobacco or other drugs) is a system of social control for obtaining drugs, learning to use them, seeking some effects and avoiding others, and for enjoying and discussing drugs in culturally appropriate ways. Consider, for example, the complex social interactions and meanings involved in the normal drinking of alcohol. These include location in space and time – the particular places where drink is consumed and times in the day, week and year when drinking is appropriate. They involve a folk or ethnoscience and history of the drug, for example how to buy, keep, prepare and drink various drinks. And they include how to drink properly – the type of container to be used, the speed of drinking, with whom drink is taken, reciprocal interactions, and accompanying activities. Drug controls can be sensitive to cultural practices and seek to modify them, or can meet them head on and seek to outlaw them.

With regard to the prevention of HIV infection, we have to consider the sort of controls we wish to promote in order to minimize the spread of this disease. HIV disease is a behavioural disease, in that it is transmitted through social, and therefore malleable, behaviours. The social interactions that make possible the transmission of HIV are bound up in mundane practices, which are embedded in social, cultural and material structures. From the point of view of the social scientist, what some people see as 'bad' (or risky) health behaviour, is not irrational or pathological. There are usually good social, cultural and economic reasons for risky and other behaviours. Furthermore, in order to influence the transmission of HIV, these everyday practices and health behaviours must change.

A wide variety of innovative practices have been introduced to help prevent the spread of HIV infection among people who inject drugs. These include increasing the supply of syringes through exchange schemes and other outlets, and facilitating access to condoms; introducing bleach and other means for syringe decontamination; attempting to make services more attractive; improving access to treatment; adopting innovative educative packages and ways of bringing health messages to people; using methadone to help people stop injecting; and reaching out to contact drug users or to encourage community changes. They all seek to introduce changes in the ways people inject drugs. In the United Kingdom, as elsewhere, these new approaches are of symbolic as well as practical significance.

ACHIEVEMENTS

Much has been achieved in a short space of time. Among long-standing regular drug injectors the message has got through that sharing syringes is an effective means of transmitting HIV. But knowledge of risks does not automatically lead to changes in health behaviour. This is well known in numerous other fields such as tobacco smoking, heart disease, and obesity: knowledge of the health risks is insufficient to cause major changes in health behaviour. In the case of drug injectors, knowledge of the risks does not necessarily lead people to see themselves as personally at risk. Indeed, the personal risk of infection is often assessed as low.

Studies in many cities including San Francisco, Sydney, New York, Bangkok, Edinburgh and Milan show that drug injectors are reporting changes in their risk behaviour. Time trend data from studies by the Monitoring Research Group at The Centre for Research on Drugs and Health Behaviour over the last three years show a steady and consistent decline in self-reported syringe sharing in the UK, both among people who attend syringe exchanges and among injectors recruited in other settings. Triangulation of data from various locations, using different methods of questioning and different kinds of interviewers, lends veracity to such claims.

In our qualitative fieldwork, we have found that many drug injectors in the south of England are no longer talking about syringe sharing as normal behaviour. There is considerable evidence that the social etiquette of drug use has changed, much as the etiquette of cigarette smoking has. Injectors tend not to offer syringes to share, just as others tend not to offer cigarettes to others. People we have interviewed have adopted a wide range of protective strategies against the risk of HIV infection and transmission. Not all of these measures make sense in virological terms – but are indicative of attempts to change. This is not to say that syringe sharing has stopped, it certainly has not, but sharing events were usually described as exceptional and occurring for a variety of untoward and unplanned situational or personal reasons (Burt and Stimson, 1990).

The picture is not the same with regard to sexual behaviour. There are some self-reported changes here – but not on the scale of those reported regarding syringe sharing. What of the hard evidence about this epidemic? Are the reported behavioural changes reflected in a changing pattern of the spread of this disease? In the case of men who have sex with men we now know that the self-reported behavioural changes that occurred in the mid-1980s have been paralleled by a reduction in sero-incidence of HIV. In the case of injecting drug users it is early to come to definitive conclusions, but there is some evidence that the epidemic is not taking off in most of England in the way it has taken off in many cities throughout the world.

Our studies show that about 50 per cent of injecting drug users have been tested for HIV antibodies. Among those recruited to our studies in London and the south-east last year and tested for HIV using the saliva test, about 4 per cent were positive (Dolan et al., 1990). The figure is on a par with data from the Public Health Laboratory Service collaborative laboratory study which showed a prevalence of 5.7 per cent in London and 1.5 per cent in the rest of England (Public Health Laboratory Service Working Group, 1989). Earlier studies in England showed rates within the same range. The high prevalence of HIV infection recorded in Edinburgh (of around 50 per cent) and the east of Scotland remains exceptional. There is supporting evidence from Public Health Laboratory Service studies that hepatitis B is declining among injectors – and because hepatitis B is transmitted in a similar way to HIV this is a good proxy indicator that behaviour changes have indeed occurred (Polakoff, 1988).

The known rates of HIV infection are low in most of the UK, apart from the east coast of Scotland. It is too soon to make the link between preventive strategies and the relatively low rates. It may be that much of the UK is still at a pre-take-off stage in the epidemic curve – that there are still insufficient people with the virus for the epidemic to gain that frightening dynamic spread that occurred in Edinburgh, New York, in Italian cities and more recently in Bangkok. On the other hand, it may be that there have been effective changes in the behaviour of many people who inject drugs.

Evidence that the epidemic may be levelling also comes from New York, Amsterdam and San Francisco, although in these cities the prevalence rate is much higher than in England. In New York the prevalence rate among injectors has levelled off at around 60 per cent, and in Amsterdam at around 30 per cent. In San Francisco, the prevalence rate has levelled off at around 12 to 15 per cent and the annual seroconversion rate has dropped to around 1 per cent (Moss, 1990). Both cities have had major AIDS risk reduction programmes.

OBSTACLES

There is reason for some optimism that it might be possible to intervene with beneficial effects. There is no reason for complacency. With HIV there is a Catch 22 situation – if things look good, governments may begin to think that less effort and fewer resources will suffice – if things look bad, resources may be forthcoming but by then it is often too late – and given the mean time between HIV infection and the diagnosis of AIDS this might be eight to ten years too late.

Despite the optimism, there are some real obstacles to future developments. The first phase of the preventive response in the UK was marked by high levels of energy and enthusiasm by many drug workers, and the rapid adoption of many innovative strategies. Moving into the second phase of our preventive response provides the opportunity to refine and develop programmes, and to look critically at what works and at what doesn't.

There are two obstacles that must lead to a review of what is being done in the UK and elsewhere. One is concerned with the resources available for services, and the second with drug injectors' drug-using practices. First the service resource obstacles. In most countries there can never be sufficient resources to offer individual services to all who may be eligible. In the United States of America the Presidential Commission on the HIV epidemic came to the conclusion that the main strategy for preventing HIV was to improve access to drug treatment and to provide treatment on demand. The Commission's own estimates are that this would require 2,500 new treatment agencies and 59,000 new treatment staff (Presidential Commission on the Human Immunodeficiency Virus, 1988). The Advisory Council on the Misuse of Drugs in its first report on AIDS and Drug Misuse (1988) made the laudable recommendation that drugs services should attract more clients. It is, however, unlikely that these services could be given adequate resources to do this task. In 1986, the Advisory Council estimated the number of injectors of notifiable drugs at between 37,500 and 75,000. On average, English drug agencies see one client per member of staff per day. If each drug injector were to come into a drug agency once every two weeks, we would need between 3,500 and 7,500 agency staff.

Some services are expensive, especially those that employ medical staff. Most drug advice and information agencies are cheaper to run than Drug Dependency Units. But even relatively low-cost programmes such as syringe exchange could not be expanded to provide adequate coverage. In the UK, to meet the needs of the estimated numbers of drug injectors, would require that case loads for the 120 existing exchanges increase to between 149 and 312 per week. Exceptionally, a syringe exchange could see numbers in the lower range. But our surveys show that syringe exchanges only see an average of twenty clients per week for syringe exchange (Lart and Stimson, 1990). The capacity is not there. Neither is it for most services currently operating in the UK. CLASH in London, a classic outreach programme, has about 500 client contacts a year – ten a week – for three or four staff. A Community Drug Team with, say, eight or ten staff will typically have a case load of 200 a year.

Whatever the programme, it is hard to imagine client-based services ever being expanded to help all the people who potentially need to be reached in an HIV-prevention strategy.

The next obstacles are found in drug injectors' drug-using practices. Among most long-term injectors there is a high level of awareness about the risks of HIV transmission, and the means to change that behaviour exist (or have improved) in many places. Why then do people continue to share syringes? It is a sociological act of faith that there are good reasons for what others view as irrational or stupid behaviour. In our qualitative research we found that syringe sharing occurred for a variety of situational and personal reasons – for example, the failure of syringe supply, the mechanical failure of a syringe, or the intoxicating effects of drugs. In another study we found that people were less likely to share syringes when they were injecting drugs at home. And in a further study, people who injected in prison were highly likely to inject with a shared syringe. Personal and social circumstances in the realm of everyday drug-using practices are all important, but the everyday factors that influence syringe sharing are well out of the reach of clinicians and drug workers.

SHARING SYRINGES AND SHARING CULTURE

How can we solve the twin problems of lack of service resources and the factors that influence drug-using practices? What is involved in helping people adopt healthy behaviours? The ability to adopt protective strategies *vis-à-vis* HIV has much in common with the ability to adopt other health protective behaviours. There are many health-promoting practices in which people regularly engage and which are integrated into their everyday lives. Personal hygiene practices – such as personal grooming and teeth cleaning – are good examples. Teeth cleaning is done by most of the population – almost without reflection. Promoting safer behaviour and healthy practices requires the knowledge about the desirability of those practices, and the means to adopt them. But it also requires personal resources and routines.

For drug injectors, the relevant knowledge is about the transmission of HIV. The relevant means to promote safer behaviour are sterile syringes, or effective means for syringe decontamination. But avoiding risky injecting practices also requires personal resources – such as a safe place to inject, a place to keep syringes or somewhere to clean syringes.

Harm minimization might therefore include the need for decent housing – using drugs at home is safer than using them in the street. Such factors also encourage, or inhibit, a life which allows for health planning and the adoption of healthy routines. It is easier to pursue healthy behaviours if they become routinized – that is, if they become part and parcel of everyday practices.

People can be helped to change through having the knowledge, means, resources and personal routines. But for people who inject drugs the routines are not only individual behaviours, but are shared with others.

Preoccupied as we have been with 'sharing' – whether in drug use or sexuality – we have yet to take on the full meaning of the term. We have focused on individual practices – the passing of a syringe from one person to another – without looking at what goes on when things are shared. As I have suggested, sharing is located in particular social and material conditions. If we wish to influence individual acts of sharing we have to influence the wider context in which that sharing occurs.

The preventive task is therefore about cultural change – about helping drug cultures to change. It cannot be done by targeting individuals for individual treatment or counselling – even though it may in part have to be done through individuals.

TOWARDS PUBLIC HEALTH AND HEALTH BEHAVIOUR

At the risk of caricature, most interventions that are being undertaken to try to help prevent HIV transmission have as their target individuals and individual behaviours. The reasons for this are found at the ideological level, and at the level of institutional sites and workplace practice. For example, in the UK most drug control measures have had an individual focus whether they are educational or treatment, and AIDS prevention has grown out of individually oriented drug advice agencies (which we have discussed elsewhere, Stimson and Lart, 1990). With their existing focus, their success will be limited by the two obstacles I have outlined – the lack of resources and the inability to reach people at the point where drugs are used.

A few interventions take a different focus. First, they are often conceived of and operate on a city- or community-wide basis (rather than at the level of an individual agency). There is a conception how all the elements of the local response fit together as a working totality, rather than existing as a number of disparate elements: the Liverpool and Amsterdam approaches are good examples. Second, they aim to enable changes in shared practices, and not just to change 'sharing behaviour'. The interventions may work through individuals, but there is a conception of how those individuals will in turn influence others. In my view, these approaches can overcome the two obstacles that have been identified.

What this suggests is the need to refocus effort to help behaviour changes within a new public health and health behaviour paradigm, in which public health helps create the conditions under which populations can lead healthy lives.

The focus now would be on enabling community and cultural change. The task would be to change cultural norms around the locus of drug use. It would sometimes be done through individuals, but the target would be other injectors who do not come into agency contact. Drug injectors would be recruited in order to help others change their behaviour.

This would lead to a rethinking of the aims of many of our current practices. For example, in the United Kingdom 'community outreach' has become a new part of the work of many drug agencies. But the term means a variety of things: it can mean agency workers engaging in peripatetic work in other agencies – for example, a drug worker going to spend some time each week in a general practitioner's surgery. It can mean reaching out to drug users in the community to bring them into contact with services. But there is a lack of a coherent sense of 'community' in much of this work done by community drug teams and other agencies. Drug services have developed on the layer of community services, but the model used is often based on casework with clients rather than being truly community focused. The rhetoric of community work may be correct – but the theory and practice are often vague.

Within a public and community health paradigm, 'outreach' and 'community' work would mean reaching out, using drug injectors or other target groups as agents of change, working through social networks to help communities change. There are some good examples of this in Liverpool, for example, using drug dealers as secondary syringe distributors and health workers. Other examples are the work of ADAPT, the bleach programmes in San Francisco, and the attempts to organize drug injectors in New York City (Friedman et al., 1990).

Another example is counselling. In a client-centred approach, counselling would seek to help individuals to change their behaviour. In a public and community health approach, the aim would be not just to influence the counselled individuals, but to enthuse those people with the need to influence others. It would entail teaching social skills in resisting risky behaviour – and would also help those people to encourage safer behaviour in others. It would entail asking them not just to refuse to share syringes, but – by offering them clean syringes to give to other people – to take the safer drug use message to others.

CONCLUSION

All drug use – whether of legitimately acquired drugs or otherwise – is, I have argued, subject to social controls that operate at a number of levels. The task for HIV prevention is the encouragement of new types of social control at the informal level of everyday drug-using practices. A public and community health approach is primarily about creating the conditions under which the social etiquette of daily drug use will change and in which new health behaviours will emerge. The aim is to put public health and health behaviour back on the map.

ACKNOWLEDGEMENTS

I am grateful to colleagues in The Centre for Research on Drugs and Health Behaviour, and in particular to Kate Dolan, Martin Donoghoe, Dr Betsy Ettorre, Dr Robert Power and Dr Brian Wells.

REFERENCES

Advisory Council at the Misue of Drugs (1988) *AIDS and Drug Misuse, Part 1*, London: HMSO.

Burt, J. and Stimson, G. V. (1990) 'Strategies for protection: Drug injecting and the prevention of HIV infection', Report to the Health Education Authority, London: Goldsmiths' College.

Dolan, K., Stimson, G. V. and Donoghoe, M. C. (1990) 'Differences in HIV rates and risk behaviour of drug injectors attending, and not attending, syringe-exchanges in England', *Sixth International Conference on AIDS, San Francisco*, Oral presentation and Abstract no. F.C.108.

Friedman, S. R., Sufian, M., Neaigus, A., Stepherson, B., Manthei, D., Des Jarlais, D. C. et al. (1990) 'Organizing IV drug users against AIDS: a comparison with outreach for producing risk reduction', *Sixth International Conference on AIDS, San Francisco*, Abstract no. S.C.733.

Lart, R. A. and Stimson, G. V. (1990) 'National survey of syringe-exchange schemes in England', *British Journal of Addiction* 85: 1433-1443.

Moss, A. R. (1990) 'Control of HIV infection in injecting drug users in San Francisco', in J. Strang and G. V. Stimson (eds) *AIDS and Drug Misuse*, London: Routledge.

Polakoff, S. (1988) 'Decrease in acute hepatitis B continued in 1987', *Lancet* 540.

Presidential Commission on the Human Immunodeficiency Virus Epidemic (1988) Report, Washington.

Public Health Laboratory Service Working Group (1989) 'Prevalence of HIV antibody in high- and low-risk groups in England', *British Medical Journal* 298: 422-3.

Stimson, G. V. and Lart, R. (1991) 'HIV, drugs and public health in England: New words, old tunes', *International Journal of the Addictions* (forthcoming).

Chapter 5

Beyond the prohibition of heroin
The development of a controlled
availability policy in Australia

Alex Wodak

REVIVAL OF A DRUG POLICY

In a matter of a few years, the issue of legalization of heroin has changed in Australia from a cause promoted by fringe groups to a campaign espoused by some of the most eminent and distinguished members of our community. The issue has found surprising supporters in recent years. In 1984, the then New South Wales Opposition leader, Mr N. Greiner, said:

> If we can bring these drug-addicted people away from having to commit crime to get the money to pay their pusher – that would mean a drop in crime. If we can wean them off the drugs in a controlled system then we are winning. If the demand is not there, the drug bosses have no-one to supply.
>
> (*Sydney Sun-Herald*)

These views have subsequently been echoed in Australia by, among others, Mr John Gorton, a former Prime Minister, and Mr Don Dunstan, a former State Premier.

It is important that we consider why this sudden interest in a previously taboo notion has arisen. One of the major factors is an increasing recognition of the high cost of restricting the supply of illicit drugs and a new awareness of the limited effectiveness of such efforts. It is generally appreciated that further intensification of law enforcement strategies will require increasing infringement of civil liberties which are already stretched close to the limits of community tolerance. The possibility that the apparent increase in corruption of the criminal justice system and among senior government officials in Australia in recent years is related to current drug policy is a conclusion drawn by many, including Royal Commissioners. But above all it is the issue of

HIV infection which has led to recent calls for a fresh examination of our national drug policies.

LINKS BETWEEN THE DRUG POLICY AND HIV INFECTION

The potential link between AIDS and the drug policy deserves careful consideration in view of the paramount need to contain HIV infection in injecting drug users (IDUs). The most likely source of HIV infection for non-drug-using heterosexuals in most Western countries is sexual contact with an IDU. The inexorable spread of the virus responsible for AIDS (HIV) in IDUs around the world is an alarming development. Within Europe as a whole it has been anticipated that there will be more injecting drug users among newly diagnosed cases of AIDS than any other risk group including homosexuals. In New York City in 1988, IDUs became the major AIDS risk group overtaking homosexual/bisexual males for the first time. By 1993, 50 per cent of all new AIDS cases in New York City will be injecting drug users with homosexual/bisexual males accounting for 33 per cent of new cases. HIV infection in IDUs is now also appearing in Eastern Europe (Poland), South East Asia (Thailand, Myanmar, India and China), South America (Brazil and Argentina) and the Caribbean.

The spread of HIV infection in IDUs in Australia must be regarded sadly as both inevitable and imminent. The most realistic national goal is to delay and minimize this development.

Policy on the spread of HIV infection must be based on our worst fears rather than our best hopes. We are entitled to hope that a vaccine against HIV will become available. But we must acknowledge the fact that many experts in this field are very pessimistic about the likelihood of ever achieving this development. A vaccine is required which must be effective against a rapidly mutating retro-virus which shares many features with other viruses against which no vaccine has been prepared previously. Experience with the development of simpler vaccines and their actual utilization in practice instructs us to be realistic about the difficulties of immunizing adults on a mass scale and accordingly modest in our expectations. The cost and logistical difficulties of deploying a vaccine against HIV are likely to be substantial. Similarly, although we can be grateful for the rapid advances in the treatment of HIV infections, it would be foolish to ignore the fact that treatment at present is still very expensive, does not return a significant proportion of treated patients to employment and probably does not reduce the risk of further HIV transmission.

It is therefore imperative that close attention is given to all efforts which offer promise in preventing the further spread of HIV infection in the critical population of IDUs. Australia already has a very substantial case load of AIDS by international comparison with the sixth highest per capita incidence of AIDS of all OECD countries. Australia is one of the few Western countries with a high incidence of AIDS but a still very low rate of HIV infection in IDUs. Full advantage must be made of this extraordinary opportunity. If the price for controlling HIV infection in IDUs requires drug policy reform, it is a price worth paying.

Containing the spread of HIV infection in IDUs

What is the role of drug policy in containing the spread of HIV infection in IDUs? The following factors deserve careful consideration:

1 In Australia, drug users inject rather than smoke or swallow drugs. This is principally because street drugs are expensive and impure. Injecting expensive, impure drugs achieves maximum 'bang for the buck'. Experience has shown that where street drugs are cheap and pure, users will often inhale or swallow drugs. Current drug policies are evaluated by their success in keeping street drugs expensive and impure. It must be acknowledged that we have little knowledge about the reversibility of drug injecting following policy liberalization although there is reasonable evidence that drug injecting becomes more likely following policy intensification. In order to stem the spread of HIV infection in IDUs, we should ensure that street drugs are cheap and of high purity to minimize the chance of drug injecting with the attendant risk of HIV transmission. Attempts to discourage users from injecting drugs should have the highest priority in drug policy. From a health view point, smoking or swallowing street drugs is preferable to injecting, which always carries the risk of needle sharing and the subsequent development of HIV infection. The extent of drug injection with associated needle sharing is, therefore, partly determined by drug policy.

2 One of the major factors in the sharing of used needles and syringes, and the consequent spread of HIV infection, is the unavailability of sterile injection equipment. In Australia at present there are an estimated 30,000 to 100,000 IDUs injecting anywhere between one and four times a day. This means there may be approximately forty to sixty million individual acts of injections of street drugs in Australia each year. Currently two to three million sterile needles

and syringes are provided by authorities in Australia annually to reduce the spread of HIV infection. It is questionable that this level of implementation can be regarded as sufficient to reduce the spread of HIV infection in IDUs in the long term. Although cost and logistical problems are important factors in slowing the expansion of the needle and syringe exchange programmes, drug policies have also been an obstacle. Drug policies in Australia have resulted in the retention of legislation concerning needles and syringes which discourages IDUs from utilizing the needle and syringe exchanges and from responsibly disposing of used injection equipment. As a result, used equipment is discarded in streets, parks and beaches and public support for the critical strategy of sterile needle and syringe exchange and distribution has declined.

3 A number of studies have shown that drug treatment reduces the risk of HIV infection in IDUs. Therefore, it is likely that HIV spread among IDUs could be reduced by increasing the proportion of drug users who are in treatment. Treatment must be adapted so that it is far more attractive to IDUs, which will require some liberalization of drug policy. The objective of containing the spread of HIV infection in IDUs must be accepted as the paramount consideration.

4 Sharing of needles and syringes and unprotected anal intercourse are common in prisons, although it is difficult to determine their frequency. There is little evidence at present to support the widespread fear that substantial HIV infection occurs in prisons. This lack of evidence may be due to the fact that few relevant studies have been performed. Studies of this kind are very difficult. The harsh conditions of US prisons mean that the few existing studies, which are American, may not apply in Australia. We must assume that substantial HIV infection does occur in prisons although we can still hope that this is not the case. If we wish to reduce the number of IDUs at risk of HIV infection in prisons, every effort must be made to divert prisoners convicted only of drug related offences from prisons to non-custodial forms of sentencing. This requires liberalization of drug policy.

5 At present, efforts to educate or otherwise modify the behaviour of IDUs is made even more difficult because the target population is ostracized and marginalized. Liberalization of drug policy will help to bring IDUs in to mainstream society so that education has a greater chance of modifying behaviour.

AIDS is not the only consideration for a national drug policy. But developing a drug policy without due consideration of HIV infection would be an act of negligence. Many options lie between the choice of retention of current policies or the legalization of all drugs. These options need to be developed so that credible alternatives are available for consideration. Australia has much more to learn about the contemporary experience in countries like the Netherlands, Switzerland and Denmark where more liberal policies have been implemented. The relative emphasis accorded to the strategies of reducing the supply of drugs, reducing the demand for drugs and treatment need to be reviewed in the era of HIV.

A number of different approaches to reducing the supply of drugs has been attempted. We need to decide which of these strategies deserve support and what level of support is required.

A 'drug free Australia' is not an achievable goal. So far, the notion of a 'drug free Australia' has scarcely been considered, even as an option.

The success or failure of control of HIV infection in the third wave of the AIDS epidemic in Australia – i.e. in the non-drug-using heterosexual community – will depend on the success or failure of efforts to control the second wave of the epidemic – i.e. IDUs. Just as IDUs are central in our efforts to delay and minimize the spread of HIV infection in the general community, so too is drug policy central to our efforts to stem the spread of HIV infection in IDUs.

THE OPTIONS FOR DRUG POLICY

The South Australia Royal Commission into the Non-Medical Use of Drugs (1979) set out five possible policy options for cannabis which can equally be applied to other illicit or even licit drugs. The first option is Total Prohibition, whereby the use, possession, cultivation and sale of drugs are all prohibited and regarded as a criminal offence. The second option is Modified Total Prohibition which is colloquially referred to as 'decriminalization'. Personal use, possession and cultivation for personal use are defined as illegal but only attract a nominal fine. Supply is regarded as a criminal offence but the minimum quantity can be varied. The third policy option is that of Partial Prohibition. In this option, personal use and personal cultivation are not considered to be offences. However, public use, commercial cultivation and sale remain illegal and are subject to a set of sliding scale fines. The fourth option is a User Licence System whereby some form of controlled use is permitted following the issue of a licence or registration. The fifth option is Free Availability commonly called 'legalization' where there are minimal or no restrictions on availability.

THE AIM OF AUSTRALIAN DRUG POLICIES

The objectives of Australia's drug policies were clearly set out at the Special Premier's Conference (colloquially known as 'the National Drug Summit') held on 2 April 1985 and attended by the Prime Minister and all State Premiers. The meeting concluded that the aim of Australia's drug policy 'is to minimize the harmful effects of drugs on Australian society' (Department of Health, 1985). The selection of the most appropriate drug policy for each particular drug should be based on a desire to maximize costs. As there is generally considered to be little benefit *per se* in a drug policy other than the minimization of harm, the cost to the individual drug user and society for each policy option for each drug is the major consideration. Although the benefits of illicit drug use are rarely considered, it is inconceivable that drug users would risk losing health, children, family and liberty if there were no benefits. Clearly it is time to admit that drug users get a great deal of pleasure from using the drugs of their choice – at least in the short term.

Drug use results in health, social and economic costs which have increased in many Western countries in recent years. Health problems associated with illicit and legal drug use cover a diverse range of physical and psychological sequelae. In Australia, AIDS accounts for only a small fraction of the health costs associated with illicit drug use at present, but may in time dwarf all other health costs associated with drug use, possibly eventually outstripping the enormous problems consequent on alcohol use. The infringement of privacy and corruption of senior public officials in the police force, judiciary and politics must be considered products of drug policies designed to reduce drug use rather than the inevitable pharmacological consequences of illicit psychoactive substances.

One of the rarely considered costs of law enforcement is the criminalization of offenders and consequent disrespect for the law arising from the fact that only a small percentage of offenders are ever apprehended. Another largely neglected cost of our present drug policies is the diversion of law enforcement resources from more important tasks. A rarely mentioned cost of our current drug policies is the extent to which international terrorist movements (such as the Shining Path movement in Peru) benefit from or depend entirely on profits from international narcotics trafficking.

THE BASIS OF SUPPLY REDUCTION

The fundamental assumption of policies designed to limit supply is that reducing drug use will reduce harm. Even if it is assumed that less drug use occurs (because of the increasing cost to the would-be-user in financial, health and legal penalties), it is by no means clear that supply reduction policies will necessarily result in less drug-related harm either to individuals or the community. This will only occur if supply reduction policies reduce consumption to a greater degree than they raise the costs of drug use.

It may be that more liberal drug policies will result in an increase in drug consumption, but this must remain an assumption until we have more evidence. Even if drug consumption does increase following liberalization of drug policy, the health, financial and legal costs to the user and the community may still fall as these are at present largely consequent on the drugs being illegal in the first place.

Heroin is a relatively non-toxic drug with almost all of the present mortality and morbidity resulting from overdoses or from chemical or microbiological contaminants. Overdoses are largely a result of uncertainty about dose which, in turn, is a consequence of the illegal status of drugs. Chemical and microbiological contamination is caused by adulteration of the drugs as they pass through the illicit distribution system. The problems of overdose and adulteration should therefore be seen as a direct result of the illegality of the drugs rather than as a consequence of their pharmacology. The spread of HIV infection among intravenous drug users may now be added to the list of health problems resulting from attempts to decrease illicit drug consumption.

Another circular aspect of our policy on illicit drugs is the effect of supply reduction on price. It has been noted that

the success of law enforcement in maintaining high prices is also its Achilles heel, creating entrepreneurs whom the law seeks to discourage by enforcement of the very laws which created profitable markets and attracted the entrepreneurs in the first place. Catch 22 if ever there was one.

(Wisotsky, 1986)

If our current drug policy is successful in suppressing supply by increasing the retail costs of illicit drugs, it can only do so by increasing the risk of arrest, prosecution and punishment. However, it also follows that if costs are increased, so too are profits, thereby attracting entrepreneurs to drug trafficking. In the long term, the volume of illicit drug trafficking may paradoxically be increased by more stringent enforcement of supply reduction policies. Although enforcement of supply reduction policies appears to reduce the availability of drugs in the short term, in the long term it is quite conceivable that existing drug policies increase the supply of drugs by making drug trafficking more lucrative.

ABOLISHING EVIL

It must be acknowledged that most drug-related problems at present are secondary to drug policy and are not a product of the intrinsic pharmacological properties of illicit psychoactive substances. Although no set of drug policies will ever eliminate drug use or drug-related harm, alternative drug policy options could possibly result in less harm than existing policies. Whether the costs and benefits of existing drug policies are greater or less than the costs and benefits of alternative drug policy options cannot be known for certain at present. The central weakness of the current debate on legalization is the fact that credible alternatives to current policies have not been sufficiently thought through so that their strengths and weaknesses can be adequately assessed and compared to existing policies. It is difficult to envisage that future research will entirely illuminate this area. Decisions will need to be based on a balance of probabilities and consideration of comparable experiences. The introduction of methadone maintenance over twenty years ago represented a major drug policy shift which is worthy of review in relation to the current drug policy impasse.

Methadone is now legally provided to over 8,000 drug-dependent persons in six of eight Australian jurisdictions. No contradiction is seen in allowing this particular opiate to find its way legally into the bloodstream of some drug-dependent citizens, while other opiates are not permitted. In the sense that methadone was first provided to known drug-dependent persons in Australia in 1969, the legalization of illicit drugs in Australia can be considered to have commenced over twenty years ago. The experience with methadone in Australia resembles that of many other Western countries. It is the most attractive treatment option for the majority of IDUs. Retention in methadone treatment is far higher than other treatment modalities. The widespread support for methadone in the community and from politicians in Australia may be an indication of the possibility of more flexible attitudes than is often supposed.

THE COST-EFFECTIVENESS OF SUPPLY REDUCTION

Increased funding for strengthened enforcement of drug policies is now being provided in Australia and overseas despite the otherwise remarkable restraint in government expenditure. At a time when all other sacred cows of government expenditure are subjected to rigorous scrutiny, resources for supply reduction have so far survived unscathed and have even been increased. However, scholarly reviews by authorities do not inspire confidence in this method of reducing drug use or drug problems. Polich concluded an examination of the U.S. situation noting 'that more intense law enforcement is not likely to substantially affect either the availability or the retail price of drugs in this country'. He added that 'nevertheless, the answer to adolescent drug use does not seem to lie with increased law enforcement' (Polich *et al.*, 1984). Reuter arrived at similar conclusions stating that :

> one cannot say that we should be spending more or less on drug enforcement overall without making assumptions about the alternative use of these funds unless it appears that some spending is either futile or likely to generate unwanted side effects of greater magnitude than its benefits.

(Reuter and Kleiman, 1986)

The curious assumption that if heroin is legalized it will inevitably be promoted is contradicted by everyday experience. For example, gelignite and other explosive substances can be legally bought and sold in Australia but cannot be promoted or advertised. There is no universal law which automatically requires advertising of any product which is legally available.

Prescription of 'take away' drugs for intravenous application by the user would be a major departure from current medical practice. Undoubtedly, changes in drugs policy will have major implications for medical practice that need to be anticipated. However, intravenous morphine, cocaine and amphetamines have been made available legally in the past in the United States and are legally available currently in parts of the United Kingdom. The consequences of a change in policy for medical practice are not a reason to reject 'legalization' but rather emphasize the importance of cautious surveillance of medical practitioners in any liberalized drug policy.

The suggestion that the federal nature of the Australian Commonwealth requires that all states (and territories) must maintain similar policies is contradicted by present-day experience with cannabis. Victoria, South Australia and the Australian Capital Territory have all recently liberalized policies on cannabis. This does not appear to have resulted in these jurisdictions becoming the 'drug capitals of Australia'. Differences in policies regarding the availability of treatment services, specifically methadone treatment, resulted in significant movement of patients between Queensland and New South Wales within the last decade. Therefore, it is reasonable to assume that this consideration is a relative factor but not an absolute consideration.

OPERATIONAL CONSIDERATIONS

Even if heroin were to be 'legalized' it is unlikely that the community would ever countenance unrestricted availability. If there is to be a change in Australian drug policy, it is likely that in the first instance government clinics will be the major outlets. Presumably, criteria for selection and exclusion will be developed similar to those which have been established for methadone.

It has been suggested that if certain people are to be refused heroin, there will be nothing to prevent their seeking to 'qualify' to receive it by intensifying their criminal involvement or increasing their dose. This consideration is also a problem for present-day methadone maintenance programmes. It has not, however, prevented the establishment or steady expansion of methadone programmes. Selection of suitable patients is still one of the many difficulties of clinical methadone management. But the real question which has to be answered is: Should the presence of some minor clinical difficulties in the operation of substitution treatment programmes involving drugs other than methadone prevent their establishment even if there are other perceived benefits?

Some argue that if heroin is legalized to undercut the black market, then all drugs will have to be legalized and made available to anyone seeking them. Consumption of illicit drugs in one country or city is not necessarily followed by the consumption of the same drugs in adjacent cities or countries. Canada and the United States share a long land border and, presumably, traffic of illicit drugs across this border would be relatively simple. Yet there are vast differences in the consumption of illicit drugs on both sides of this border. As discussed above, the decriminalization of cannabis in some Australian states does not seem to have led to a discernible population shift. And even if, after the introduction of controlled availability of heroin, it was decided to extend the policy to other drugs, the question is not whether this would be a 'good' or a 'bad' thing, but whether this would be a lesser evil than the current system.

Currently, heroin of unknown concentration, adulterated with every imaginable and dangerous impurity, is readily available to anyone of any age with sufficient cash throughout Australia twenty-four hours a day, without supervision, on a take-home basis and at high cost to user and the community alike. The present system must be compared with an alternative whereby pure heroin and other drugs of known concentration and purity are carefully provided to selected users with the possibility that some diversion will also regrettably occur. Which scheme is preferable – the status quo or controlled availability?

At present, Australia imports an estimated 1,000 kg of illegal heroin per year of which 5–10 per cent is intercepted. This leaves 900–950 kg of illegal heroin left to supply the illicit market. If an additional 50 kg of licit heroin were to be diverted to the illicit market to add to the 900–950 kg illegally distributed, would this be an unmitigated evil, especially if a benefit was achieved in improving the health of drug users, reducing corruption, reducing the spread of HIV infection, and reducing law enforcement costs?

The 'appropriate dose' of heroin is determined at present by drug users buying an uncertain quantity of unknown concentration of illicit drugs of unknown purity. If the consumer stops breathing following injection of heroin, then the 'appropriate dose' has been exceeded. If the consumer does not feel an adequate effect from the product, a further sample is consumed. Which system is to be preferred? A clinical system with some inherent uncertainty or an illegal system which is totally uncontrolled and unsupervised? Presumably, there will be some individuals who will continue to consume heroin for their lifetime if this option is made available through legal channels, just as there are presumably some individuals who wish to use illegal heroin throughout their lifetime. Again the question is whether it is preferable for a person to obtain contaminated heroin of unknown concentration through illegal channels over which the government has no control, or pure samples of known concentration through a government-sponsored clinic?

MORE OBSTACLES TO DRUG POLICY REFORM

Proceeding from a set of familiar but apparently ineffective policies to an alternative set of options which might be more effective is not an easy matter. In the case of drug policy reform, alternative options are generally considered to lack credibility. In part, this displays a lack of awareness of the historical experience of controlled availability in the United States, the United Kingdom and, more recently, with contemporary experience in some European countries. In part, there are legitimate concerns regarding appropriate safeguards and regulations to ensure that legal, pharmaceutical and medical practice remains reputable. Drug policy reformers have an obligation to develop these areas so that the potential costs and benefits of alternative options can be compared against existing policy.

International considerations also represent an obstacle to drug policy reform. Although it is often considered that commitment to international treaties may prevent any experimentation with controlled availability of illicit drugs, it is by no means certain that this is the case. In fact, the Single Treaty, to which Australia is a signatory, permits the controlled dispensing of specified substances (including heroin) under medical supervision.

A series of false comparisons and misunderstandings have also obstructed adequate consideration of drug policy reform. Controlled availability of illicit drugs is often interpreted as unfettered availability and compared by critics to a halcyon state where illicit drugs are unknown. Confusion also often arises because of the inappropriate comparison with legal drug availability. In the case of the legal drugs alcohol and tobacco, the correlation between the risk of negative consequences and quantity ingested holds good for both individuals and communities. The effects of a reduction in the intensity of law enforcement policies on illicit drug use is unknown. But even if consumption of these drugs was to increase following a relaxation of policies, it is conceivable that drug-related problems would still decline as these are more closely linked to supply reduction policies than to intrinsic pharmacological toxicity.

THE TIMING OF CHANGE

The rapid and widespread adoption in Australia of pragmatic HIV prevention policies, including sterile injection equipment programmes and changes to methadone programmes, has stimulated a lively debate on drug policies. Although initially opposed to a debate on drug policy, the Commonwealth Minister for Health acknowledged publicly in late 1989 his support for a vigorous public discussion of drug policies.

As economic considerations are now pre-eminent in most policy areas in Australia, it is likely that the final decisions on drug policy will be made by accountants and not by advocates for public health.

It would be misleading to describe the debate in Australia in the early 1990s as having reached the 'pre-contemplation level'. On the other hand, it is undeniable that there has been a major shift in public opinion as demonstrated by opinion polls. Australia's relative isolation has not been sufficient to prevent drug trafficking but may be enough to allow the drug policy debate to be resolved earlier than in many other countries.

REFERENCES

Department of Health (1985) *National Campaign Against Drug Abuse*, Canberra: Australian Government Publishing Service.

Greiner, N. (1984) *Sydney Sun-Herald* (10 June).

Polich, J. M., Ellickson, P. L., Teuter, P. and Kahan, J. P. (1984) *Strategies for Controlling Adolescent Drug Use*, Rand Corporation.

Reuter, P. and Kleiman, M. A. R. (1986) 'Risks and prices: an economic analysis of drug enforcement', in M. Tonny and N. Morris (eds) *Crime and Justice, An Annual Review of Research*, Vol 7.

South Australia Royal Commission into the Non-Medical Use of Drugs (1979) Final Report (Professor Sackville, Chairman), Adelaide: The Commission.

Wisotsky, S. (1986) *Breaking the Impasse in the War on Drugs*, New York: Greenwood Press.

© 1991 Alex Wodak

Chapter 6

International law
The final solution?

Simon Davies

The quest for a solution to the drug problem has evolved into what can only be described as a poorly but passionately defined debate between supply reduction and demand reduction. Both poles compete spiritedly for public support and public funding. And while each side spouts platitudes about the need for balance, the end result, inevitably, is a humiliating fracas in which truth and dignity are stretched to the limit.

Throughout this unfortunate battle for drug policy supremacy, the more credible arm of the demand reduction lobby focused its attention on science, logic and reason. It sought answers through pragmatism and scientific enquiry. It implored humanity and common sense. And it lost the war.

Over the last twenty years, while well-meaning professionals bickered over the definition of harm reduction policy, a massive chain-reaction of events was setting the world irrevocably on its present path to global prohibition. While educators, rehabilitation experts and normalization advocates fought over crumbs from the local or national funding cake, the prohibition lobby – whose philosophy was far better defined and far less parochial – were influencing the development of embryonic international law.

Now, as the world enters the final phase of universal regulation, most demand reductionists still carry on the old game, oblivious that the rules have all changed. Domestic drug policy is now an integral part of a much wider international arrangement. Sovereign policy is, in a legal and tangible sense, less possible now than at any time in history. A reformist drug policy may now no longer be possible.

This chapter is a very brief attempt to outline the events leading up to this new international situation, and the extraordinary impact that it will exert on the domestic drug policy of all nations.

The creation of a global community has been made more feasible in the twentieth century largely because the pace and nature of technological developments in transport, communications, and data processing have allowed economic and trade relations to occur with speed, precision and accountability. The technology was affordable, widely available and relatively easy to master. Of equal importance was the nature of this new technology, which meant that major and complex international arrangements could be conducted without the establishment of obvious cultural supremacy. All the events of significance happened discreetly and with a degree of subtlety. As communications technology expanded through the twentieth century at a hyperbolic pace, economic relations between nations developed like Topsy. In its wake, a plethora of international laws sprang up, representing global interest in a vast array of issues.

Following the turbulence of the 1939–45 war, many of the world's nations set their sights on the creation of a formal infrastructure to deal with many emerging international issues. In years to come some people came to know this vision as the Global Village. Others knew the scheme more conspiratorially as the 'New World Order'.

By whatever name it was known, this new attempt to harmonize the international community succeeded in establishing a real impact on the relations between countries. The new United Nations, through an astoundingly complex web of conventions and treaties, obliged much of the international community to apply a range of protocols, accords, proclamations, standards and agreements. Many of these obligations were ultimately translated into domestic law. The external affairs powers of some national constitutions allowed the direct incorporation of international treaties into sovereign law. This all took place with little public debate or awareness, despite the fact that it occurred outside the usual democratic process.

The conventions grew by the thousands throughout the 1960s and 1970s. And they covered virtually every aspect of human activity. By the mid-1980s, these various conventions had created a legislative net that influenced sovereign decision-making in all principal aspects of the economy, trade, cultural relations, the environment and human rights.

The formal process of harmonization established by the United Nations is bolstered by an extensive (though not necessarily interlinked) mass of other international organisations, ranging from the 'International Commission of the Cape Spartel Light' to the 'Central Bureau of the International Map of the World on the Millionth Scale'. These groups are represented, in turn, by the 'International Union of International Associations'.

But international organizations are subject to a far greater gravity –
that of international organization. International organization is a
process, a formula, a philosophy, that by its very nature throws up
structures. International organization is a fundamental approach to
dealing with and seeing the world and its development (Claude, 1964).
It is a way of seeing that will determine the future of drug policy for
virtually all the world's nations.

This process is not new. It has been developing on and off for more
than two thousand years. Every time the Roman, Ottoman or British
empires exported another reform to an alien culture, another brick was
laid in the foundation of an entirely new and synthetic legislative net.

But now, as we enter the 1990s, the New World Order has reached
a handsome adolescence. In the first year of the decade the strength of
the Global Village was tested on two issues: the Gulf Crisis, and the war
on drugs – both with substantial success. It can be argued that the
mobilization of global opposition to Saddam Hussein, President of Iraq,
came about as much as anything by happy coincidence. The same
cannot be said of the growing success in creating universal support for a
war on drugs. That victory is being achieved as a result of a far greater
precision and planning.

The downside of global drug mobilization is that virtually all the
international unification concentrates on supply reduction. While well-
meaning professionals in the harm reduction and demand reduction
professions go about the business of seeking real answers at a human
level, a massive amalgamation of interests at an international level are
determining the real fate of world drug policy. While drug professionals
see the solution in very precise and specific terms, the supply
reductionists view the problem more and more in the way communism
was widely seen ten years ago – supra-national, supra-disciplinary, and
beyond definition.

If there is any reason why the widespread adoption of rational drug
policy is less and less likely, it is because drug professionals tend to be
reductionist and analytical, while their antagonists in law and order
operate on the basis of motherhood positions.

If any event stands testimony to this unfortunate dichotomy, it can
be seen in the recent 'World Ministerial Summit to Reduce the
Demand for Drugs and to Combat the Cocaine Threat', held in
London in April 1990.

The conference, comprising senior government representatives from
130 countries, divided into two committees – one for demand reduction,
and the other for cocaine elimination. From the outset it became clear

that demand reduction would lose out. To start with, the demand reduction committee adopted an 'informal' structure; a fatal decision, particularly when their sister committee made no such declaration.

The demand reduction committee produced a series of resolutions similar in nature to countless committees that preceded them. The committee agreed that the problem was complex. It agreed that solution would not be found in the actions of governments alone. Nor would they be found in the actions of individual nations. In a word, the chairman's statement said nothing new and proposed nothing of substance.

The statement of the cocaine committee, on the other hand, was entirely sexy. It made exhilarating reading. Rather than adopting an 'informal' approach, the committee members had clearly decided from the outset to agree on a precise position. Accordingly, the resolutions were framed in specific terms. They proposed a definite schedule of action with regard to UN Conventions. Members of the conference could thus take something home with them.

It should hardly come as a surprise that the result was thus. Although the preamble to the conference spoke altruistically about 'balance' between demand and supply reduction, the final communique from the conference came down squarely on the side of supply reduction. It described the international drug problem as a 'plague', and described with great colour the new UN Convention against narcotics as a 'vital weapon against those who ply the drug traffickers' evil trade'. Such imagery, implying that certain drugs and drug traffickers are somehow innately evil, has provided the fuel for prohibition for centuries (Szasz, 1975).

Margaret Thatcher created quite a coup by organising this conference. She succeeded in elevating drugs to the status of a first level international bartering chip. There are very few such chips. Defence support, monetary assistance, trade pacts, telecommunications and postal liaison are among the few that exist on a universal scale.

International conventions fall vaguely into two categories: those which are supported by all, or nearly all, nations (such as postal arrangements), and those which are supported, for whatever reason, only by countries with a common interest (such as conventions on monetary arrangements). Until the Thatcher conference, international drug strategy, controversial as it was, still remained squarely in the upper echelons of the second category along with terrorist control and environmental law. Now, the message has clearly been transmitted that the drug war is about to be elevated to the universal status of such conventions as shipping, postal services and telecommunications. Like the conventions applying to the Law of the Sea, which took many years to establish, the war on drugs will now embrace a significant element of reciprocity between nations.

This shift in the status of drugs is critical to international relations. It means that compliance with the drug war is a fundamental component in the relations between countries. This new arrangement means that countries which fail to comply with the status quo are likely to be excluded from other international monetary and trade agreements.

It is with this gloomy backdrop that we should now turn to the 1988 United Nations Convention Against Illicit Traffic in Narcotic Drugs and Psychotropic Substances.

The 1988 Convention, which was adopted unanimously by the Thatcher conference, supersedes the 1972 convention in several important respects. The 1988 arrangements are far more specific and demanding. They require compliance with extradition and with freezing the assets of drug criminals. They go at least part of the way to requiring minimum sentencing. More important than all these is the requirement of the Convention that signatory states maintain a state of criminalization over the lengthy and growing list of substances listed in the annexures of the document.

This development takes on a more substantial dimension if you consider for a moment the number of countries which are moving into a 'democratic' phase, and which are signatories to many of the UN Conventions. Their embryonic legal systems will be influenced as much by international agreements as the extremities of the British Empire were influenced by the Westminster system of government. The pattern is consistent. Watch over the next few years how the more Westernized of the Eastern European nations, as they become members of the Council of Europe, will become influenced by the structure and directives of the European Commission.

All this means that the war on drugs can only intensify and broaden in the coming years. Moreover, it can only be argued convincingly that the international strategies against illicit drugs may replace some initiatives by the West to defeat communism. Whether by coincidence or conspiracy, there is little doubt that the focus of drug strategy initiatives by a growing number of Western nations has taken a military perspective. Through direct pressure from President Bush and Dick Cheney, the US military has been placed on a tangible war footing in Central and Latin America. The imminent merging of the NATO and Warsaw Pact nations means that Western military and intelligence forces might need to find other useful targets. With the war on drugs elevated to a primary bartering position, the UN might effectively approve military action against countries which contribute to the trade in drugs.

As if these circumstances were not sobering enough, consider the following scenario.

During the 1970s, the West embraced a rosy view of the world's future. Population and family planning programmes were in place. Agricultural reform was proceeding on target, and economic growth in many developing nations had surpassed expectations. It took less than ten years for the optimism to fall flat on its face. Fertility programmes in India collapsed. Population control programmes in China were revised upward. Meanwhile, in Africa, family planning never even got off the ground.

The crops failed. Grain production during the 1980s actually fell in half the developing nations. In 1988, the grain harvest of North America failed, causing a massive drop in the world grain reserves.

Now the world's population is rising sharply – by more than ninety million a year (more than the entire population of Scandinavia, Belgium and Great Britain). Within forty years, there will be twice as many people living on this planet, eating three times as much food and consuming four times as much energy (Harrison, 1990).

How will these people live? From present calculations, many will survive precariously in polluted, cluttered and underdeveloped Third World cities. Places like Mexico City, which by the end of this century will have a population of 25 million – one-third of them under the age of ten. The UN estimates that places such as this will need to improve their infrastructure by 65 per cent in the next ten years just to maintain present conditions.

Forests will be cleared to make way for the expanding population. Currently, an area the size of Austria is mowed down each year for this reason. Water supplies will diminish. It is predicted that within ten years, Egypt will be able to supply less than half a bucket of water per day for each person. By 2025, Third World countries alone will be churning out three times more carbon dioxide per year than the whole world does now (United Nations, 1990).

This sad but seemingly unrelated set of events will bear a direct consequence for international drug policy. First, many developing nations which currently have embryonic drug problems are likely to agree to (or push for) hard line drug strategies in return for concessions on such matters as environmental and population controls. It is at this level that drugs become a bartering chip. The bargaining may occur at a bi- or trilateral level, but under the aegis of the international anti-drug conventions, the effect will nonetheless be the same as if these narrower deals were an across-the-board global arrangement.

There is a second strong connection between this impending population, environmental and resources crisis, and the likelihood of an increasingly hard line drug strategy by the international community. The United Nations, like many of its member states, is turning more to economic rationalism in an attempt to overcome complex problems. Within the process of conservative economics, anything that exists outside the conventional formula (that is, the grey or black economies) is considered a threat to the stability and growth of the economy as a whole. This purely economic view provides a hard and tangible edge of the war on drugs. It expedites the seizure of money and assets of drug criminals and provides justification for the wholesale destruction of underworld economies. Moreover, an economic rationalization allows the widespread intrusion into domestic affairs of countries which, for whatever reason, are singled out as contributing to the drug economy. Whatever its other merits, such a well-defined economic view provides an articulate justification for blind prejudice.

The view of the economic rationalists is likely to find more favour as economies grow towards union, and as the share of corporate foreign investment expands. The growth of foreign investment among all countries is slowly eroding sovereign economies, and is thus providing a much sharper and more real focus for international economic policy (*The Economist*, 1990).

There is, of course, a remote possibility that the international community could take the other path. They might go against the grain established in the past, and adopt the view that in an era of diminished resources, the world simply cannot become obsessed with a matter as trivial as drug consumption. It seems more likely, however, that the view of the rationalists will prevail, convincing nations that monetary growth, tax revenues and productivity are being sacrificed.

Ironically, other less conventional economic studies have shown that current drug control strategies impose significant costs and barriers to an economy (Marks, 1989; Cleeland Report, 1989). Such reports, however, invariably publicize the authors' conviction that prohibitionary policies are not necessarily the cornerstone of social policy. They are therefore rejected out of hand by the establishment.

But despite the dubious claims of rational economic theorists to represent a real picture of the negative impact of liberal drug policies, conservative calculations conveniently omit several key factors. One of these is the growing problem of sharing injecting equipment in the transmission of HIV, and the health consequences of a prohibitionary approach. The experience of the New York health care system is eloquent testimony to the economic disaster that can be wrought on the public sector when the third wave crashes. Similar problems are being experienced the world over, in places as culturally remote as Bangkok and Edinburgh. The relationship between prohibitionary drug policies and the spread of AIDS has been all but ignored by conventional drug policies economists.

~ The Thatcher conference affirmed the necessity of bringing intravenous drug users into contact with health care and treatment facilities to minimize the spread of AIDS. In the same breath, however, the conference communiqué rejected out of hand the legalization of 'unauthorized or uncontrolled' supply or possession of narcotic drugs. In reaffirming the UN treaties, the Thatcher conference had again closed off intelligent consideration of harm minimization or normalization strategies.

As with so many conferences at this level, there existed an atmosphere of warm mutual support – an environment in which all past international conventions were taken as absolute. At no point were the presumptions and principles of the UN Conventions called into question. Not one article. Not one word. It is against this background of global action that we should scrutinize the worthy efforts of the harm minimization lobby.

The harm minimization sector has developed a focus that could only be described as the precise reverse of the focus being adopted by the prohibition lobby. Each passing year, the drug helping profession becomes more local, more autonomous, and more clearly focused by industry and discipline. Each year the harm reduction sector strives for greater democracy and accountability. They seek cooperation rather than confrontation. They seek the reasonable middle ground – even worse – for consensus. And worst of all, the drug helping profession is almost entirely reliant on recurrent governmental support. They are held hostage to their funding bodies. The prohibition lobby, on the other hand, has no such pretensions or restraints. They can operate on imagery, on mysticism, and on a variety of well-executed motherhood positions. The law and order lobby can achieve funding on the basis of what they have not achieved. They can obtain public support on a foundation of fear rather than logic.

Drug helping professionals have not learnt that logic is a more or less useless weapon against the machinations of the global position. We have, for instance, adequate evidence that intensification of police activity in any district always directly drives up the local price of drugs, and thus escalates attendant crime (Davies, 1986). The production of such evidence consistently appears to have a counter-productive effect. It seems to prove, in the mind of the prohibitionist, the precise reverse of reality. It's almost as if a pathology is at work.

It could be argued, of course, that this position is far too pessimistic. We might postulate that the war on drugs could dissolve in much the same way as did the war on communism. Maybe so, but I ask myself four questions:

1 Has there ever been a time in the history of humankind when across countries people and governments have acted rationally about the majority of substances?
2 Has there ever been a time when logic has consistently triumphed over fear?
3 In our noble efforts to inject a little renaissance thought into this arena, a little rational thinking, a touch of scientific reason, are we gaining any ground whatsoever?
4 Is there any likely event on the horizon that might turn the tide?

The answer to all four questions is, of course, a clear No. The verdict is bad news for the future of rational drug policy.

Internationalism, by its very nature, must be conservative.

The premise of the drug helping profession is that reason will prevail. The premise of the antagonists is that evil will prosper when good men do nothing. While these two positions are maintained, the current trend to prohibitionism is sure to continue.

REFERENCES

Claude, I. L. (1964) *Swords into Plowshares*, London: University of London Press.
Cleeland Report (1989) 'Drugs, crime and society', Parliamentary Joint Committee on the National Crime Authority, Canberra: Australian Government Publishing Service.
Davies, S. (1986) *Shooting Up: Heroin in Australia*, Sydney: Hale and Iremonger.
Economist, The (1990) 'The myth of economic sovereignty' (23 June).
Harrison, P. (1990) 'Every beat of your heart, two babies are born', in *The Correspondent Magazine*, UK.
Marks, R. E. (1989) 'The economics of drug policies' (unpublished), University of New South Wales.
Szasz, T. (1975) *Ceremonial Chemistry*, New York: Anchor Books.
United Nations (1990) 'United Nations Population Funds Report on the State of World Population', New York.

Chapter 7

US drug policy
Public health versus prohibition

Ernest Drucker

My purpose here is to describe the ways in which the US drug policy, based as it is on drug prohibition and criminalization, explicitly contradicts the development and implementation of effective harm reduction approaches to drug use and severely limits the potential of public health programmes aimed at dealing with AIDS. To illustrate this point, I shall describe the context of the public presentation – the climate which currently prevails in the US – and discuss some of the limitations that this image places on our practical and policy options.

The first part of this climate is the public representation of the drug problem in the United States. There is little discrimination between the different types of drugs and the wide spectrum of drug use. The uncontrolled or addicted user of hard drugs, i.e. the most desperate and troubled segment of this population, is portrayed as the typical user and the model for what will happen to people who use drugs. Drug-related advertisements and newspaper headlines frequently greet the subway rider each morning on his way to work. 'The Partnership for a Drug Free America', a heavily endowed corporate anti-drug consortium, will spend over $30,000 for a one-day ad in the *New York Times*. The most famous shows a fried egg in a pan ('This is your brain on drugs'); another, a businessman crouched in a toilet stall fumbling with a spoon of cocaine ('Welcome to the glamorous world of drugs'). *The Daily News* and *New York Post*, more proletarian papers in New York City, feature schoolroom 'show and tell' 1980s style, headlining the eleven year old bringing 411 phials of crack to school, or the school principal busted buying crack – tried and sentenced in the press.

But the spectrum of drug use is acknowledged to extend beyond the inner city core to some other areas of American life, especially to sport. The baseball star Dwight Gooden, of the New York Mets, is a twenty-two year old earning over one million dollars per year and spending some of it on cocaine. When this became public (headlines of 'SHAME' and 'SAY IT AIN'T SO') it was dealt with by 28 days of treatment at the highly regarded $1,000-a-day Smithers Center at New York's Roosevelt Hospital. But, following his 'rehabilitation', Dwight was taken back and embraced by the team: 'The only thing that really mattered', said the team management, 'was his health.'

Then there is the public campaign to blame drugs for all of America's problems. Drugs are undermining America. It is drugs that are making it impossible for us to do anything well – from controlling the behaviour of our children, to competing with Japanese electronics. Drug use in the workplace must be ferreted out by widespread programmes of drug testing – often bordering on the unconstitutional.

But the hard core of American drug policy is criminalization. The intent is to identify as many drug users as possible and to lock them up. Presently in the US, 3.7 million people are under the control of the criminal justice system – 1.2 million in prison on any given day, and another 2.5 million on probation or parole. It costs approximately $40,000 per year to keep someone in prison in the US – so that bill alone is over $60 billion a year. Over 50 per cent of those who go to jail these days are there in association with drugs – not necessarily for drug possession or use, but for drug-related acquisitive crime – typically robbery. As a result, the US prison system has expanded by 100 per cent in the last ten years to accommodate the increased pressure for arrest of this population. So at least $30 billion is being spent on this side of the drug war. In times of restricted budgets, little is left for other approaches – e.g. treatment or the prevention of AIDS.

Of course, as you extend and enforce this policy more efficiently, you begin to see a sharp increase in the number of drug arrests and the proportion of arrests associated with drugs comes to dominate, then flood, the criminal justice system. The inevitable delays in trial, and the inability of many drug defendants to raise bail, clogs the city jails. New York's Rikers Island jail processes over 140,000 cases per year – more than half for drug-related offences. These are, overwhelmingly, minorities from the poor areas of the city. They are the prisoners of drug war campaigns waged with military enthusiasm. Heavily armed SWAT squads block off both ends of the street and make a sweep taking every young male, and some young females. They spread-eagle them up against the walls and search them for drugs. These are all Black and Hispanic neighbourhoods, of course, and the police deliberately do this in full view of everyone in the neighbourhood – a shock tactic meant to convey a strong message. In New York last year we spent $169 million on SWAT teams, which made around 9,500 arrests. That works out to about $17,000 per arrest – more than the annual cost of most residential drug treatment centres.

The racial and class aspect of this war must not be overlooked. The target population is inner city, youthful, minorities – groups with poor education, health and social support. Their drug use patterns are the most visible and destructive and they are easy to round up. Today, more than 25 per cent of all Black men in the US between the ages of twenty and thirty have been arrested and convicted of a crime. They tend to remain in the control of the criminal justice system – either in prison, on probation or on parole, with recidivism rates of 80 per cent. The lifetime expenditure on arrest, prosecution and imprisonment of each such case exceeds $1 million.

With this immense effort of local law enforcement and its disruption of the street drug trade, we should expect some diminution of availability or increase in the price of the commodity. But the reverse is true. The multiple avenues of supply in New York City and the inventiveness of drug smugglers are quite formidable. A recent example is the Colombian airliner which crashed in a New York suburb because it ran out of fuel before making it to Kennedy Airport. But, since it had no gasoline left, it didn't burn when it crashed. Although half the people on board were killed, about 100 survived and were sent to hospital – where two were found to have intestines full of cocaine. Each had swallowed about thirty or forty double condoms, containing about an ounce of cocaine. If this is a true random sample of South American airline traffic into New York, and just one plane had 4 kilos of cocaine, then three flights per day from Colombia alone would provide 4,380 kilos of pure cocaine annually to New York City. From this example, one can see the scale and the range of options for people bringing drugs into the US, which has over 10,000 miles of (mostly) unguarded border. So the market is continuously fed from outside with only the occasional bust of big-time distributors. Most of the drug-related crime and arrest stems from sales and distribution at the lowest street level – i.e. of users.

The pattern of vastly increased seizures of large quantities of drugs in every category across the years is something that would normally be considered evidence of great success in an interdiction programme. Yet the economy of the international drug trade seems to grow with time, diversifying and extending to new areas. As the seizures increase, the basic supply from producer countries increases to take those seizures into account and the increased profits that the pressure produces induce new countries and regions to enter the game (keep your eye on the Soviet Union). And this 'industry', once it is established, becomes the major economic support of many inner city communities. We estimate the drug trade in New York City to be about $4–5 billion a year – most of it taking place in communities that have a 50 per cent unemployment rate and little prospect for change. Thus the drug trade provokes entrepreneurial activities – an American virtue now turned to a new purpose. It also leads to political corruption. The major money associated with drugs attracts attention and becomes a part of the context of larger scale political corruption – from pay-offs of cops to multi-million dollar bank money laundering schemes. Every major political figure in the Bronx was either indicted or jailed between 1980 and 1990. That includes the Borough President, two United States Congressmen (one of whom represented the most devastated area of the South Bronx), a State assemblyman, and the leader of the County Democratic party for the Bronx. People from other countries who visit the Bronx ask, 'How could this devastation possibly be prevented? Where are your political leaders?'

But these days it is the violence associated with the US drug trade that captures most public attention. You can hear the guns going off every night in the South Bronx and Harlem; everyone knows someone who was killed in this battle. New York City will have over 2,000 murders this year – perhaps half of them 'drug related'. The crack trade plays a central role in this violence – but not in the way one might think. A study by NDRI's Paul Goldstein (1989) of 500 drug-related homicides in five police precincts in New York City revealed that 96 per cent of those murders were associated with the structural or economic characteristics of the drug trade – as opposed to the pharmacological properties of the drug. While crack is often described as a drug that makes crazed killers out of the single-time user, it is in fact the political economy of it that seems to drive the violence, i.e. the battle for lucrative and powerful turf in the absence of other economic or social opportunities. Ansley Hamid, an ethnographer, has looked very closely at the way in which a Jamaican community in Brooklyn, previously involved in marijuana importation and distribution, has recently moved into crack dealing (Hamid, 1990). This has proved quite destructive in part because the sporadic or binge use of crack-cocaine is far less stable than the regular use of marijuana – or even of heroin. A street level user-dealer may take $100 worth of crack on consignment, but instead of selling it he smokes it, and so he gets into trouble with his distributor. This economy is at the core of a lot of the disruption and violence associated with the crack trade in New York.

This then is the background of the drug problem and the way in which US drug policy is perceived by most Americans: The Drug Wars. Drug users are people who shoot, kill and maim others; they sell crack to eleven-year-olds and undermine the performance of some of our most revered sportsmen and political figures. This is the daily meal fed to the American public and forms the infrastructure of public support for the war on drugs. In 1989, 65 per cent of Americans saw drugs as the most serious national problem. A similar proportion of Americans agreed that no search and seizures warrants should be required for drug raids and that the military should be able to go into houses and search for drugs, while many were willing to forfeit some of their own fundamental rights to support the war on drugs. Of course, most believe that it is someone else who is going to be thrown up against the wall and have their bodily cavities searched But politicians are very aware of this enormous support, and drugs have been an extremely serviceable political issue in the US throughout the 1980s.

Then along comes AIDS, which begins to create a pressure to re-examine our drug policy. Some of the original panic about the epidemic (i.e. the feeling that everybody could get it, indiscriminately), has begun to fade. But in the US, we do have one million people infected: 150,000 have already been diagnosed with AIDS, and over 80,000 have died, making it the worst epidemic in the US in the twentieth century. The characteristics of the epidemic in the US are important for understanding who is at risk and what that risk means for the future of the epidemic in this country. The bulk of infections in the gay communities in San Francisco and New York, and in the IV drug users in New York, took place before 1985, prior to our really knowing anything about the AIDS epidemic. Recall that it wasn't until 1985 that we first had a test that enabled us to detect antibodies to the virus.

Further, AIDS presents itself differently in different places, leading to different impressions of the epidemic. The ratio of male to female cases of AIDS in the country as a whole is about 1 : 10. In New York City as a whole it is 1 : 5, and in our hospital (where we have seen over a thousand AIDS patients) it is 3 : 2. Between 17 and 20 per cent of national cases are now drug related. But in New York, since August 1988, the monthly report of new AIDS cases among drug users (by the NYC Department of Health) has outstripped those of gay and bisexual men. In our own hospital it is now up to about 60 per cent IV drug users. And, by 1992, there will be more new cases among women than

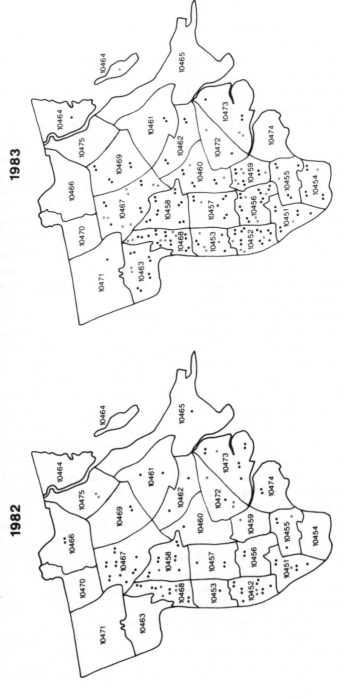

Figure 7.1 Hospital admissions for immune disorders in the Bronx by zip code among people aged 25–44

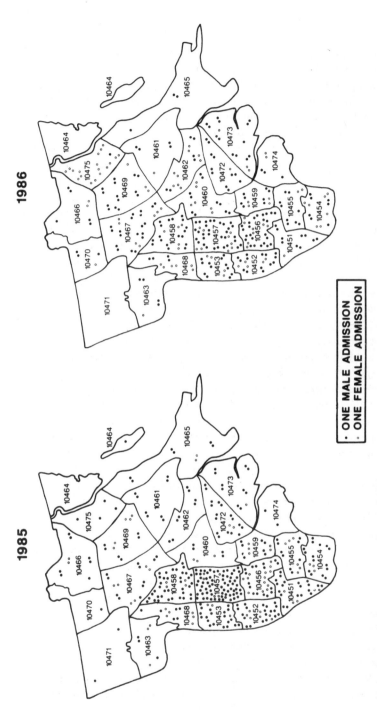

1985   1986

• ONE MALE ADMISSION
○ ONE FEMALE ADMISSION

(*Source*: New York State Department of Health)

among gay men. This indicates the significance of drug use in the US AIDS epidemic. The fact that some people were infected through sharing needles is significant, but the fact that they are also sexually active heterosexual individuals living in a community with a high rate of HIV infection has implications for the future of the epidemic independent of the original drug use.

One of the ways to observe that is to look at the physical geography of New York and see how AIDS relates to it. For any epidemic, geography is destiny – and that is certainly true of the AIDS epidemic in New York. In fact, there are really two AIDS epidemics in New York, the one among gay men and the other among drug users. The astonishingly separate maps in Figure 7.1 denote the areas of New York where gay men live – lower Manhattan, Greenwich Village, Chelsea and Murray Hill, some areas of Manhattan, and a small area of Brooklyn, Brooklyn Heights – as compared to the IV drug use epidemic of AIDS which is seen in distinct neighbourhoods, the South Bronx, Central Harlem and the core of Brooklyn.

Other related factors follow the same geographic pattern. If we consider teenage pregnancy in the South Bronx, we see close to 30 per cent of all births involve women below the age of nineteen. Teenage pregnancy is not a health problem, but it is certainly an indication of early unprotected sexual exposure to anything from pregnancy to sexually transmitted diseases. And the map of teen pregnancy is exactly in accordance with the map of the AIDS epidemic in New York City among heterosexuals. As is the map of segregated neighbourhoods. The Black and Hispanic communities, which correspond to the poor areas of the City, are those same high AIDS districts. So it's not surprising that 80 to 90 per cent of drug-related AIDS cases are among minorities and over 90 per cent of AIDS babies are born to Blacks and Hispanics in New York. And finally, of course, the map of drug-related events – crimes, arrests, overdose deaths – is identical.

Looking more closely at the Bronx in Figure 7.2, you can see how, over time, the AIDS epidemic settles into a community and develops. In 1982, the first year in which we had AIDS data, there were about a dozen cases. In 1983 you can see the rapid growth. Also in 1984...and 1985. You don't need a PhD in epidemiology to know what's going on here. The way this looks to people within these communities is that, soon, everybody knows somebody who has AIDS. There are large families with four or five people with AIDS.

What are these communities like, in which about 2 million people are living? They are burnt-out stores and buildings; 200,000 units of

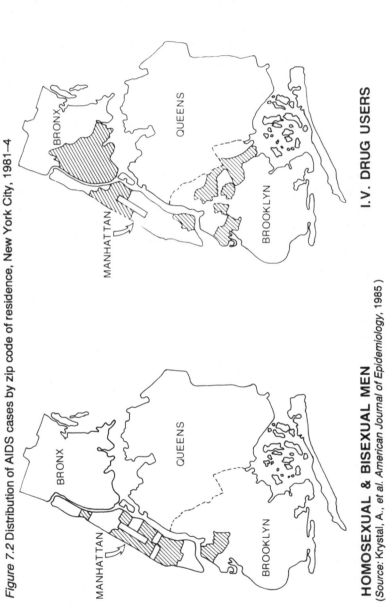

Figure 7.2 Distribution of AIDS cases by zip code of residence, New York City, 1981–4

HOMOSEXUAL & BISEXUAL MEN
(*Source:* Krystal, A., et al. *American Journal of Epidemiology,* 1985)

I.V. DRUG USERS

houses destroyed by fire in New York over a ten-year period from 1970 to 1980; vast areas of destruction and social dislocation, with many children growing up in these conditions.

Within this lethal environment, the AIDS map quickly becomes a map for the drug wars, and a guide for the assault on that same population. Not surprisingly, AIDS has become a major feature in the prospects of drug users – the major cause of death among addicts. The baseline mortality rate for drug use associated with adulterated drugs and dangerous injection practices prior to HIV was always high. Now, more and more deaths appear to be HIV related, with AIDS *per se* accounting for a five-fold excess of deaths. Other causes are HIV-related pneumonia, tuberculosis and endocarditis – infections which addicts always endured, but which have become lethal because of HIV.

Drug treatment and other public health measures (street outreach, bleach, needles) should clearly be of great interest in New York at this time. It has been demonstrated quite clearly that methadone helps – injection stops over time, there is a reduction in IV drug use clearly related to dosage and time on the programme – as well as decreases in arrests associated with drug acquisition, and decreasing criminal complaints. In New York, during an earlier time (when we had the political will to take care of business), New York City went from having no drug treatment slots in 1968, to having 35,000 by 1974. Changes in drug-related mortality rates clearly show that methadone in New York City worked in this period. Yet, we have been unable to open any new drug treatment programmes since 1976. There is increased hostility in most communities to drug programmes – which are seen as importing drug users or treating them too well.

Dr Stephen C. Joseph, the NYC Health Commissioner from 1986 to 1989, opened a small needle exchange program, only to have it closed in 1990 by the new Mayor, David Dinkins. Elsewhere in the country, there are attempts to promote AIDS risk reduction programmes such as 'Bleach Man' from San Francisco (Pappas, 1989) – but he has never walked the streets of New York. In the face of this hostility, it is increasingly difficult to get bleach programmes in New York where the teams that are doing it are being severely cut by budget reductions. Increasingly, AIDS activists are being arrested for giving out needles. Jon Parker was exonerated by a court in Boston, only to be arrested in New York (and in ten other cities) for continuing to defy the laws prohibiting needles. What is happening more and more around needle distribution, drugs information and access programmes is civil disobedience. Gay activist groups (e.g. Act Up) have set the tone for confrontative AIDS politics as one way of getting attention for clinical trials and AIDS care resources. But this approach does not diminish the perception of the rest of America that AIDS is not their problem. Thus, in combination with the drug wars and their huge criminal justice apparatus, the climate, or tone, for a discussion of drug policy in the US is hardly a civil one. The agenda is not public health, but prohibition – Just Say No, Zero Tolerance.

CONCLUSIONS

There is an intimate relationship between a drug policy based on prohibition and criminalization of drug use, and the difficulties in development of effective preventative and treatment approaches to addiction. And by our failure to develop and offer effective treatment and preventive approaches, we are ultimately bound to fail in our public health approaches aimed at reducing drug-related harm. The response to AIDS is just one example.

We are at a critical juncture in the US regarding people's consciousness about drugs. There is now a sense that the war on drugs is failing. Drug Czar William Bennett has resigned. Even if the USA is a country that was crazy enough to institute alcohol prohibition in 1920, it was also a country that was sane enough to repeal it fifteen years later. I believe it is the repeal of drug prohibition policies that we must seek. Unless we repeal drug prohibition and all the baggage of public attitude it carries with it, things will continue to deteriorate. We must work for the availability of funds for a range of drug treatment services appropriate to the population that needs help, and end the marginalization not only of the drug user, but of those professionals who would choose to work in this area. But moving drug issues into the mainstream of medicine and public health will be impossible as long as criminalization policies continue.

REFERENCES

Goldstein, P., Brownstein, H., Ryan, P and Belluci, P. (1989) 'Crack and homicide in New York City in 1988', *Contemporary Drug Problems* 16: 651–8.

Hamid, A. (1990) 'The political economy of crack', *Contemporary Drug Problems* 17.

Pappas, L. G. (1989) 'Bleachman: A superhero teaches AIDS prevention', presentation at V International Conference on AIDS, Montreal, Canada, June 4–9.

Chapter 8

Cocaine users' perceptions of their health status and the risks of drug use[1]

P. G. Erickson, V. Watson and T. Weber[2]

INTRODUCTION

One of the issues posed by the organizers of the conference on harm reduction, which generated this collection, was how to reach the 'hidden sector' of drug users – those neither in prison nor registered in treatment centres or other official agencies. Why is it important to study this less visible fraction of the drug-using population? As other contributors have pointed out, many drug users are satisfied with their lives for some time, and indeed, some do 'retire early' before developing serious problems. Clearly, not all drug roads lead to addiction.

We need to know more about the process that leads to different types of outcomes of drug use, not just the most destructive, in order to promote the occurrence of less harmful outcomes. Moreover, risks associated with drug use are not absent from even experimental or recreational use. Risks may be reduced by personal and social controls.

All drug use is subject to some form of social control, including the formal threats of punishment and the informal controls transmitted through peers and other social groups. Users who are less visible to enforcement agents and not in treatment are likely to be more influenced by personal and informal controls, including knowledge, beliefs and advice available in their social networks (Maloff *et al.*, 1979). Their perceptions can contribute to the development of a harm minimization approach that is based on the reality of the drug use milieu.

The topic of this chapter is the user's perspective on risk and other health-related factors found in a sample of 100 cocaine users in Toronto, Ontario. This analysis includes three groupings of cocaine users: those who had used powder only, intranasally (*N*=22); those who had used powder and also smoked crack cocaine (*N*=52); and those who had snorted, smoked and injected cocaine (*N*=21).[3] Thus their experiences reflect a continuum of risk according to mode of administration, one dimension to be considered in a harm reduction strategy.

SAMPLE AND DESIGN

A sample of adult cocaine users, aged eighteen years or more, was recruited directly from the community by means of advertising and referrals. The field period extended for twelve months and was completed by the end of March 1990. Designed as a prospective study, follow-up interviews will be conducted with respondents after one- and two-year intervals, in order to detect changes in cocaine use patterns and perceptions over time. The results presented here reflect the baseline data from the first wave of interviews.

The sample's demographic profile was as follows. The majority of respondents were male (70 per cent) aged thirty years or less (72 per cent), single (71 per cent), not university educated (74 per cent), employed full time (57 per cent), lived in shared or rented accommodation (62 per cent) and had a personal income of $30,000 or less (62 per cent). This community-based sample shared similar age, sex, education and employment status characteristics with a representative sample of cocaine users from an Ontario provincial survey (Adlaf and Smart, 1989).

As drug users more generally, most had lifetime experience with a wide range of drugs, licit and illicit. While all but one respondent had ever used cannabis, over 80 per cent had experience with LSD, other hallucinogens, and other stimulants from non-medical sources. In addition, about half of respondents had ever used narcotics other than heroin, barbiturates or tranquillizers from non-medical sources; one-third had used phencyclidine (PCP) and nearly one-quarter had used heroin. Tobacco and alcohol were the first drugs tried, at a mean age of thirteen years. Cannabis was next, at nearly fifteen years on the average, followed by amphetamines, barbiturates, hallucinogens, tranquillizers and narcotics other than heroin, all before a mean age of twenty. In the early twenties, heroin was tried next, then cocaine and finally crack at the average age of twenty-five. With the exception of alcohol, cannabis, cocaine and crack, use of any of these other drugs in the past year was restricted to a minority of the sample.

As cocaine users, just under half reported the use of cocaine in the past month, and about one-quarter had used crack in the same period. Just over one-third had not used cocaine in the past year. The amounts of cocaine used per occasion were fairly small: 0.84 g in the first year of use, 1.81 g in the period of heaviest use, and, for those who were still using, 0.92 g in the last three months. This sample tapped a broad range of experience with cocaine, not only in its various modes of administration but also in frequency and patterns of use.

RESULT 1: SATISFACTION WITH HEALTH AND WELLBEING

Respondents were asked a series of questions related to physical and mental health and wellbeing and asked to indicate how satisfied they were with these various aspects of their lives. In Table 8.I, their responses are shown, according to their experience with three modes of administration of cocaine: snorting powder cocaine only, intranasal use plus smoking crack, and snorting and smoking crack and intravenous use. Although, in general, respondents in these subgroups expressed quite a high degree of satisfaction on all of these measures, the group with powder, crack and intravenous experience with cocaine showed the lowest scores on all of the items except coping with stress and solving problems. The powder-only group was highest on six of these (accomplishments, solving problems, decisions, enjoyment of life, self-confidence and worth as a person). The powder plus crack group had greater satisfaction than the other groups on four aspects of their lives (health, day-to-day activities, coping with stress, and attractiveness).

Table 8.1 General health and wellbeing of cocaine users

In the past twelve months, how satisfied or dissatisfied have you been with the following aspects of your life?

Percentage responding extremely, very or fairly 'satisfied' to each of these items*	Powder only (N=22)	Powder and crack (N=52)	Powder, crack and IV (N=21)
(a) Health	73	90	71
(b) Accomplishments	77	64	52
(c) Day-to-day activities	68	71	57
(d) Coping with stress	64	69	65
(e) Solving problems	91	71	76
(f) Decisions	86	79	67
(g) Attractiveness	77	80	67
(h) Enjoyment of life	77	76	52
(i) Self-confidence	86	75	67
(j) Worth as a person	91	80	71

* (N=95) Excludes five cases of 'crack only' users.

Table 8.2 Indicators of problems or health concerns in past twelve months

Percentage responding 'yes' to each of these items*	Powder only (N=22)	Powder and crack (N=52)	Powder, crack and IV (N=21)
(a) Rate my overall physical health as very good or excellent	50	52	14
(b) Have felt in good spirits or very good spirits mostly	46	39	38
(c) Seen a doctor for routine medical visits	59	71	81
(d) Seen a doctor for a medical problem or emergency	59	65	76
(e) Spent one + nights in hospital	0	21	19
(f) Taken days off work/ school because of drug use	54	58	67
(g) Sought medical attention for physical reason because of cocaine use	5	18	43
(h) Sought medical attention for psychological reason because of cocaine use	5	29	19
(i) Sought medical attention because of use of alcohol or drug other than cocaine	23	23	35
(j) Cocaine has changed life for the worse	27	44	43

*(N=95) excludes five cases of 'crack only' users.

The differences between the three groups were, however, small on nearly all of the items and attain no or marginal significance.

Respondents were also asked more specific questions about any problems or health concerns which they had experienced in the past twelve months. Their responses are shown in Table 8.2, again according to their experiences with three modes of administration of cocaine. Those who had snorted, smoked and injected cocaine indicated the lowest overall rate of physical health (14 per cent as very good or excellent, compared to about one-half of the powder/crack groups). In addition, this multi-mode group reported the most visits to doctors (whether routine or emergency), missed the most work or school, and was far more likely to have sought medical attention for the physical effects of cocaine use. In contrast, powder plus crack users were most likely to have sought medical attention for psychological reasons related to their cocaine use. Powder-only users were least likely (27 per cent) to say cocaine had changed their lives for the worse, whereas nearly half of the other two groups said that it had.

RESULT 2: CONTROLS ON USE

Four types of controls which may discourage or limit the use of cocaine will be described: availability, legal deterrence, risk perception, and informal guidelines operating in user networks. The first two can be disposed of quickly, since they had little impact. Availability was perceived to be *high*, as over 90 per cent of the respondents generally found cocaine easy to obtain. Deterrence, or the perceived risk of punishment, was *low*, in that over 90 per cent thought it was unlikely or very unlikely that they would be caught for a cocaine offence in the next year. Actually, 7 per cent reported a prior arrest for cocaine, and many more had friends who had been arrested, but still regarded the risk of arrest as remote.

Table 8.3 Perceived 'great' risk in trying, occasional use and regular use of cocaine, crack and heroin

	Trying			*Occasional*			*Regular*		
	Coc. (%)	Cra. (%)	Her. (%)	Coc. (%)	Cra. (%)	Her. (%)	Coc. (%)	Cra. (%)	Her. (%)
(a) Powder only (N=22)	32	68	77	32	90	82	82	100	100
(b) Powder and crack (N=52)	29	54	60	40	69	78	87	94	98
(c) Powder, crack and IV (N=21)	33	52	47	48	57	63	82	81	95

Perception of health risks has been shown to be one of the key factors explaining persistent and different patterns of drug use. In this study, respondents were asked the extent to which people risked themselves by trying, occasional use and regular use of cocaine, crack and heroin. The data reproduced in Table 8.3 show that the percentage in each of the three subgroups of cocaine users (according to experience with different modes of administration) perceive a GREAT risk in different use levels of cocaine, crack and heroin.

For *trying* each of these substances, it is evident that the three subgroups in our sample are very similar in their perception of a fairly low risk for cocaine, as less than one-third saw the risk as great. In contrast, about twice the proportion viewed the risk of trying crack or heroin as great. Powder-only users saw a higher risk for these latter forms of drug use than did those whose experience with cocaine extended to crack and intravenous use.

Occasional use of crack and heroin is viewed as much more risky than occasional use of cocaine by powder-only users. The contrast is not nearly as great for those who have used powder plus crack, and even less so for those who have experienced all three modes. Both of the more intensive cocaine-using subgroups viewed occasional use of heroin as more risky than occasional use of crack, while the opposite was indicated by powder-only users.

A very high proportion of all cocaine user subgroups, 80 per cent or more, see a GREAT risk in *regular use* of all three substances. Again, heroin on a regular basis is viewed as even more risky than crack, particularly by the group with intravenous experience with cocaine.

Since not all members of this sample had tried crack or injected cocaine, despite ready availability and little fear of arrest, it was instructive to ask them: Why not? Those who had never smoked crack said either that they were not interested, and were satisfied with the intranasal effects, or were concerned that crack was too addictive. Those who had never injected cocaine offered a variety of reasons, including a fear of needles, of AIDS, of overdosing, and simply that injecting was too dangerous.

Respondents were asked if they had ever encouraged someone to try, or discouraged someone from trying, cocaine. More reported that they had taken a negative rather than a positive stance towards cocaine with friends or acquaintances. About two-thirds said they had actively discouraged someone from trying cocaine. Other than not trying it, respondents offered this advice to novices: limit the amount you take, only snort it, and do it with friends.

The advice offered to daily cocaine users, in order of frequency, was: get help, quit, use less, talk to them; however, one-quarter of respondents said they had no advice to offer to daily users, principally because advice would make no difference or be disregarded. When asked how they kept their own cocaine use in control, a wide range of responses was elicited. A majority expressed some concern about addiction as a possible result of their use, while a minority said they did not try to control their use because they had no need to. Others said they controlled use by avoiding people and situations where cocaine would be found, by limiting the amount used or the money spent, by abstaining or by exerting self-control.

CONCLUSION

We would make three points in conclusion. First, how can 'harm minimization' be enhanced in a group of experienced drug users? A realistic view is that many, if not most, will probably not become addicted to cocaine or otherwise harm themselves. Informal and personal controls will operate to minimize the risks involved. This is, of course, dependent to some extent on the accuracy of available knowledge and its dissemination among users. As in earlier studies of cocaine users, these respondents displayed quite high levels of concern regarding the health risks of cocaine and its addictive potential (Erickson and Murray, 1989). For others who have a higher threshold of risk, there might be points of intervention that would support healthier drug use practices. For example, self-perceptions of satisfactory mental and physical health were quite high among all users, yet the more quantitative information on seeking medical assistance (e.g. nights in hospital) indicated a fairly poor health profile in a group of young adults. This suggests that primary health care workers might have the most access to such users and be attuned to potential problems.

Second, what are the implications of drug policies for conducting such research as this on low-visibility drug users? This study has illustrated the difficulties of doing community studies in the midst of a 'war on drugs' mentality that has characterized the media and police activities in the Toronto area (Cheung et al., 1991). It is difficult to get early stage and lighter users of illicit drugs to volunteer for research at any time, but especially when the newspapers are full of stories of increased enforcement targeting cocaine and crack. Also, the willingness of those who are interviewed to provide referrals to other users is reduced. Furthermore, we are concerned that the success of the follow-up component of the study will also be compromised by a perception of greater vulnerability to arrest among drug users. The result is that knowledge about the development or avoidance of risky outcomes of cocaine use, and the factors that influence these paths, will be compromised.

Third, and more broadly, it is also important to recognize that policies for 'safer' cocaine and crack use should encompass not only users' health, but also must include the minimization of harm to the public at large. Long-range policies, within a harm minimization perspective, ought to involve less stigmatization of the drug users themselves and decreasing criminalization of users. This is not to be equated with legal and widespread availability, as examples of irresponsible and self-destructive behaviour abound for both alcohol and tobacco. Rather, we need a 'new public health' approach that encourages responsible use of all psychoactive substances. This may mean *no use* in some settings and for some individuals, and *restrained use* in other contexts. As the chapters in this collection attest, the first steps in conceptualizing and implementing harm minimization are underway. Research and evaluation are part of the next crucial phases in the shift towards a more comprehensive public health policy for the prevention and control of substance misuse.

NOTES

1 This research was funded by the National Health Research and Development Program, Ottawa, Ontario. The research assistance of Tammy Landau and Joan Moreau is gratefully acknowledged.
2 Any views expressed in this chapter are those of the authors and do not necessarily reflect those of the Addiction Research Foundation.
3 A fourth subgroup, consisting of five respondents who had only used crack, was excluded from the analysis because of the small number and because there was no clear-cut rationale for including them in one or other of the larger crack-using subgroups.

REFERENCES

Adlaf, E. M. and Smart, R. G. (1989) *The Ontario Adult Alcohol and Other Drug Use Survey, 1977-1989*, Toronto: Addiction Research Foundation.
Cheung, Y. W., Erickson, P. G. and Landau, T. (1991) 'Experience of crack use: Findings from a community based sample in Toronto', *Journal of Drug Issues* 20.
Erickson, P. G., and Murray, G. F. (1989) 'The undeterred cocaine user: Intention to quit and its relationship to perceived legal and health threats', *Contemporary Drug Problems* 16 (2): 141–56.
Maloff, D., Becker, H. S., Fornaroff, A. and Rodin, J. (1979) 'Informal social controls and their influence on substance use', *Journal of Drug Issues* 9 (2): 161–84.

Chapter 9

Police policy in Amsterdam

Leo Zaal

As a police officer of the Amsterdam narcotics squad, I find that the treatment of drug addicts and the police policy against drug trafficking are often at variance. The Dutch might have a tolerant attitude towards drug users, but this tolerance does not extend to criminal activities involving drugs. To illustrate this, I shall explain the national Opium Act (which forms the basis for many police enquiries), the local drug policy of Amsterdam, the position of the police in the Amsterdam drug policy, give some results of this approach, and comment on the involvement of the police in the drug problem.

The Netherlands Opium Act came into force in 1976, with an addition concerning conspiracy being added in 1985. The Opium Act divides all drugs into two categories, 'hard' and 'soft'. The group of hard drugs includes heroin, cocaine, amphetamines, methadone and LSD. Marijuana and hashish are categorized as soft drugs. The distinction between the two kinds of drugs is based upon the health risks associated with their use. In the Netherlands, we are convinced that the use of soft drugs is less harmful than the use of hard drugs. However, the Opium Act does prohibit the import, manufacture, distribution, possession, sale, transport and export of all kinds of drugs.

The only difference between the two groups of drugs is that the possession of less than 30 grams of soft drugs is classed as a misdemeanour, a minor offence. Also, the punitive measures for soft drugs are lower, because of the health risks.

The Opium Act applies to the entire country. The interpretation of the law can differ in several areas, however, because the Public Prosecutor has the right to prosecute but not the obligation. Since 1986 we have used an integrated hard drug policy in Amsterdam. This policy has two main objectives: (a) to create humane conditions for the users of hard drugs, with no threat to public health, which can also lead to drug users becoming more socially acceptable; and (b) to limit any public nuisance which may be caused by the use of illicit drugs. The second goal is the basis for police activities, which include:

- promoting good community relations in areas where drug use and drug trade is concentrated;
- using an active tracing policy for drug-related crimes, thereby minimizing the attraction of Amsterdam to foreigners;
- combating the illegal trade in hard drugs.

HARD DRUGS

In 1985, when the drug policy came into effect, the narcotics squad of the Amsterdam police was expanded to sixty-five officers. To emphasize police efforts towards local policy, a special unit of thirty-five detectives was assigned to this task. Since then, the statistics have shown an enormous increase in seizures. Internal criteria in handling drug cases are used. Dealing in or around schools has the highest priority and when information concerning this is received, immediate action is taken. However, during the two years that these criteria have been in use, we have only had one notification that a dealer was active in the neighbourhood of a school. Dealing from houses is the next priority, but the important condition is that there has to be some public nuisance. If information is received about dealing which does not involve any kind of nuisance, this house receives less priority. If there is a concentration of dealers and junkies on a street, we try to move them. This usually has a positive effect on the perception of local residents.

The Amsterdam police is also interested in persons or groups who supply the area between the wholesale and retail sides of the drug market. After nearly five years, a decrease in the number of arrests has been noted, as well as a decrease in the number of houses causing nuisance. This is not to say that the market has collapsed, or that fewer drugs are available. It is more likely that dealers and buyers have found more acceptable ways to continue their activities without disturbing others in the neighbourhood. For example, instead of one dealer supplying eighty addicts each week from one point, he may now use eight separate distribution points, causing less disruption and less risk of police intervention. In this way, we also receive fewer complaints from local residents. The outcome of this strategy is that there has been a reduction in the number of detectives attached to the local unit, as they have their assignments changed to deal with more international oriented investigations.

Consequently, the Amsterdam police is not interested in drug users as such, as they are at the lowest level in the system from source to customer. In order to obtain evidence, the statements of users may be needed, but the Amsterdam police does not use programmes simply to arrest drug users, but always in connection with other objectives. After all, as police it is not our job to help addicts through treatment and our criminal process is not equipped for large-scale arrests, which would soon become overwhelmed by this type of criminal.

SOFT DRUGS

Towards soft drugs, especially for possession and low-level sale, we use a more refined policy. In order to remove the soft drug user from the criminal justice system, we permit the sale of marijuana and hashish by coffee-shop owners. As police we shall not take action if coffee-shops follow some basic rules – only sell on a small scale, no hard drugs are allowed, no selling of drugs to juveniles and no price lists displayed in the shop. Coffee-shops are also forbidden to advertise, e.g. by means of marijuana leaves on the window or any other kind of advertisements. Some coffee-shops have recently been closed by the police, because they refused to abide by these rules.

But what is the result of this attitude? First of all, cannabis users don't have to fear arrest by the police if they are simply smoking a joint. Consequently, there is no illicit behaviour by this group, because they can obtain their drug of choice in the same way you or I can buy other drugs, such as alcohol. This leaves the police free to focus attention on the drug trafficker, instead of tracing minor drug users. From an economic point of view, we have to conclude that this is more cost-effective.

This is also beneficial from the users' perspective, as they can get good-quality products for reasonable prices, so they do not need to resort to criminality to be able to buy hashish. They can even afford it from their social security money! The police statistics reflect this, as soft drug users are rarely part of the criminal figures.

IMPORT, EXPORT AND DISTRIBUTION

The other part of the Amsterdam narcotic squad focuses its efforts on import, distribution and export of drugs. Again, the Amsterdam police is not merely interested in the drugs themselves, but more in the group that is responsible for the drug trafficking. It is police policy to eliminate the supply from source countries, such as Thailand, Turkey, Pakistan and South America, to the Netherlands and, in addition to this, to arrest persons involved, eliminate the organization and forfeit their possessions. Although it is not expected to have a major influence in the drug market, the Amsterdam police has the obligation to enforce the rules and values of our society. It is unacceptable for criminals to have influence in our society because they have power and money from organized crime.

If we analyze the policy of the drug squad and compare it to the soft drug approach, there is a certain contradiction. To 'decriminalize' the user of soft drugs, we permit the small-scale trade of hashish and marijuana. However, the supply of this market is in the hands of criminals, who are our main interest. This may seem paradoxical, but the Amsterdam police policy is to concentrate on the organized crime which goes hand in hand with the profits. Consequently, persons who limit their activities in this area, have less risk of arrest. So it is a mistake to believe that legalizing soft drugs will then reduce criminal activities, as criminals will only change to another profitable illegal activity. Recent research into the economics of drug addicts has shown that only 22 per cent of their income is provided by criminal activities, and not 80–90 per cent as was previously thought. Dealing drugs to provide for one's own use is not seen as a criminal activity (18 per cent). Other main sources of income are social welfare (28 per cent) and prostitution (22 per cent). This conclusion means that drug addicts are not the only ones responsible for the crime figures, but that other disadvantaged groups pose major problems too.

Drug use and the drug trade influence the perception of socety as well as politics. We are aware that drugs are not the only problem. Using drugs is one expression, social misbehaviour (like stealing and extortion) are others. What we define as the drug problem is a society-related problem, which cannot be solved by law enforcement. The police contributes in the overall policy, but it cannot be the only group responsible.

OTHER ASPECTS

Police action is not merely confined to law enforcement. All police stations in Amsterdam are involved in the needle exchange programme. Intravenous drug users can obtain a new needle in a police station, if they hand over a dirty one, which also means increased safety for police officers. The police also contribute to educational programmes at schools and universities, as well as participating in the local drug advisory group which prepares new policies for the mayor and local authorities. Last year, the police and Municipal Health Service developed a programme called 'Srteetjunk', which involved approximately 120 addicts. Upon arrest, the addicts are invited to make a choice between participating in a treatment programme or being prosecuted. The aim is to try to convince the addicts that help is available if they want it. If not, jail awaits them. The results, though not outstanding, are encouraging. Another programme allows doctors from the Municipal Health Service to supply methadone to addicts in jail, and supplies access to social assistance groups who visit the addicts in police cells.

What are the results of this approach? Since 1985, we have seen the number of addicts decrease to approximately 6,500. Also, the average age of the drug user is rising, which means that fewer youngsters are using drugs. The number of deaths caused by overdose has been stable over the last few years, and there is no extension in arrests. There have also been more successful developments in the area of drug trafficking. More cocaine has been seized, the shipments are larger than those of heroin, and the price at wholesale is going down while the quality remains good.

The Amsterdam police drug policy has made it possible to contact addicts and give them alternatives. This policy also has an influence on drug use, and has made it less attractive for youngsters. Society's acceptance of drug users has increased, but drug trafficking still continues.

© 1991 Leo Zaal

Chapter 10

The criminalization of pregnant and child-rearing drug users
An example of the American 'Harm Maximization Program'

Loren Siegel

INTRODUCTION

I am convinced and find that a child who is born but whose umbilical cord has not been severed is a 'person' within the intent and meaning of Florida law...I am convinced and find that the term 'delivery' includes passage of cocaine or a derivative of it from the body of the mother into the body of her child through the umbilical cord after birth occurs.

So spoke the Honourable O. H. Eaton, Jr, of the Seminole County Circuit Court, before passing sentence upon Jennifer Johnson, a twenty-three-year-old mother of four, a cocaine abuser, and the first woman to be convicted by an American court under a drug-trafficking statute for delivering drugs to her infant through the umbilical cord. Johnson was punished for her transgression with a sentence designed to keep her from future temptation: one year of house arrest and fourteen years of closely supervised probation, during which time she is forbidden to possess controlled substances, associate with others who do, or enter a bar without the permission of her probation officer. If Johnson should become pregnant again during those fourteen years, she must follow a pregnancy care programme approved by the court. She will also be subject to random urine drug tests and warrantless searches of her home during her first year of house arrest.

George Orwell was only a few years off the mark when he selected 1984 as his symbol of state-sponsored social control. America's contemporary War on Drugs has spawned an impressive array of counter-productive measures to curb the demand for illegal drugs. But the persecution of pregnant users is perhaps most emblematic of America's 'harm maximization' approach to its drug problem.

THE CASE AGAINST JENNIFER JOHNSON

Jennifer Clarice Johnson, at the time of her arrest, was a cocaine abuser and had been for about three years. Although she sought treatment for her addiction during her pregnancy, she was unable to find a programme that would accept her. On 23 January 1989, Johnson gave birth to a baby girl. Her labour and delivery were normal and, in the words of the attending obstetrician, the baby 'looked and acted as we would expect a baby to look and act'. Johnson told the obstetrician that she had used cocaine during her pregnancy, a fact which was confirmed by urine drug screens administered to both mother and infant. The hospital then notified a state child protection investigator of the birth of a 'cocaine baby', and the investigator in turn notified the County Sheriff's Office who initiated a criminal investigation which led to Johnson's arrest.

The case was assigned to Jeff Deen, a publicity conscious county prosecutor in need of a theory upon which to base his novel drug-trafficking case. Since under Florida law a foetus is not a person, he could not charge Johnson with delivering cocaine during the pregnancy itself. So instead, he argued that the 'delivery' occurred after the birth during the sixty to ninety seconds before the umbilical cord was clamped.

Judge Eaton was, as he put it, 'convinced', and concluded the sentencing hearing with these uncharitable words:

> The fact that the defendant was addicted to cocaine at the time of these offences is not a defense. The choice to use or not to use cocaine is just that – a choice. Pregnant addicts have been on notice for years that taking cocaine may be harmful to their children. This verdict puts pregnant addicts on notice that they have a responsibility to seek treatment for their addiction prior to giving birth. Otherwise, the state may very well use criminal prosecution to force future compliance with the law or, in appropriate cases, to punish those who violate it.
>
> State of Florida v. Johnson (Circuit Court, 13 July 1989)

OTHER CASES

While Jennifer Johnson is the first to be convicted, she is not the only victim of the 'pregnancy police' (McNulty, 1987). By last count, at least fifty women in sixteen states have, in recent months, been arrested for drug use during pregnancy. In South Carolina, where cultivation of lethal tobacco is the major agricultural endeavour, eighteen women have been charged with criminal neglect of their foetuses. Following a protocol developed by the public hospitals, the police, the department of social services, and the prosecutor, these women, all of whom tested positive for drugs, were, within days of giving birth, arrested, handcuffed and taken to jail until they could make bail. Their babies have been taken into 'protective custody' by the state (Goetz *et al.*, 1990).

CIVIL PROCEEDINGS

Less dramatic than the criminal prosecutions, but far more prevalent, are civil proceedings against drug-using new mothers. Hundreds of women have lost custody of their newborns based upon a single positive toxicology at birth.

Typically, these proceedings are triggered by the hospital's report of a positive toxicology to the local or state agency charged with providing services to neglected or abused children. An increasing number of states are enacting laws that redefine 'neglect' to include prenatal exposure to controlled substances. The State of Oklahoma, for example, recently enacted a statute defining 'a deprived child' as 'one born in condition of dependence on a controlled, dangerous substance'. The same law requires the hospital to report chemically dependent children to social services, which in turn must give any evidence of drug abuse to the district attorney. Failure to report constitutes a crime (Okla. Stat. Ann. Tit. 10, Sec. 1101, 1988).

POOR AND MINORITY WOMEN ARE TARGETS

Despite the fact that illicit drug use crosses all income levels and races, poor Black women are by far the predominant victims of the pregnancy police. In a recent study conducted in a Florida county, 380 pregnant women in public clinics and 335 in private care were drug tested. The rate of positive test results was 15.4 per cent among White women and 14.1 per cent among Black women. Yet a Black woman was nearly ten times as likely to be reported for substance abuse as her White counterpart (National Association for Perinatal Addiction Research and Education, 1989).

This bias can be attributed to two factors. First, public clinics and hospitals that primarily serve low-income, often minority women, comply with reporting regulations to a far greater extent than do private hospitals and doctors serving the middle and upper classes. Second, doctors are influenced, either consciously or unconsciously, by a drug user profile based on racial stereotypes and are, therefore, much more likely to test the urine of poor, Black women than of middle-class, White women, in spite of empirical evidence showing comparable patterns of drug use. In South Carolina, one element of the profile used by public hospitals to identify probable drug users is no prenatal or late prenatal care (after twenty-four weeks). This is highly discriminatory since Medicaid (medical insurance for poor people) does not cover prenatal care before nineteen weeks of pregnancy (Goetz et al., 1990).

LACK OF TREATMENT

Judge Eaton's admonition to Jennifer Johnson that 'pregnant addicts have a responsibility to seek treatment' is indicative of either shocking ignorance or indifference to the plight of poor women in need of medical care. In fact, Johnson had sought drug treatment but failed to find it. She testified at her trial that she had, on several occasions during her pregnancy, called for an ambulance out of concern for the baby: 'I thought that...if I tell them I use drugs they would send me to a drug place or something.' But her pleas for help were ignored. As for her prenatal care, as Johnson put it, 'It wasn't much, but it was enough that I had been checked by the doctor and I know I didn't have any diseases or nothing like that.'

NO PRENATAL CARE FOR THE POOR

In spite of the universal belief that prenatal care is essential to healthy pregnancies and healthy babies, such care does not exist for millions of American women. In fact, access to prenatal care and delivery services has diminished in recent years for poor women, and at the same time the addiction problem has worsened. For example, in San Diego, California, clinics turned away 1,245 pregnant women during a recent three-month period because of limited resources.

The lack of prenatal care has been particularly disastrous for drug-abusing women who are already at special risk. Indeed, quality prenatal care is probably more essential to a good outcome for these women than drug treatment. As one expert has put it, 'In the end, it is safer for the baby to be born to a drug-abusing, anemic or diabetic mother who visits the doctor throughout her pregnancy than to be born to a normal woman who does not' (St Petersburg Times, 1986).

UNAVAILABILITY OF DRUG TREATMENT

Drug treatment for poor, pregnant women is even scarcer than is prenatal care. And the need is enormous. Surveys indicate that the incidence of maternal substance abuse has tripled since 1981, and in this drama, crack cocaine has played a leading role (Chavkin, 1989). Fifteen per cent of 3,000 infants born at Harlem Hospital in New York City were prenatally exposed to cocaine. A study at Boston City Hospital revealed that 17 per cent of delivering women had used cocaine during their pregnancies (Brody, 1988). (It should be borne in mind that the urine screens do not indicate frequency of use or dosage, and there is anecdotal evidence that some women take cocaine during labour in order to speed up delivery; many of these women may not be chronic users.)

It is extraordinarily difficult, even for highly motivated pregnant women, to find drug treatment programmes that will accept them. In New York City, of seventy-eight drug treatment programmes surveyed in 1989, 54 per cent refused to treat pregnant women, 67 per cent refused to treat pregnant women on Medicaid, and 87 per cent had no services available for pregnant women on Medicaid who wanted to stop using crack. Moreover, less than half of the handful of programmes that did accept pregnant women provided or arranged for prenatal care (Chavkin, 1989).

This, then, is the backdrop against which these prosecutions are taking place: no prenatal care, no drug treatment, and no mercy.

THE PROSECUTORS' MISGUIDED THEORY OF DETERRENCE

Deterrence theory is based on the premise that if you punish people for engaging in certain behaviours you will prevent others from doing so. It is clear from their own statements that the prosecutors in these cases believe that their actions will deter not only the defendants, but pregnant women in general, from using drugs. As District Attorney Michael Ramsey of Butte County, California, put it: 'We intend to send a strong message not only to mothers, but to the community at large, that Butte County will not allow drug abuse to affect its babies' (Dell, 1988).

Those directly involved in the care of substance-abusing pregnant women differ with D.A. Ramsey over the effects of his so-called message. They are concerned that such punitive actions will not deter addicts from using drugs during pregnancy but will deter them from sharing important information with their doctors and, indeed, from using the health care system at all. Last year a Florida newspaper reported that :

> After uniformed officers wearing guns entered Bayfront Medical Center to investigate new mothers suspected of cocaine abuse, doctors reported that they could no longer depend on the mothers to tell them the truth about their drug use because the word had gotten around that the police will have to be notified.
>
> (*St Petersburg Times*, 1989)

The head nurse at Greenville Memorial Hospital in North Carolina, which was the site of similar police actions, was blunt in her appraisal: 'I think these prosecutions are dangerous. The mothers won't seek medical help. If they don't seek medical help, we're going to have a lot of dead babies' (Garloch, 1989). There is some anecdotal evidence that more women are giving birth in abandoned buildings in order to avoid detection by the health care system.

But it seems that many of the prosecutors, who are after all elected officials, are animated more by concern for votes than concern for the welfare of 'their' babies. And these 'get tough' measures, in spite of their obvious and extraordinarily counter-productive consequences, do enjoy a considerable measure of popular support. In one poll, 46 per cent of respondents thought that 'prenatal abuse' should be a criminal offence (*Glamour Magazine*, 1988).

SOURCE OF POPULAR SUPPORT

How is it that in the final decade of the twentieth century in the advanced industrialized nation of the United States of America, the body politic can so utterly fail to be outraged by these ignorant and barbaric practices? Even our civil rights organizations have been uncharacteristically silent in spite of the policy's blatant racism.

The answer lies in the unfortunate convergence of two powerful social movements: the anti-abortion movement and the anti-drug movement.

These forces on the New Right came to ascendancy during the two-term presidency of Ronald Reagan and continue to wield considerable political power. With fundamentalist Christian groups at its core, the New Right seeks a return to what it calls 'traditional family values'. Drug-taking and sex outside heterosexual marriage threaten these values and are therefore condemned as morally unacceptable, sinful and deserving of strong condemnation and punishment (Reinarman and Levine, 1989).

THE ANTI-ABORTION MOVEMENT AND FOETAL RIGHTS

The American anti-abortion movement has been a potent political force in the country for more than a decade. Central to the philosophy of the anti-abortion movement is the pseudo-legal concept of 'foetal rights'. In fact, anti-abortion activists describe themselves as civil rights advocates on behalf of 'the unborn'. It has been an uphill battle because firmly embedded in the nation's common law is the 'born alive' rule: a foetus must be born alive in order to secure legal personhood (McNulty, 1987). Traditionally, the law has viewed mother and foetus as an indivisible unit whose legal interests are the same. The anti-abortion movement has been trying to drive a legal wedge between mother and foetus for years.

One of the movement's tactics for establishing foetal rights is to support legal actions that raise the issue, even in the non-abortion context. The criminal prosecution of drug-using pregnant women provides just such an opportunity. Ann Louise Lohr of Americans United for Life Legal Defense Fund had this to say about the prosecution of Kimberly Hardy, a Michigan woman who was charged with delivering cocaine to her baby via the umbilical cord:

> You do not have an absolute right to do with your body what you want. The state can require you to have vaccines. There are seat-belt laws, motorcycle helmet laws. Here's a class of people that aren't getting any protection, and it's the unborn.
>
> (Kennan, 1989)

The 'right-to-lifers' reason that if you can criminally prosecute pregnant women for harming their foetuses by ingesting cocaine, then you can prosecute them for 'killing' their foetuses by aborting.

THE ANTI-DRUG MOVEMENT

The origins of America's anti-drug movement were contemporaneous with the anti-abortion movement and also grew out of a backlash against the hedonism of the 1960s (Reinarman and Levine, 1989). The movement, which came into being in the late 1970s and had strong religious overtones, was a loose confederation of drug abuse professionals, parents' groups, individual 'moral entrepreneurs' and government officials (Zimmer, 1990). Their guiding principles were total intolerance of all illegal drug use and strong support for criminal sanctions. Just after Ronald Reagan took office, Nancy Reagan, on the advice of her public relations advisers, decided to adopt the anti-drug crusade as her own, and met with leaders from the National Federation of Parents for Drug-Free Youth, a coalition of over 4,000 parents' groups (Reinarman and Levine, 1989; Zimmer, 1990). Soon she was riding the circuit, delivering the anti-drug message she coined in that insufferably simplistic sound bite: 'Just Say No.'

The early anti-drug movement's efforts at arousing the American public were not very successful. In fact, as late as 1986, only 2 per cent of the population regarded drugs as the nation's most important problem (Zimmer, 1990). But, in the spring of that year, several events changed everything: two famous young athletes, Len Bias and Don Rogers, died after ingesting cocaine, and crack arrived in our inner cities and was noticed by the media. In a relatively short period of time, the anti-drug movement became an all-out national crusade, and by 1989 a staggering 64 per cent of Americans named drugs as America's most critical problem, the highest percentage ever received by a single issue in any public opinion poll (Zimmer, 1990). The drug scare was in full flower.

The government's response

In 1982 President Ronald Reagan declared his war on drugs. His principal war strategy was supply reduction. Enormous sums of money were poured into interdicting illegal drugs entering the country. But billions of dollars and thousands of drug seizures later, the government was forced to concede that 'Despite interdiction's successful disruptions of trafficking patterns, the supply of illegal drugs entering the United States has, by all estimates, continued to grow.'

Demand reduction

When George Bush entered office, the country's drug control strategy had already begun to shift from supply reduction to demand reduction. Official rhetoric talked less about seizures of cocaine shipments, and more about drying up domestic demand. In his inaugural speech, Bush, referring to the drug problem, stated grandiosely, 'This scourge will stop'. When queried later by the press, he elaborated: 'The answer to the problem of drugs lies more on solving the demand side of the equation than it does on the supply side, than it does on interdiction or sealing the borders.' A new catch-phrase was coined to capture the essence of this strategy: user accountability. If you use drugs, any drugs, you must pay the penalty.

In the autumn of 1988 Congress passed the Anti-Drug Abuse Act, which, among other things, established hefty civil fines for casual users and the denial of government benefits to convicted drug offenders. The Act also mandated the new president to appoint a so-called Drug Czar to oversee and coordinate national drug policy.

The Drug Czar

In William Bennett, the Bush Administration found the ideal person to direct the new demand reduction programme. As Secretary of Education under Reagan, Bennett had demonstrated his harsh, neo-conservative views admirably. One of his favourite aphorisms was, 'after love, what children need most is order'. As Drug Czar he waged a punishing moral crusade against all drug use and all drug users:

> Anyone who sells drugs and anyone who uses them is involved in an international criminal enterprise that is killing thousands of Americans each year...we should be tough on drugs – much tougher than we are now. Whatever else it does, drug use degrades human character...drug users make inattentive parents, bad neighbors, poor students and unreliable employees – quite apart from their common involvement in criminal activity.

Bennett's blame-the-user ideology captured popular imagination just as the drug problem was becoming more and more identified with underclass minorities. Although a very occasional newspaper article will remind us that White suburbanites take illegal drugs too, that message is overwhelmed by the far more common depiction of drugs as an inner city, minority problem. Today's imagery of the 'drug problem' is of gun-toting Black teenage gangs, ghetto crack houses where unspeakable horrors take place, and depraved Black women who prostitute themselves to raise money for their crack, and who give birth to tiny, drug-addicted babies whose pictures are plastered all over our subway cars in extravagantly graphic public service messages warning of the dangers of drugs.

Given this political environment, the criminal prosecutions of Jennifer Johnson, Melanie Green, Marcelle Denise Bruce, Toni Suzette

Hudson, Kimberley Hardy, Cassandra Gethers, and other poor Black women are not surprising.

LEGAL AND ETHICAL COMPLICATIONS

We need to be concerned about these women's plight. But the harms caused by criminalizing their pregnancies extend far beyond the women themselves to their families, the medical profession, and the causes of women's rights and civil rights.

Destruction of families by the state

With the lodging of criminal charges, the defendant's newborn is immediately removed from her custody and placed in foster care. Older children may suffer the same fate. For example, when Kimberley Hardy of Muskegon, Michigan, was charged ten days after giving birth, her baby and her two older children, who were five years old and fifteen months old, were all seized and sent into foster care. There were no allegations of child abuse or neglect against Hardy. Her children were taken away from her based solely on the results of the drug test administered by the hospital and on the assumption that Hardy was an unfit parent because she used drugs.

Turning doctors into medical cops

The pregnancy prosecutions are usually triggered by a hospital's report of a positive toxicology to a state agency. This practice violates both the woman's right to non-disclosure of private information and the physician's ethical obligation to protect doctor–patient confidentiality (Moss, 1989). Only a confidential and trusting relationship enables a physician to learn from the patient all the facts necessary to make a diagnosis and provide appropriate care. Knowing this, many practitioners are simply not reporting drug dependency at birth. But under the laws of some states, the failure to report constitutes a crime. Thus physicians now face the dilemma of either violating the privacy rights of their patients and their own ethical obligations, or running foul of the law.

An attack on women's rights to privacy and autonomy

The US Supreme Court's 1973 decision in Roe v. Wade (410 US 113), that women have a constitutional right to abort a pregnancy, corrected the more than 100-year-old denial of a woman's right to personal autonomy and privacy. It freed women from unwanted pregnancies and thereby afforded them options in life previously reserved for men. The pregnancy prosecutions, by creating an adversarial relationship between the woman and her foetus, return to the state the power to control her behaviour during pregnancy (Johnsen, 1986).

The concept of foetal rights robs women of child-bearing age of rights retained by all other citizens. It also completely ignores the fact that fathers too have a powerful effect on foetal development. We know now that alcohol and drug use have an effect on the quality of a man's sperm (Cohen, 1986). And a man's behaviour can have a powerful effect on the course of a woman's pregnancy. In the United States, one in twelve women are beaten during pregnancy. Yet violent husbands are not being charged with foetal abuse (Pollitt, 1990).

Under Judge Eaton's ruling in the Jennifer Johnson case, women in Florida who smoke or drink alcohol during pregnancy could be prosecuted, since delivery of alcohol and cigarettes to a minor are criminal offences in that state. A woman in Wyoming was recently charged with criminal child abuse for endangering her foetus by drinking while pregnant, although the charges were subsequently dismissed (Wyoming v. Pfannensteil, County Court of Laramie, 1990). These events conjure up images from Margaret Atwood's prophetic novel, *The Handmaid's Tale*, in which the story's protagonist protests: 'We are two-legged wombs, that's all; sacred vessels, ambulatory chalices.'

Selective prosecution based on race

It is clear that Black women are being singled out for prosecution. Indeed, the American 'war on drugs' is permeated through and through with the racial biases of its 'generals'. Street level enforcement of the nation's drug laws is disproportionately targeted at minority residents. The prison population in the US is close to one million, the highest it has ever been. Fifty per cent of those prisoners are Black men, even though Black men constitute only 3 per cent of the country's population. The war on drugs is primarily a war on people of colour.

Cruel and unusual punishment

The Eighth Amendment to the Bill of Rights of the United States Constitution prohibits the imposition of 'cruel and unusual punishment', a flexible concept that should change to reflect contemporary standards of decency. As long ago as 1925, the United States Supreme Court ruled that drug addiction was, in and of itself, not a crime but a disease (Linder v. United States, 268 US 18, 1925). Then in 1962, in the case of Robinson v. California (370 US 660) the Court struck down a California law that made the mere status of being an addict a crime punishable by a prison sentence. Ruled by the Court: 'We forget the teachings of the Eighth Amendment if we allow sickness to be made a crime and sick people to be punished for being sick. This age of enlightenment cannot tolerate such barbarous action'. The pregnancy prosecutions, while nominally based on trafficking and child abuse laws, in essence punish women for their status as addicts.

CONCLUSION

The criminalization of pregnant and child-rearing users is the complete antithesis of a harm reduction approach to drug abuse. It greatly magnifies the potential harms to both mothers and infants by driving drug-using women away from the very health care providers who could assist them in having normal pregnancies and healthy babies. It aids and abets the reactionary and anti-woman foetal rights movement. It destroys doctor–patient confidentiality and turns caring physicians into medical cops. It cruelly punishes drug abusers for their chemical dependency. It is blatantly racist in its application.

Worst of all, by blaming victims, the government gets itself conveniently off the hook. Pointing the finger at 'bad mommies' diverts people's attention away from the scandalous shortage of treatment facilities for all drug abusers, the dismantling of social welfare programmes, the ever-widening gap between the haves and the have-nots in America. It is 'cruel and unusual punishment' that scapegoats society's most vulnerable members.

REFERENCES

Anderson, P. (1986) 'Taxpayers pay for lack of pre-natal treatment', *St Petersburg Times* (3 November).

Brody, J. (1988) 'Widespread abuse of drugs by pregnant women is found', *New York Times* (30 August).

Chavkin, W. (1989) Testimony presented to House Select Committee on Children, Youth and Families, 27 April.

Cohen, F. (1986) 'Paternal contributions to birth defects', *Nursing Clinics of North America* 21 (1).

Dell, T. (1988) 'DA to prosecute moms of addicted new-borns', *Chico Enterprise-Record* (28 October).

Garloch, K. (1989) 'Four accused of drug use during pregnancy', *Charlotte Observer* (17 August).

Glamour Magazine (1988) 'This is what you thought: 46% say prenatal abuse should be a criminal offence' (May).

Goetz, E., Fox, H. and Bates, S. (1990) 'Poor and pregnant? Don't go to South Carolina...', Initial report on RFP's South Carolina Investigation, *ACLU Reproductive Freedom Project*, Memorandum.

Johnsen, D. (1986) 'The creation of fetal rights: Conflicts with women's constitutional rights to liberty, privacy and equal protection', *Yale Law Review* 95.

Kennan, M. (1989) 'The birth of a felony', *Detroit News* (21 December).

McNulty, M. (1987) 'Pregnancy police: The health policy and legal implications of punishing pregnant women for harm to their fetuses', *New York University Review of Law & Social Change* XVI (2):277.

Moss, K. (1989) 'Substance abuse during pregnancy', *Harvard Women's Law Review* (winter).

National Association for Perinatal Addiction Research and Education (1989) Newsletter update.

Pollitt, K. (1990) 'Fetal rights: A new assault on feminism', *The Nation* (26 March).

Reinarman, C. and Levine, H. (1989) 'The crack attack: Politics and media in America's latest drug scare', *Social Problems and Social Issues*, Hawthorne, NY: Aldine de Gruyter.

Zimmer, L. (1990) 'Drug testing and the war on drugs' (unpublished manuscript).

Chapter 11

Clarifying policy options on drug trafficking
Harm minimization is distinct from legalization

Nicholas Dorn

INTRODUCTION

This chapter applies the principle of minimization of harm to the response of the criminal justice system to drug trafficking. Four alternative directions for the future of drug control are discussed: escalating penalties for trafficking; decriminalization of possession for personal use while maintaining severe penalties for trafficking; full legalization of drug markets; and reduction in penalties for trafficking. The escalation in penalties, up to and including life imprisonment and in some countries death, is described as being more effective in expressing disapproval than in restraining trafficking. Tendencies towards decriminalization of possession for personal use are noted as being perfectly compatible with severe yet ineffective measures against traffickers. Legalization proposals are criticized as confusing the principle of a legal ban on trafficking with the way in which that ban is currently put into practice; also legalization is questioned on grounds of the development implications for 'producer countries'.

On balance, the best way to minimize negative outcomes, including drug market-related harm, is by continuing a ban on trafficking but with a switch of resources within the criminal justice system, from incarceration to investigation. There is a need to distinguish and distance harm minimization proposals from proposals for legalization.

1 THE PATH OF RIGHTEOUSNESS

The first and most obvious path for the future development of drug control, illustrated most clearly by the United States, would involve focusing in particular upon drug use associated with minority groups, and a rapid escalation in penalties for trafficking offences. The two points, about race and punishment, go together. As Helmer convincingly showed in a Drug Abuse Council-funded study, it is historically at times of labour surplus within the United States, as poor Whites have been forced to compete more fiercely with ethnic minorities for the jobs available, that the drugs associated with those minorities (in reality or, more importantly, in the popular imagination) have become a focus for increased control (Helmer, 1975). That is to say, the minorities themselves have become a focus for increased controls, via drug control.

During the 1980s, it has been cocaine use and cocaine dealing among young Black males that have taken up the historic role of providing reason for enhanced policing of populations facing economic blight. Of course, such a policy response is also articulated in other ways, for example through the promotion of terminology such as 'mugging' in the 1970s (translation – street crime is Black-on-White) and 'wilding' in the 1980s (translation – vicious and sexual assaults are the responsibility of Blacks, not of Whites). But it is in the area of drug policy that the vision of the WASP (White Anglo-Saxon Protestant) has been most eloquently articulated:

> The drug crisis is a crisis of authority – in every sense of the term 'authority'. What can be done to combat this crisis of authority? Two words sum up my entire approach: consequences and confrontation. Those who use, sell and traffick in drugs must be confronted, and they must suffer the consequences. By consequences, I mean that those who transgress must make amends for their transgressions. Consequences come in many forms. In terms of law enforcement, they include policies such as seizure of assets, stiffer prison sentences, revocation of bail rights, and the death penalty for drug kingpins. On these points I find general agreement...
>
> We need to do more. We need to reconstitute authority. What those of us in Washington, in the states, and in the localities can do is to exert the political authority necessary to make a sustained commitment to the drug war. We must build more prisons. There must be more jails...
>
> (Bennett, 1989: 4)

Quite so. You know it makes sense. We really must build more jails! And who are we going to put in these facilities? Everybody appreciates that ethnic minorities are over-represented in the prison systems of most developed countries, and also that drug trafficking throughout the 1980s provided the most dynamic motor of incarceration. For the United States, the Assistant Comptroller General reported to the House of Representatives in 1989 that the rapid increase in federal prison populations is largely driven by the increase in the number of drug violators who are being incarcerated. Whereas the population of drug offenders increased by 31 per cent in the two years from September 1986 to September 1988, there was only a 5 per cent increase for all other offenders combined. Another measure of the relative effect of [the incarceration of] drug offenders is that they account for 79 per cent of the total increase among those sentenced to prison over that two year period.

(Chelimsky, 1989)

The report makes it clear that it is US drug control policy that is primarily responsible for the increase in incarceration.

The relationship between sentence length and the extent of prison overcrowding is direct. For example, if the increasing number of drug offenders were disproportionately sentenced to short sentences (less than one year), then the growth in prison population might be short-lived. If, however, the majority of new [drug] offenders were being sentenced to longer stays in prison, the prison population could be expected to grow.

(Ibid: 13)

A similar, if in some respects less extreme, state of affairs obtains in many other countries. In Britain, for example, drug trafficking is one of the few crimes for which penalties rose sharply in the 1980s (Dorn *et al.*, 1991: ch. 10), as the judiciary followed the dominant social sentiment to apply higher sentences and as legislation changed in the mid-1980s: maximum penalties of life imprisonment (and possible fine) plus asset confiscation replaced a maximum of fourteen years (and possible fines). Even in Holland, widely regarded as 'liberal' in its drug policies, prison sentences for trafficking offences are high *relative to the tariff for most other offences*, and so an increasing proportion of the prison population is made up of traffickers, many of them couriers and of foreign nationality.

2 THE PATH OF HOLLANDIZATION

The second path, illustrated in differing ways by British, Dutch and other European drug control policies, involves an attempt to reconcile increasingly heavy penalties for trafficking with some harm reduction for users. It is particularly the Dutch who represent this approach at the level of policy rhetoric, and for this reason the term 'Hollandization' is being heard on the European conference circuit, although the path they follow is shared with others.

Broadly speaking, this policy amounts to a *de facto* partial decriminalization of cannabis possession (and, in restricted circumstances, retail sale of cannabis), with an emphasis upon health measures (treatment and syringe exchange, in particular) in preference to a purely crime control perspective on other drugs. In the Netherlands itself, the policy on cannabis extends from a toleration of possession and retail sale to a broader concept of 'market separation', where the aim is to keep markets in cannabis separate from markets in substances with 'an unacceptable risk'. This aspect is not favoured in most other countries, but police officers in parts of Britain take the view that cannabis trafficking is beyond their effective control. This does not mean that they do not attempt to police cannabis (indeed the greater proportion of criminal justice-generated drug statistics relate to cannabis) but it does reflect a practical police view on the need to focus primarily on other, less widely spread but more dangerous drugs.

As far as the Dutch emphasis on health policy rather than crime control is concerned, it can be said that such a policy is, to varying degrees, also shared by other European countries (and not by the United States). Even in Germany, sometimes taken in contrast to the Netherlands, health policy plays a part. In the southern European countries, there are pressures for decriminalization of personal possession and use in Italy, a well-developed response to HIV in Spain and France, and although resource difficulties restrict the Greek approach, health concerns are well to the fore there in terms of policy formulation. Most of the ex-communist countries are in movement from a denial of drug problems, through control responses sometimes involving psychiatry in a repressive mode, towards community-based and social responses to users. To find a European country that remains firmly against any hint of tolerance to drug users, we have to go to Norway.

To summarize on decriminalization, we can say that although it is seldom legislated, it is informally practised by many countries, if only partially and for practical reasons. Why not, some say, push harder in this direction, and link public health and civil liberties issues in a coalition for legalization of the trade in all drugs currently proscribed?

3 THE PATH OF THE FREE MARKETEERS

The third path is that proposed by the advocates of legalization of the trades in drugs such as heroin and cocaine.

There seem to be three perspectives that are commonly taken on the likely consequences of legalization of drug trades. These are: (a) perspectives on the potential impact on levels of consumption; (b) perspectives on the impact upon various indices of harm; and (c) perspectives upon the consequences for those developing countries within which psychoactive plants such as the opium poppy, coca bush and marijuana are grown.

Of course, we are all familiar with (a), the arguments about the possible impact of legalization upon levels of consumption. It is quite common for government spokespersons to predict that legalization would result in an 'explosion' in drug use. Legalizers deny this, saying that drug consumption would probably remain at about the same level or perhaps fall. Who is right is probably one of those many questions which are context-dependent. Legalization in a situation of hitherto quite tight policing would probably have different (greater) impact upon availability than legalization in a situation of hitherto *de facto* loose control.

Perspective (b) is a bit more subtle, since it refers to levels of market-related and user-related harm and suggests that these would be reduced by legalization. For example, a legal market might mean less corruption of banking systems, enforcement agencies and government officials; legal consumption would mean few arrests, and so on. This is a very interesting argument that deserves to be articulated more clearly, but it does have a major problem. Advocates of legalization sometimes have a tendency to talk as if the various negative side effects of the *present* set of controls in the USA or elsewhere are inevitable consequences of *any* system of criminalization, yet that is obviously not the case. Clearly, a country's legal system can proscribe trafficking without having maximum penalties as high as they are today (as described above, up to life imprisonment plus asset confiscation in many developed countries, death penalty in some other countries, particularly in South East Asia).

Twenty years ago, penalties were nothing like what they are today. At the end of this chapter I shall return to this point, suggesting a radical reduction in penalties for trafficking as a cost-effective approach to minimizing market-related harm, but within a clear commitment to continuing proscription of trafficking. But here let us simply register that there is a distinction between support for the *principle* of legal ban, and support for any specific penalty. Supporters of legalization seem all too easily to gloss over this distinction.

Let us turn now to perspective (c), which asks about the probable impact upon plant drug producing countries of a free market in the production of drugs. Here, we have to enquire into the present social and economic conditions of production of psychoactive plants and consider the likely future scenario under legalization.

At present, most psychotropic plant production is carried out by peasants and small tenant farmers who grow these crops on a proportion of the village lands as a cash crop, the remainder being given over to food crops for familial consumption and/or local sale. Although, as has often been observed, the farmgate price is low in comparison with the prices at higher levels of the market, and minuscule compared with the price of the finished product as purchased by consumers, *nevertheless* the farmgate price is sufficient to provide farmers with cash that they would otherwise find difficult to raise.

Indeed this is one of the difficulties facing crop substitution programmes. The standard problem with such programmes is that the prices offered to farmers for the 'substitute' crops (wheat, fruits, tobacco, etc.) are generally not sufficient to offset the loss of income entailed in giving up psychotropic crops, especially when the farmer has to purchase special seeds, fertilizers, transport, or storage – expensive 'inputs' that were not required by the previous pattern of cultivation. It is not surprising that farmers who agree to take part in crop substitution programmes may show resistance to their full implementation as the implications emerge. It is widely recognized that, although crop substitution programmes may succeed on a local basis if sufficient outside funding is poured in and if enforcement is vigorous enough, these conditions cannot be achieved on a global basis. The best that can be achieved, for example, is the partial displacement of poppy cultivation from parts of Pakistan to less accessible Afghanistan, as happened in the 1980s; and a resurgence of cultivation in the Far East, as seems to be happening in the early 1990s. The world is just too big and the authority of many states too fragile to overcome completely the economic motivation of cash cropping.

Thus, paradoxically, illegality guarantees this form of production and its *relatively* good returns.

The plantation solution

Let us now ask what would happen if cultivation were to be made legal. The obvious result would be that peasant cultivation would no longer constitute the main form of production. As an advocate of the free market 'solution' describes, competition occurs between existing and new producers.

> In the production of drugs, natural and synthetic, there are no scarce factors such as special land, or patented technical information, which would hinder entry into the market. Quotas [restricting the market

to existing players] would be difficult to enforce, and the power of Third World producers would be further reduced from producers of natural and synthetic drugs in consumer countries. It would be likely, therefore, that the legal drug industry would be competitive at the production stage.

(Stevenson, 1990: 661)

The entry into the market of big farming interests and multinational corporations – at present excluded by the legal sanctions which only geographically and economically peripheral producers can evade – would transform the present situation. Consider the ways in which legal commodities such as tobacco, tea, cocoa and sugar are produced. Typically, cultivation takes place in large farming units, specializing in one such commodity only, and using labour hired by the week or month. This would become the general pattern of cultivation of psychoactive plants, if legalized.

The exact consequences would vary with the nature of the crop. In the case of cannabis, for example, labour needs are low, with little to be done before harvesting except some weeding, which could be done manually or mechanically. In the case of poppy, the extraction of the juice from seed heads is a process that might be difficult to mechanize, thus necessitating a large labour input for a few weeks only. Otherwise, all the labour that is required is weeding between the seedling plants. In the case of coca, labour is needed to harvest the leaves about four times a year, assuming that machinery capable of stripping the leaves mechanically would not be developed. Regardless of the crop, however, the lessons of history of production of licit commodities strongly suggests that legalization of production of plant drugs would see large-scale monoculture cropping expand at the expense of small-scale, mixed crop peasant production.

What would be the consequences? Seasonal, low wage and partly migrant labour would accelerate at the expense of settled self-employment. Economic dependency would deepen as self-sufficiency became further eroded. The combination of increased competition, a fall in the farmgate price, seasonal demand for wage labour and aggregation of lands into large units would, together, intensify existing pressures on peasant small-holders – especially in those (common) situations in which tenants would have difficulty in proving or defending a right of land-use against landowners and officials keen to help 'modernize' the countryside. This is hardly an attractive development path.

Better the present situation, which involves a slower process of eroding of local self-sufficiency, than the implementation of the plantation solution. Proposals for legalization of trade in psychoactive plants can only be justified by an indifference to, or romantic misreading of, the development implications.

4 HARM MINIMIZATION AND DRUG MARKETS

The fourth and final policy path to be discussed involves an application of the concept of harm reduction/minimization to the drug market as well as to the user. I want to suggest that reduction of maximum penalties for trafficking offences would help to reduce drug market-related harm such as violence, would improve information flows to the enforcement agencies and hence would improve levels of apprehension and deterrence. A switching of resources from prisons to policing would increase the overall cost effectiveness of the criminal justice system in drug control.

Let us review the historical record. Two decades ago in Britain, when drug *dealing* had only recently been legislatively distinguished from drug possession and drug *trafficking* had yet to be described as such, a person found guilty of supplying or intending to supply a kilo of a drug such as heroin might go to jail for about two or three years. By the early 1980s, penalties were creeping upwards, and the same crime might attract a sentence of around five years. In 1984, the Hodgson Committee recommended asset confiscation (seizing the proceeds of crime) as an alternative to longer prison terms: already, there was concern about prison overcrowding, cost, and lack of rehabilitative value of escalating imprisonment (Hodgson, 1984). In 1986 the Drug Trafficking Offences Act did bring in asset confiscation, but imprisonment showed no downturn. Quite the contrary: the judiciary chased prison sentences further up. This trend was legitimized by Parliament in its 1985 Controlled Drugs Penalties Act, which for the first time provided for maximum penalties of life imprisonment. Our trafficker caught with a kilo might now expect a sentence approaching ten years, *plus* asset confiscation. The intention of Hodgson, that asset confiscation should partially replace imprisonment, was forgotten in a blaze of 'get tough' rhetoric.

Has the escalation of prison sentences had any impact upon the problem? Of course, this is difficult to tell for sure. But longer sentences evidently have not provided a level of deterrence sufficient to reduce the extent of trafficking, as evidenced by the *increase* in trafficking in

Britain, in Europe, and on a global level. This is hardly surprising from a criminological perspective, since it is the likelihood of being caught, rather than the penalty that one aims to escape, that is generally understood to provide deterrence. Heavy prison penalties may be symbolically important (see Moore and Kleiman's 1989 discussion of law enforcement measures as 'expressive' of social disapproval) but they are not effective in any other way and they cost a lot of money.

How, then, should we proceed? Perhaps we need to go back to general principles, and ask what it is that we are trying to achieve. The general principle behind anti-trafficking policy should be similar to the general principles behind policy on drug consumption. Such an approach would lead us to pursue measures congruent with (a) minimization of the extent of trafficking and (b) minimization of the various forms of harm that are contingently associated with drug markets and control measures (cf. ACMD, 1984; Pearson, this volume; Dorn *et al.*, 1991).

Harm minimization is a well-understood concept in relation to management of the drug *user*, whereby policies and practices are adjusted so as to minimize the extent to which users and those around them suffer in terms of health problems, social problems, legal problems and financial problems that may be contingently related to drug consumption but are not inherent in it. The best-known example is the attempt to limit the spread of HIV by provision of sterile injecting equipment and injection advice, but the practice of harm minimization has developed along social, legal and financial dimensions as well as the more familiar health dimension. To take an example familiar to students of the early so-called 'British system' of prescribing injectable heroin, one of the aims of that system was to prevent or slow the emergence of an illicit market and hence keep users away from the legal, social and financial harms that it might present. This policy had been all but abandoned by the early 1980s, but by the middle of the decade there was a resumption of short-term prescribing to lure people into contact with counselling facilities and syringe exchange schemes. In the field of criminal justice, the British police are increasingly giving formal warnings to minor drugs offenders rather than taking them to court, the aim being to minimize unnecessary criminalization. So, one way or another, the concept of harm minimization in relation to users is well understood, if patchily adopted.

How might harm minimization be understood in relation to drug markets? Of course, one way of reducing the various types of harm that may be associated with trafficking, purchase and consumption is to hold down the market in quantitative terms: minimum market, minimum amounts of drugs, and minimum harm, other things being equal. But other things may not be equal, in the sense that certain strategies that look as if they reduce the market might actually make it nastier. Consider, for example, the US police practice of shooting at fleeing suspects who fail to stop when challenged. Might this not provoke suspects to carry weapons more frequently, whereupon they are more likely to use them against police and others in the market? We are fortunate in Europe that our enforcement agencies are less gun-happy than their US counterparts. Consider proposals for the death penalty for trafficking; might this not also motivate even more traffickers to take desperate steps to escape arrest?

Whatever powers are given to the police and to the courts, it is very clear that the illicit drug market will continue to exist to some extent. So, public policy has to be concerned with reducing – or, at the very least, not exacerbating – forms of harm that are only *contingently* associated with the market. This should be the criterion against which all policy proposals be evaluated: to what extent would they tend to hold down the market in quantitative terms *and* minimize the harm (legal, social, financial, etc.) associated with it.

To take the British context, a halving of maximum prison sentences, returning us roughly to the 'tariff' of the 1970s, may be a useful proposal for the purposes of debate. It is time to consider reform of the Drug Penalties Offences Act. A halving of prison places currently taken up by trafficking offenders would save millions. The financial resources thus freed would then allow considerable enhancement of policing, especially in respect of financial intelligence, precursor intelligence, surveillance operations and other means of investigation and case-building. The enhancement of these sophisticated elements of enforcement would result in a higher rate of apprehension of traffickers (though the increase would be modest, according to Wagstaff and Maynard, 1988), hence rather more deterrence, slightly less trafficking and, as a consequence, lowered availability of drugs. In other words, a re-allocation of resources from unproductive incarceration to modern forms of investigation would go some way to meeting the first element of prevention – there would be a smaller drug market.

Another important bit of legislation that needs critical scrutiny is the Drug Trafficking Offences Act (DTOA) of 1986. This Act made it obligatory for the courts to order a financial investigation of *every* person found guilty of a trafficking offence, so that an estimate of proceeds of trafficking could be made and an asset confiscation order made in the case of conviction. Of this requirement, Michael Zander has said

> Drug trafficking conjures up the image of fabulous profits. But most drug trafficking offenders are probably fairly small time... This does not mean that the existing power of confiscation is unnecessary. But it does help to put into perspective the call for yet more draconian penalties. It may even raise the question whether the scarce expert skill of detection available to the police would not be better deployed in the more serious cases than in pursuing so many minor offenders. It may actually be more productive, in every sense, to restrict confiscation in drug trafficking cases (as under the Criminal Justice Act 1988) to those involving sums of more than £10,000.
>
> (Zander, 1989: 52)

Yes, why not bring the DTOA into line with the 1988 Criminal Justice Bill, which in relation to crimes *other than* trafficking calls for confiscation of proceeds *only* above £10,000? This would bring anti-trafficking legislation into line with legislation on other areas of gainful crime. It would also release financial specialists, currently tied up with the implementation of confiscation orders in minor trafficking cases, to initiate new and more substantial investigations. Here, as elsewhere, a 'liberal' reform in relation to punishment could be a plank in a more effective anti-trafficking strategy. Sadly, although the DTOA was due to be discussed in Parliamentary circles during 1991 and may eventually be reformed, the chances of change along the lines suggested by Zander are at best uncertain.

Radical reductions in prison sentences might well reduce other problems, too. First, the motivation to use violence to avoid arrest might be reduced, since it would hardly be worth risking a long sentence for a violent act if abstaining from violence and getting caught resulted in a relatively short sentence. This would be a worthwhile outcome in its own terms.

Furthermore, a reduction in the lengths of prison sentences facing traffickers might reduce their motivation to threaten or use violence against suspected informants. At present, the degree of intimidation induced by the desire to escape 'exemplary' sentences has so reduced the flow of high-quality leads from frightened informants that large rewards are being offered in an attempt to restore the situation. It is widely accepted in policing circles that the motivation of good informants is far more complicated than financial greed (Dorn *et al.*, 1991). There is the danger that big rewards will induce some traffickers to intervene more forcefully against potential informants. If we want to reduce the market-related harm of violence, then we need to reduce every incentive for the drug trade to be further 'hardened'. At the very least, we must avoid further escalations in penalty.

CONCLUSION: SOME OBSTACLES

The escalation in penalties for trafficking has coincided with worldwide expansion of the drug market and its transmutation into a nastier form than previously. The intensity of punishment threatened does not guarantee the effectiveness of deterrence. Rather the reverse may be the case. What, then, drives the punishment motive, if prevention does not?

Domestic policies are part of the answer, as I indicated at the beginning of this chapter. But we should also accord some role to foreign policy. If we look at the foreign policy of the US, in particular, we find that whenever this country has a problem with part of the developing world, drugs that come from that region become described as particularly dangerous, traffickers in them are targeted as particularly evil, and problems of the inner cities become blamed on consumption of those drugs. In the post-Second World War period, as the US attempted, unsuccessfully as it turned out, to take the place of the departing French in the Far East, so heroin traffickers became dramatized – ironically, since it seems that it was those 'friendly' to the US rather than its enemies that were most involved in that trade (McCoy, 1974). Later, a similar pattern emerged in the Afghanistan/Pakistan region. As Latin America showed signs of independence, cocaine was re-positioned by US authorities, from being a relatively harmless drug to the worst drug imaginable.

It is interesting to speculate about the future, given the troubles that emerged in 1990 in the Middle East, one region for cultivation of psychoactive plants other than coca. If this region becomes even more of a sustained focus for US and European foreign policy, may we expect that cannabis will become re-described as possessing previously unrecognized dangers? Watch this space! Drug policy may for some time retain its characteristic of throwing up the most spectacular visions.

Such observations are not intended to imply that drug control policy is *only* an effect of broader foreign or domestic policies. We should not forget that the United States was prepared to 'lean on' Turkey to persuade that country to discontinue opium cultivation, even though such pressure was not especially desirable from a foreign policy point of view. Similarly, Mexico became the recipient of considerable pressure when that country supplied the bulk of US heroin. In these cases, it seems fair to describe drug policy as helping to shape foreign policy. But, having made these specific acknowledgements, it does also appear that domestic circumstances and foreign policy quite often have large and complicated parts to play. We should not generally expect a discussion of drug policy *per se* always to be taken strictly on its merits.

In closing, I hope that I have managed to convey some of my dis-ease over the two main 'solutions' being touted for drug problems – heavier penalties and legalization. Heavier penalties can only make drug markets 'heavier'; indeed there is a case for reducing imprisonment and re-directing the money saved to the policing side. Legalization of production and marketing will no doubt remain a pipe dream – which is a good thing, because it would provide a poor development path in regions of countries in which psychoactive plants are currently cultivated as a cash crop in conditions of peasant semi-self-sufficiency. It may seem a little unheroic and uninspiring, but the best option may be the middle course of fine-tuning the criminal justice system through a general reduction in penalties for trafficking.

ACKNOWLEDGEMENTS

The author thanks Karim Murji, Pat O'Hare, Jasper Woodcock and Lorraine Olver for criticisms and suggestions on an earlier draft.

REFERENCES

Advisory Council on Misuse of Drugs (1984) *Prevention*, London: HMSO.

Bennett, J. (1989) 'Restoring authority', *New Perspectives Quarterly* 6 (2): 4–7.

Chelimsky, E. (1989) Assistant Comproller General, in the Introduction to US General Accounting Office, *Federal Prisons: Trends on offender characteristics*, Gaithersburg, Maryland: GAO.

Dorn, N., Murji, K. and South, N. (1991) *Traffickers: Drug markets and law enforcement*, London: Routledge.

Helmer, J. (1975) *Drugs and Minority Oppression*, New York: Seabury.

Hodgson, D. (1984) *The Profits of Crime and their Recovery*, London: Heinemann.

McCoy, A. W. (1974) 'The politics of the poppy in Indochina: A comparative study of patron–client relations under French and American administrations', in L. Simmonds and A. Said (eds) *Drugs, Politics and Diplomacy*, Beverly Hills: Sage, pp. 112–36.

Moore, M. and Kleiman, M. (1989) *The Police and Drugs*, Washington, DC: National Institute of Justice.

Stevenson, R. (1990) 'Can markets cope with drugs?', *The Journal of Drug Issues* 20 (4): 659–66.

Wagstaff, A. and Maynard, A. (1988) *Economic Aspects of the Illicit Drug Market and Drug Enforcement Policies in the United Kingdom*, Home Office Research Study 95, London: HMSO.

Zander, M. (1989) *Confiscation and Forfeiture Law: English and American Comparisons*, London: Police Foundation.

Chapter 12

Self-injection education for street level sexworkers

L. Synn Stern

Many street sexworkers in the Bronx, New York, 'stroll' to support a drug habit. To say that these individuals are at risk for HIV may be correct, but they have more immediately threatening occupational risks: harassment, assault, rape, robbery and arrest due to the visible and unprotected nature of their employment; plus the skin and vein infections, trackmarks, and circulatory damage common to poorly managed IV drug use. AIDS education as it is normally delivered in New York City will not satisfy the needs of this population as it focuses only on AIDS and does nothing to address the more visible, stigmatizing and damaging aspects of their lives. Appropriate health education for this group needs to include lessons in safer professional sex and proper needle use. An individual can be taught to secure as much money as possible in as short a time as possible, thereby lessening the sexual risks and the possibility of coming to the attention of law enforcement personnel. The more attractive sexworkers appear, the more likely they'll be approached by clients, and the more money they make per trick, the less tricks they'll have to turn. Teaching needle sterilization is not always well accepted because it is an extra step, but teaching trackmark prevention and more competent injection techniques requires no extra time, can be taught in a few simple lessons, and provides information that most IV drug users desire. AIDS education, offered in this context, is more meaningful to the drug user and facilitates better connections with health care professionals. This chapter will focus on a simple course in self-injection, abscess prevention, and safer professional sex that has been found effective with a mostly homeless group of sexworkers in the South Bronx.

This chapter describes street outreach work[1] in the Bronx, New York City (NYC). The work has been conducted among a group of homeless injecting (intravenous or IV) drug users who support themselves by selling sex. They live in abandoned cars, trucks, and buildings in a warehouse district of the South Bronx. At dawn, the area is an active market supplying NYC with most of its meat and produce. Once the markets close at midday the area is abandoned to drug sales, sex sales, and police. The outreach worker has met with over four hundred IV drug-using sexworkers; they are Bronx natives, gay and straight, teens and adults, male and female.

Many sexworkers in the South Bronx have threatening occupational risks both from the visible and unprotected nature of their employment and from poorly managed IV drug use in a city with minimal access to new needles. In NYC, prostitution is a crime and a status offence, meaning that sexworkers can be arrested merely for being prostitutes, as well as for soliciting customers. Just as the majority of the arrests for drug use are in the more visible and less wealthy segment of the population, the majority of the arrests for sexwork are of street hustlers. Drug-using hospital staff, with access to sterile injection equipment and pharmaceutical drugs, seldom face the same law enforcement attention (or health risks) as the user, and buyer, of street drugs and needles. Men and women who sell sex indoors or through agencies frequently escape the police attention the poorer, mostly non-White, street sexworkers arouse.

There is a certain amount of outreach to the street sexworking population, but its focus traditionally has been 'rescuing' men and women from the life, and more recently the prevention of HIV (with funding coming from agencies more interested in the protection of the buyer). The rescue-style outreach teams frequently alienate or insult those they seek to engage because they refuse to assist with the concrete problems of street life. AIDS education programmes, while generally more comfortable dealing with sex and drug issues, frequently make the mistake of only talking about AIDS, condoms and bleach. Handing out bottles of water and bleach is both necessary and useful, but bleaching syringes is an extra step that some fatalistic and demoralized IV drug users will not take, and properly bleached syringes do not in any way prevent the skin and vein damage many drug users do to themselves and the others they inject.

There is a myth that IV drug users are hard to engage and that they are not interested in health care issues. Whether or not people actually like their jobs, they are usually very willing to talk about them. And most students do best in the subject they find most interesting. Street hustling is a job. Maintaining a drug habit is a job. Engaging addicts is no different from engaging anyone else, provided that you are not assumed to belong to the police force. The outreach worker has not yet met an addict who didn't want to talk about getting high, or an active user who wasn't interested in learning ways to perfect their drug-using technique. With the constant threat of arrest, no housing, and little income, AIDS just isn't the biggest problem on the block.

While some drug dealers require that potential customers display their trackmarks as proof that they are safe to sell to, there are no other circumstances in which tracks are desirable: police harass you, shop clerks follow you in stores, unless hidden they make finding straight employment difficult, and johns use the knowledge that a sexworker is addicted as a point from which to bargain for unsafe sex, or prices well below the local standard. The very nature of sexwork demands that workers appear enticing and highly visible (conditions that will also assist in getting them arrested) but there is no reason for drug use to be so. With careful education and a minimal attention to detail, trackmarks, abscesses, oedema, cellulitis, missed injections and venous collapse can be almost totally avoided.

When insulin-dependent diabetes is first diagnosed, the patients are shown how to inject themselves safely and with minimal damage and pain. They have access to sterile syringes and inject themselves subcutaneously, which requires less skill. Although NYC claims belief in a disease model of addiction, addicts are not taught even the basics of IV injection. They may be shown how to use bleach the outreach teams supply, or may be given alcohol swabs to clean the injection site, but programmes either assume that drug users already know how to inject properly, or are unwilling to take this step in health education. Poor injection technique is not only the cause of a host of unsightly and dangerous physical conditions, but is to blame for missed and stolen shots.

Possession of injection equipment is a misdemeanour and using it is a felony. Shooting galleries get a lot of press, but in the Bronx they also routinely get burnt down. Persons without homes or cars in which to inject their drugs, frequently do so on the street where they risk not only arrest, but theft of their drugs by other users. To avoid this a user needs to be quick: quick at finding a vein to prevent another user from snatching the loaded syringe, and capable of getting all the drug into a vein and not spilling it into the surrounding tissue where it has less effect and may ulcerate – street drugs often contain strange, inflammation-producing active cut. Even in the shooting gallery a less deft user risks having his or her drugs stolen.

Once a week for the past year the outreach worker has joined a team that makes nightly visits to the Bronx strolls. While distributing condoms, bleach kits, AIDS literature and clothing to the young people who live and work on the street, the worker spoke with the IV users among them and taught everyone willing to spend a few minutes how to give better, cleaner injections. While most of the men and women approached were mistrustful, they were also very grateful for an opportunity to discuss the problems they were having, not only with drug use, but with the work involved in using drugs.

The easiest and most dramatic thing to teach is the rotation of injection sites. This saves veins, prevents tracks, takes no extra time and requires no real change in individual behaviour. The use of alcohol and bleach is stressed, but not its HIV-preventing properties; rather, bleach use is recommended as a way to keep a constantly reused syringe flowing smoothly, and alcohol as a skin-freshener. A dull needle can be carefully resharpened with the striking surface of a matchbook, as most people are pleased to learn, but needs to be flushed several times prior to use to prevent the introduction of graphite or metal particles into the bloodstream. Knowing how much liquid to cook or mix drugs with, and at what speed to introduce it into the body, helps cut down the risk of abscessing, and teaching people how to get quickly and smoothly into and out of a vein cuts down on bruising and the likelihood of arrest. In a lesson or two a person can learn to give a quick, painless, competent injection that will leave little trace. It is made clear to everyone that the worker can be approached with questions relating to abscesses, ulcers, or other drug-related accidents. Even though these are exactly the things the outreach worker hopes to help people prevent, it would be unreasonable to expect total compliance, and total freedom from mistakes. Topical haemorrhoid preparations are wonderful healers of swollen overburdened veins, may help prevent tracks, can take the pain and puffiness out of a missed injection and their emollients provide some surface protection for dry, exposed skin.

In NYC, heroin and cocaine are the most frequently injected drugs. Heroin melts at boiling point and cocaine dissolves at room temperature. Some users enjoy injecting these drugs simultaneously but, in doing so, risk having the liquid solidify when the cocaine suspension heats up and the heroin solution cools down. To avoid this frustrating event it is recommended that users inject these drugs separately.

Although most IV users seldom have access to a wide variety of needles, it is often helpful to convince people to pay the extra dollar for a two-piece needle and syringe rather than buy the insulin syringes with the needle permanently attached. Should the needle on one of these clog, there is no way to recover any of the drug that may remain in the barrel, and they become dull and unserviceable more rapidly from constant banging of the point into the cooker.

Because the IV users are also sexworkers, the outreach worker ensures that these men and women have a good understanding of the ways in which professional sex could be made safer, and teaches those who did not know how to sneak condoms onto male customers during oral sex and to fake vaginal and anal sex when they could by taking it in their hand. Street sexworkers hustle to make money, and the addicted among them use their money to buy drugs. The better they look, the more money they can make. The higher their asking price, the less tricks they have to turn. And the less time they spend on the streets, the less exposure they'll have to law enforcement personnel, to violence, and to the health risks related to selling sex, like bladder infections, fissures, and sexually transmitted diseases (including HIV).

Street life is as exhausting as it is exciting, and many people are glad to learn ways in which they can make their drug money for the day or the week quickly, and with as few encounters with johns as possible. Persons who cannot be enticed to use bleach for its viral prevention properties are still generally interested in making drug money, in getting everything they paid for into their bodies, and in learning skills that will keep them from immediate physical harm. In addition, a person who is able to find veins has a talent for which less capable others are willing to pay. In the last year, the outreach worker has watched men and women already drug-sick and anxious, miss shots that they had worked several hours to pay for, and then in desperation enter cars with two or more men – a near guarantee of robbery, assault and rape – or agree to intercourse without condoms. Men and women often work five hours or more at a time just to make enough money to get straight, and then still have to work in order to have money to bring home. The hustlers who manage to hide their IV drug use have less hassle with johns and police officers alike. The fact that they also may experience a general improvement in health, and usually gain at least a few hours of free time each day, comes as a bonus. The reasons why people get high are enormous, societal, and individual. The outreach worker may have done little to change the clients' consumption of drugs, or their relationship to drugs, but has been able to provide them with skills that will make their IV drug use less apparent. With that comes some protection from addictophobia, from infection, and the hours that people had spent waiting for johns or digging for veins can now be used to do other things.

Self-injection education does nothing to change New York City's inhumane drug and needle policies, to change the community's perception of drug users who prostitute, or to provide clients with much needed housing. But it has helped them to a little more privacy, control, money, and time. And they have shared more of their lives with the worker than they might have if talk had only been about AIDS, or rehab, or detox, or condoms.

NOTE

1 Opinions expressed in this chapter do not necessarily reflect the policy of the supporting organization.

© 1991 L. Synn Stern

Chapter 13

HIV and drugs
Handy hints for women

Sheila Henderson

INTRODUCTION

Some providers of services for past or present users of illicit drugs are becoming more conscious of the needs of women in the HIV context (DAWN, 1991; Ryan, 1990). This chapter[1] addresses some of the issues from a British perspective.

WHY WOMEN AND HIV?

In January 1990, during a period of some speculation over the 'myth of heterosexual AIDS'[2] in the UK and the USA, the World Health Organization (WHO) announced that World AIDS Day 1990 would focus attention on 'Women and AIDS' – aiming to heighten awareness of the risk of HIV infection among women, highlight the increasing impact of risk of HIV infection among women and the role they play in HIV prevention and care. The WHO estimated at that time that at least six million people were infected with HIV worldwide, of which approximately two million were women. It is also predicted a cumulative total of 350,000 cases of AIDS among women by the end of 1992, or three times as many as had occurred by the end of the 1980s.

In Britain, the number of women reported to be infected with HIV at the end of June 1990 was 1,408 (HIV total for both sexes 14,090) and the number of women with AIDS, 138 (AIDS total for both sexes 3,433). These figures are likely to be underestimates. Previously, women with the virus were mainly injecting drug users but the number of reported cases of AIDS acquired heterosexually almost doubled last year. At the end of 1987, 147 women were known to have contracted HIV sexually, compared with 567 in September 1990. The reported number of women infected through injecting drug use rose from 168 to

615 in the same period. Positively Women, the organization for HIV-positive women, currently reports that nine of ten women who now contact them have acquired the virus heterosexually. Meanwhile, current medical knowledge indicates that women are more likely than men to contract HIV through an infected sexual partner.

These details underline the importance of thinking about women in the context of HIV prevention work and service provision – women are increasingly becoming infected as well as affected by the virus.

WHY DRUGS?

The official June 1990 HIV figures put the number of reported cases of heterosexual transmission at 7 per cent of the total and injecting drug use at 14 per cent. Nearly half of these heterosexual people with the virus were women. Add to this the fact that reported cases are likely to be under-representative, that there is now some suggestion that women drug injectors are becoming infected through heterosexual sex and that, despite some recent changes, drug services are less likely to attract women – and there is a considerable case for initiatives which will shift drug policy and practice accordingly.

The need for change was stated in *AIDS and Drug Misuse, Part 2*, the Report of the Advisory Council on the Misuse of Drugs (ACMD, 1989) on the implications for services of HIV infection and related illness in drug users.

Research suggests that although proportionately fewer female than male drug misusers attend drug services, services which make a particular effort to gear what is offered to the needs of women can be successful in attracting a much higher proportion of women clients. Drug services should review their policies to ensure they are receptive to the needs of women (ACMD, 1989: 41).

The reports suggested reasons why women may have reduced access to services.

...because they find the service off-putting and not understanding of their needs; because it is difficult to find somebody to look after their children; or because they are frightened that their children will be taken into care if they admit to having a drug problem. Evidence indicates that women are far more likely to attend services which consciously aim to attract them; unfortunately many services inadvertently deter them.

(Ibid.: 23-4)

The suggestion made by the report for overcoming these barriers included women-only sessions, availability of women doctors and counsellors, provision of creche and child care facilities, good family planning advice and well-informed counselling for pregnant HIV+ women. The need for social services departments to counteract the fear that drug use *per se* is a reason for separating parents and children was also emphasized, as was the need for a change in attitudes which assume that certain types of sexual behaviour and drug misuse are less acceptable in women than in men.

WOMEN, HIV AND HARM MINIMIZATION

With the ACMD report's recognition that 'HIV is a greater threat to public and individual health than drug misuse' (ACMD, 1988), some official support for the adoption of a general harm minimization approach (previously or otherwise known as harm reduction, risk reduction) within drug services was forthcoming. As such, HIV legitimized, to some degree, approaches to drug treatment which have safer or controlled drug use in various forms, rather than total abstinence as their only goal. The development of a new kind of service – needle and syringe exchange schemes and the provision of condoms – has been the most graphic illustration of this shift. Concern over the spread of HIV infection has consolidated and also boosted expansion in community-based services and multi-agency approaches to service provision.

Almost certainly, more than any other single factor, AIDS and the threat of transmission of HIV both within the drug-using population and beyond has forced a fundamental rethink of drug services (Ettorre, 1990).

Focusing on women in the context of HIV underlines the need to continue this rethinking process. Despite the move towards community-based information, advice, counselling and treatment services and the emphasis upon 'user friendliness' and upon maximizing contact with drug users, women still do not figure large as consumers of drug services. Even needle and syringe exchange schemes – where women might have been expected to fall into a 'shopping' role – would not appear to be attracting more women. The 1989 figures for those attending needle and syringe exchanges in England showed no improvement on 1987–8 – an overwhelmingly male attendance of 79 per cent (Donoghoe, 1990). This failure to provide the kinds of drug services which women feel able to use would suggest a need to abandon any remaining isolationist approaches to the provision of drug services, to realize the limitations of 'clients must come to the service' assumptions, and to broaden the concept of harm minimization. 'Harm reduction is not just about clean needles and syringes, methadone, etc., but also about ante-natal advice, child care issues, etc.' (Roulston, 1990). The concept could also be usefully broadened to take account of women's health aside from their role as mothers and to include Positively Women's view of the key issues facing women with HIV/AIDS – 'a roof over our heads, food in our stomachs, stability and information on treatment' (London Voluntary Services Council, 1989).

WOMEN AND DRUG USE

Women who use illicit drugs are beyond the moral pale. Their behaviour goes against people's expectations of the feminine and is typified as selfish, deviant, criminal, etc. Greater horror is expressed at women users than men, as men are expected and 'allowed' to be aggressive, self-indulgent and so on, although they are punished for it. This is particularly clear from the enormous concern about mothers – never fathers – using drugs .

(DAWN, 1980).

The different social perceptions and personal experiences of women drug users have been acknowledged in some quarters of the drug field for over a decade. Addressing their needs is no new idea – even if it is an idea still awaiting widespread practical application. Drug-using women have long contended with the social sanction which constructs them as 'failed' and often 'fallen'. However, HIV has added a new dimension. Apart from the more obvious threat it holds for their lives and wellbeing, HIV-positive women drug users and ex-users report being confronted by a triple layer of stigma: the association of drug use with deviance and self-destruction, the images of sexual deviance associated with AIDS and the now double departure from socially prescribed behaviour worthy of the 'good woman', which connection with the previous two factors apparently signifies.

ISOLATION

Positively Women, the organization for HIV-positive women, report that women are frequently reluctant to approach often unsympathetic services, living instead in fear and isolation. A negative association between Africa and AIDS in the public mind makes this particularly acute for Black women, but also for women from other minority ethnic backgrounds. Stigma and fear of the authorities is particularly relevant to women involved with drugs. The fact that women's multiple social roles – especially informal caring and child care roles – can result in a tendency to defer meeting their own health needs has also been suggested as a contributing factor.

REPRODUCTION

It is often the case that a woman's first response to a positive HIV antibody test result is one of loss. This feeling can include many things – one of which is a sense of loss of the possibility of becoming a mother, even though having a child may never have been seriously considered. Scientific findings may be of little support in this emotional situation but current research puts the risk of an HIV-positive mother infecting her baby at between 25 and 33 per cent – less than or similar to some genetic diseases. Early research findings in the US, however (based on a small cohort of women already ill), suggested a high likelihood of transmission and the onset of illness among HIV-positive new mothers. The unfortunate result of the combination of this now revised information with the general panic over AIDS has been a tremendous pressure upon HIV-positive pregnant women to have abortions. This practice, unaccompanied by clear and accurate information enabling women to make an informed choice, has not – despite major improvements in specialist services in recent years – disappeared. HIV-positive women can now also receive excellent treatment throughout the process of childbirth, but again, cases of unnecessarily punitive responses from medical staff are still reported, with many HIV-positive women made to feel 'like murderers with no social conscience'.

SEX AND SEXUALITY

Discussion of sex and sexuality in the drug and HIV literature tends to be reduced to questions of prevalence of condom use as an indicator of (lack of) behaviour change among drug users. This is a limited view by any account, particularly as it relates to women in the HIV context. Positively speaking, HIV has opened up the possibility for women to pursue the non-penetrative sexual pleasures the sex surveys have indicated they often prefer. However, many women are personally and socially unable to exercise control over their lives, even if they wish to.

HIV-positive women are surrounded by negative images. Negative assumptions, previously attached to women who use drugs and now to HIV-positive women, are often based upon an historical persistent association between active female sexuality and deviance. A departure from traditional heterosexuality can still invite social sanction. Or a step into activities considered deviant can also be associated with sexual deviance. It is, for instance, often assumed as a matter of course that women drug users are involved in prostitution. ISDD's research and other reports suggests that HIV-positive women tend to be seen as promiscuous or in some way deviant no matter what their lifestyle (Dorn et al., 1991).

For women involved in prostitution, HIV has prompted an increase in official scrutiny based upon fear over the spread of HIV infection. The race to establish the rate of HIV infection among them emphasized the threat to the consumers of these sexual services rather than the providers. Later self-help and outreach initiatives have attempted to reverse the focus, emphasizing the risks for the women involved, including the risk from offers of higher rates of pay for unsafe sex.

Much of public health education on HIV/AIDS geared to heterosexuals has placed the responsibility for promoting safer sex, as birth control, upon women. Research shows that women are more inclined to want to practise safer sex. However, apart from the fact that carrying condoms still cuts across the grain of female respectability in the eyes of many, the social circumstances of women's relationships often prevent them. Recent reports suggest that articulate and advantaged women, well informed about HIV, still have difficulty in negotiating safer sex. Questions such as betrayal of trust, failure to demonstrate love, destruction of 'spontaneity' complicate the issue. For women who inject drugs the difficulties may be more acute – since, for instance, they may take up additional positions of dependence upon men, such as sharing injecting equipment, following and being injected by a male partner. The wish for a child in a long-standing relationship also works against the notion of practising safer sex. The popular (and inaccurate) status of lesbian sex as 'no-risk' sex, although contradictory to another popular association between HIV and all homosexuality, also combines with it to hinder consideration of safer sex practices among women.

CHILD CARE

For many women, living with the virus is complicated by the responsibilities of child care. The consequences of the parenting role for health and general wellbeing can be depleting as well as rewarding at the best of times. HIV can bring with it fear of infecting children, fear of their treatment by others or the task of caring for an infected child. Contact with services is likely to be increased for mothers and with it the possibilities of experiencing disservice. Informing her children of her (and possibly their own) HIV-positive status can be a particularly difficult decision (some women have less choice by dint of obvious illness). Any impetus for a straightforward and honest approach can be complicated by fear of the internal impact upon the child – especially the burden of the information and the consequences of any breaches in confidentiality. Concern over the future of children in the event of illness and/or death is complicated for women by the lack of child care support in general, and of respite and residential care geared to mothers and of 'safe' fostering systems in particular.

CONCLUSION

Many issues surrounding drug use, HIV and women have yet to be fully addressed. Those competing for attention include the lack of practical forms of support available such as cash help, housing, dealing with welfare benefits, legal problems, etc., and the lack of clear and accurate information on the clinical manifestations of the virus in women. (It has, for example, been suggested recently that opportunistic infections that may be a part of the spectrum of AIDS-related diseases in women may go unrecognized.) Meanwhile, there is no dimension to the range of issues which requires more attention than that of race. The major rethink of drug services predicated by the advent of HIV/AIDS may yet provide the impetus for the dramatic change required to make drug services in Britain attractive to the majority of black people who may require them.

In this country, there are initiatives to support and make contact not only with women who inject drugs, but also with other women drug users and non-drug-using female partners and relatives of drug users. Much of this innovative work is under-publicized but includes: establishing specialist drug services in women's health centres and other generic health services; detached work in supermarkets and launderettes; multi-agency work involving family planning, obstetric and gynaecological staff; residential units for women drug users wishing to maintain custody of the children and streetwork with women involved in prostitution (Henderson, 1990). Such work is in its infancy and those involved in its development would not profess to know all the answers. However, it does point the way forward in the important process of developing services which cater for the specific needs of women – an essential consideration for harm minimization strategies which all too often have been gender blind.

ACKNOWLEDGEMENTS

Special thanks go to Mary Treacy of the Standing Conference on Drug Abuse (SCODA) for invaluable advice, comments and support throughout the production of the book that forms the basis of this chapter. Thanks also to my colleagues at the Institute for the Study of Drug Dependence (ISDD) and in the Women and HIV/AIDS Networks in Lothian and the Thames Region. This work was supported by the AIDS Unit of the Department of Health.

NOTES

1 This chapter has been an edited version of the introduction to *Women, Drugs, HIV: Practical Issues*, a paperback edited by the author, in which practitioners from a range of services discuss the issues as they arise in their specific areas of work.
2 In November 1989, *The Sun* picked up on the latest wave of attempts to sway the official line on HIV/AIDS away from the notion that it affects us all and sweep it to the margins. Headlines such as that of 18 November 1989, 'AIDS: The Hoax of the Century', were sparked off by words attributed to Lord Kilbracken (a member of the All Party Parliamentary Group on AIDS) to the effect that 'straight sex can't give you AIDS'. This, together with coverage of Michael Fumento's book, *The Myth of Heterosexual AIDS*, cast previous campaigns to prevent the spread of AIDS through heterosexual sex as a phoney war.

REFERENCES

Advisory Council on the Misuse of Drugs (1988) *AIDS and Drug Misuse, Part 1*, London: HMSO.
——— (1989) *AIDS and Drug Misuse, Part 2*, London: HMSO.
DAWN (Drugs, Alcohol, Women, Now) (1980) A report from First DAWN Symposium, November 1980.
——— (1991) *Women, Drugs and Alcohol: A national survey of service provision*, London: HMSO. (in press)
Donoghoe, M. (1990) *National Syringe Exchange Monitoring Study. Interim Report on Characteristics and Base-Line Risk Behaviour of Clients in England, April–September 1989*, London: Monitoring Research Group, Centre for Study of Drugs and Health Behaviour.
Dorn, N., Henderson, S. and South, N. (1991) *AIDS: Women, Drugs and Social Care*, London: Falmer Press. (in press)

Ettorre, B. (1990) 'Service development for AIDS and drugs', paper presented at a seminar on AIDS and Drugs at Birkbeck College, London, May.

Henderson, S. (1990) *Women, Drugs, HIV: Practical Issues*, London: Institute for the Study of Drug Dependence.

London Voluntary Services Council (1989) 'Linking up. Voluntary and statutory collaboration on HIV/AIDS', report of a seminar held by the London Voluntary Services Council, London.

Roulston, J. (1990) 'Women in perspective', paper presented to the NOVOAH Conference, Birmingham, April.

Ryan, L. (1991) 'Desperately seeking services? A directory of service provision for women by the Women's HIV/AIDS Network', London: Health Education Authority.

Chapter 14

Smack in the eye!

Mark Gilman

In 1987 the North West Regional Health Authority gave the Lifeline Project, a Manchester-based drug advice service, £5,000 to produce HIV prevention information for drug users. This chapter provides an overview of the production, distribution and evaluation of the resultant HIV prevention initiative that takes the form of an adult comic book for drug users called *Smack in the Eye*. The aim of the comic is to 'promote' safer drug use and safer sex. This approach is an alternative to health education 'warnings of danger' that seek to tell people what not to do without suggesting possible alternatives. In short, this is a practical initiative borne out of 'harm reductionist', as opposed to 'abstentionist', theory and philosophy. Whereas the central goal of abstentionist initiatives is to reduce drug use, the central goal of harm reduction initiatives is to reduce the harms (such as HIV/AIDS) that can arise from drug use. *Smack in the Eye* 'nudges' drug users towards safer drug using practices in the manner described by Stimson (1990) and targets drug users for information and advice on safer sex as suggested by Newcombe (1987, 1988) and Klee *et al.* (1990).

This harm reduction initiative is primarily aimed at the injecting drug user 'community'. It is designed to encourage a reduction of drug-related harm, with specific reference to HIV and AIDS. As there is no cure for AIDS and no proved method of preventing drug use, the Lifeline Project has attempted to develop a strategy that both accepts and works within this reality. Some commentators have been quite shocked by the use of a comic book format to address such a serious issue as HIV and AIDS. However, it has been pointed out that the emergence of HIV among injecting drug users has given a legitimation to the harm reduction approach that was previously unthinkable. Similarly there is a growing recognition of the successful use of comic books in many different areas of public education and information.

To begin this project we arranged a series of meetings with a group of drug users with a view to establishing some basic principles that could guide our harm reduction initiatives. In-depth conversations with this group suggested that just as advice on contraception has to start from an acceptance of sexual activity as 'normal', so harm reduction messages and advice have to come from a user-friendly and non-judgemental agency which accepts drug use as an activity that may lead to problems but is not in itself pathological behaviour.

Attempts at primary prevention have often tried to scare people away from drug use. In these attempts, balanced, factual information about drugs has often been abandoned in place of an emphasis on the 'possible' dangers of drug use. This has created a 'credibility gap' between those sending messages about drug use and those drug users who receive them. Current attempts at harm reduction have to win back the confidence of drug users who have been socialized into a subculture used to discounting warnings of danger from well-intentioned but ill-informed professionals (Gilman, 1989).

The consultation process revealed that drug users had grave reservations about the majority of standard drugs and HIV information. These reservations concerned both content and style. These drug users saw standard drugs and HIV education as falling into one of two categories: 'bullshit' or 'boring'. For example, a poster that merely informs you that 'DRUG ABUSE KILLS!' is an example of the bullshit variety. It is bullshit because it tells you nothing. It tells you that drug abuse can kill, but so can rock climbing, potholing or driving a motorbike too fast. In other words, a whole variety of exciting activities contain a potentially lethal risk factor. We are informed by those in high political office that the only thing that drug users can look forward to is despair and degradation. Subsequent mass media campaigns here in Britain have pursued this theme. However, such is the appeal of the 'wasted look' in youth culture that the 'HEROIN SCREWS YOU UP!' posters, featuring a suitably wasted young man, have been seen nestling beside the latest pop stars on the bedroom walls of British teenagers. Those with a more wry sense of humour have altered the wording of these posters, replacing the word heroin for unemployment so that they now read 'UNEMPLOYMENT SCREWS YOU UP!'

The 'boring' variety of standard drugs and HIV education came from well-intentioned individuals who produced materials in a style which reflected their chosen daily reading material – The Guardian (one of the 'quality' British daily newspapers). In true Guardian style, the information in these materials is thorough and accurate but very difficult to get excited about. Drug users accepted the information in these materials yet described reading these materials as 'hard work'. In other words, the information is not bullshit but the style of presentation is 'boring'. Had we not gone out and consulted drug users I suspect that we too would have produced worthy but boring materials. The result of our consultations was quite clear, we had to produce drug and HIV information in a format that was both credible and entertaining.

In relation to HIV prevention it became increasingly clear that harm reduction messages about not sharing injection equipment need to be supported by the provision of easy access to clean injecting equipment. Official exhortations to reduce or eliminate the sharing of injecting equipment will be ignored if access to the practical means of achieving this behaviour change are absent. The establishment of a needle exchange scheme, for example, can be presented as a symbolic and practical indication that, 'The spread of HIV is a greater threat to individual and public health than drug misuse' (Advisory Council on the Misuse of Drugs, 1988). The absence of such schemes will see drug users dismiss the HIV/AIDS 'scare' as just another attempt to scare people away from, and out of, drug use.

A comprehensive approach to HIV prevention among drug users should address the three variables of Knowledge, Attitudes and Behaviour. Provision must be made to increase factual 'knowledge' about HIV transmission and encourage an 'attitude' whereby it is fashionable to 'know' about HIV/AIDS. Perhaps the most important is easy access to the equipment (e.g. clean injecting equipment and condoms) necessary to alter 'risky behaviour'. It should be noted that the knowledge – attitude – behaviour relationship is not a linear one. An increase in knowledge will not necessarily lead to a change in attitude. A change in attitude will not necessarily lead to a change in behaviour. *Smack in the Eye* attempts to address all three of these variables simultaneously. We give factual information about HIV transmission, show that it is 'cool' to 'wise up' about HIV and advertise outlets where users can obtain the practical means (e.g. clean injecting equipment and condoms) for changing behaviour.

Having reviewed existing, contemporary material we began to look at how drug users had traditionally been informed about safer drug use. In this context we recognized the contribution made by the underground press of the 1960s and 1970s. The underground press did a better job of delivering drug education than '...an army of drug educationalists' (Lewis, 1985).

We also looked at how other agencies at home and abroad were 'selling' their safer drug use and safer sex messages. Experience from the Netherlands suggested that a more 'active' approach needs to be adopted with our target group than with general public education which makes information material freely available to be picked up or ignored. Anecdotal evidence from drug agencies and needle exchange schemes confirmed that drug users had to be strongly encouraged to take HIV/AIDS leaflets and even then these leaflets were often found discarded in adjacent streets.

The first task therefore is to produce materials that drug users themselves actually want to see and pass on to their friends. Our consultations with drug users revealed that adult comics were far more prevalent than quality newspapers among our target audience. The most popular of these comics is a publication called *VIZ*. The success story of *VIZ* is quite remarkable. It began life as a number of photocopied sheets sold around pubs and clubs in the north-east. It is now one of the most widely read publications in England, whose readership eagerly await each issue. *Smack in the Eye* is clearly within the *VIZ* genre which has provided us with a model to guide our efforts. *VIZ* characters and plots are wide and varied, ranging from the classic schoolboy toilet humour of 'Johnny Fartpants' to the more acidic style of humour as seen in the character of 'Postman Plod – the miserable bastard'. *Smack in the Eye* contains a similar range of styles and characters.

In the pilot issue we counter-posed some cartoons that originally appeared in a Dutch Aids leaflet with a depiction of cartoon characters of our design. The Dutch cartoons are headed 'The Wise Guys', because they practise safer drug use and sex, whereas the other cartoons depict 'The Daft Bastards' who do not. We chose, and have continued with, this counter-position in an attempt to ally a prevention message to positive attitudes and behaviour already evident in some drug-using subcultures. In our experience one should not underestimate the importance of variety and fashion in the lives of many of today's drug users.

The depiction of unsafe ('untogether') use as being the preserve of 'daft bastards' seeks to reiterate and reinforce the general theme of the comic that unsafe drug use and sexual practice is anti-social and damaging to the drug user's own subcultural group. Those who refuse to share injection equipment are obviously 'Wise Guys', whilst the users of their unwanted needles are clearly 'Daft Bastards'. The targets for humour are the attitudes and behaviour of the character who wants to share someone else's injection equipment.

We have devised a character called 'Tough Shit Thomas', a cat with nine lives who is a 'Daft Bastard' of the first order, but who is always ready to learn. 'Tough Shit Thomas' has appeared in every issue of *Smack in the Eye* and has been used as a vehicle for general advice on: safer drug use and safer sex, overdose, dangers of injecting benzodiazepines and your rights when arrested by the police.

The practical experiences and tactics of people who already practise safer drug use could be of benefit to other users. Given the lack of organization among drug users it is quite likely that the 'successful' user may never encounter novices or 'unsuccessful' users whose practices may involve regular high-risk activities. Comics can be employed to portray scenarios where such meetings do take place and the successful user passes on harm reduction advice. Alternatively, the comic may just give us a glimpse into the lives of 'together' users. We have devised a character called 'Grandpa Smackhead Jones: The Oldest Junkie in the World' who passes on harm reduction advice to younger, less experienced users. 'Grandpa Smackhead Jones' has given advice on: safer injecting, dangers of injecting dextromoramide ('Palfium'), crack cocaine and amphetamine use.

From the outset of this project it was felt to be crucial that the comic carry messages about safer sexual practice in tandem with safer drug use advice. This is particularly important as many drug injectors who do use their own equipment feel that by doing this they have 'done their bit'. For many drug users 'AIDS' is about not sharing injection equipment. Having taken this message on board they appear to regard themselves as sufficiently 'inoculated' and carry on practising unsafe sex. This is evidenced by the fact that by no means all the drug users who collect injection equipment from needle exchange schemes take up the offer of condoms. In this context we are faced with all the problems inherent in encouraging safer sex among the heterosexual population in general.

Homosexuals and lesbians who use drugs can benefit from the high level of organization among the gay and lesbian community where safer sex messages and information are clearly evident.

While carrying out the research for the comic we were informed by gay men that, in conducting their sexual relations, they have traditionally chosen from a wide range of sexual activities that do not involve penetration and as such are examples of safer sex. Many of these acts provide all the satisfaction of penetration and are often seen as more exciting. Because many heterosexuals choose their sexual activities from a much more restricted repertoire, penetration is still of paramount importance. One of the problems with social advertising is its negativity. Because of their negative emphasis, social advertisements are perceived as threatening by the audience – they seem to substitute less attractive activities for those which are more hazardous but nevertheless more enjoyable. This means that such advertising can induce anxiety and defensiveness which prompts a dismissal of the message. The humour of the comic format clearly distances the messages contained within it from the standard serious messages which create such defensiveness.

A central aim of the comic is to promote the theme that safer sex allows pleasure without regret. The comic format is a suitable vehicle from which to sell a safer sex message and avoid a negative, moralistic attitude which informs drug users (already engaged in an activity outlawed by society via the criminal justice system) of something else that they should not do. Comics can begin to explore an alternative approach that does not insist on a reduction in sexual activity or the use of condoms but rather promotes examples of safer sexual activities as exciting alternatives to the monotony of penetration.

One of the difficulties we have experienced in encouraging the formation of drug users' organizations in the past is that both users and workers are unclear about what such a group would do. Drug users' groups can organize around a specific activity such as the distribution of relevant information. The distribution system for *Smack in the Eye* was designed with this in mind.

The comics were initially distributed to drug users in contact with services (including the needle exchange schemes) and then passed on by them to their drug-using friends and acquaintances. We put a small cover charge on the comic to give the drug users who distribute the comic the option of selling the comic to other users thereby utilizing the well-documented entrepreneurial skills of some drug users. The inclusion of a cover price was simply to assist distribution of the comic. As an organization we make copies of the comic freely available to our drug-using customers and expected other organizations to do the same.

Unlike the one-off leaflet that can be perceived as a single exercise in inoculation against HIV, the comic format can be produced regularly to repeat and reinforce harm reduction messages using different characters and scenarios. This is an important feature of the comic. Much contemporary health education draws heavily on the 'Health Belief Model', which clearly identifies the need to continue to re-inform and re-inforce 'appropriate patient beliefs'. A research team from the Pentagon has found that people retain information far longer when it is presented in comic book form; and that the more dramatic the images, the better the comic succeeds.

Given drug users' dismissal of the more formal health education material, the style and content of a comic has to reflect aspects of the social milieu of groups of drug users which may be unpleasant to some; however, there is a significant lobby arguing that the presence of HIV infection poses such a fundamental threat to society that no risk reduction option should be rejected because it conflicts with our own feelings and attitudes to drug use.

However, such laudable intentions pose real dilemmas for all those who attempt to produce harm reduction materials. The producers of *Smack in the Eye* were not immune from this. We, too, had to find out what we were and were not prepared to publish. That meant we had to confront our own personal value systems, those of Lifeline as an organization, and those enshrined with legislation. Brave statements about risk reduction are much harder to translate into reality.

Producing *Smack in the Eye* has proved to be an exercise in 'boundary clarification'. By this we mean that we have had to decide what is acceptable, and more problematically, what is not. Putting together a comic that aimed to be different from all other HIV information/prevention materials meant that we were consciously aiming for a style and tone that would make the comic stand out – that would make its readers remember both the medium and the message.

In this attempt to highlight the risk of the transmission of HIV we have deliberately employed the language of the street and explicit portrayal of sexual activity and drug use. The use of explicit 'street language' clearly distances the material from more traditional health education approaches. Similarly, there is well-documented evidence that humour is evident among drug users even when the most serious of issues are being discussed. The use of humour stands in direct contrast to the traditional use of 'fear arousal', the shortcomings of which have been well documented.

Humour can be very effective, but is very often a double-edged tool as it often requires a target. The problem is to create humour with a 'sting in its tail'. Within a comic format humour can be employed to attract attention yet leave behind a meaningful harm reduction message. In identifying targets for humour one should focus on examples of unsafe practices and the attitudes that accompany them in an attempt to stigmatize these attitudes and behaviours. However, one has to be very careful that the characters depicting these target behaviours and attitudes do not develop into anti-heroes, proud of their kamikaze attitude and behaviour.

Having distributed a pilot issue of *Smack in the Eye* we conducted thirty in-depth interviews with drug users who had read the comic. Although our exploratory research with drug users, prior to the production of the comic, highlighted a credibility gap between those sending messages and the drug users that receive them, we have been genuinely surprised at the extent of the suspicion of official messages. We have been similarly surprised at the fond memories that today's drug users still have for the 'head comics' of the underground press.

The dominant discourse on drug issues makes much use of the terminology of war. It is our experience that a war on 'drugs' can very easily become a war on drug 'users'. Evaluative interviewing has shown that drug users perceive the production of *Smack in the Eye* as a positive step by the Lifeline Project to 'take sides' with them. If the target audience for health education messages 'trust the messenger' they are more likely to 'trust the message'.

In order to maintain the trust and respect of drug users we are committed to act on behalf of those who were concerned about issues of stereotyping in the pilot issue. In many ways the stereotyping issue has been the most problematic. Although we have made every effort to avoid stereotypical images in the production of *Smack in the Eye* it is very difficult to portray characters and scenarios that are recognizable and familiar in a cartoon format without running the risk of stereotyping. Having been made aware of this concern, however, we have taken great care to avoid any offensive stereotypical imagery in subsequent issues.

The British Advisory Council on the Misuse of Drugs (1988) report, *AIDS and Drug Misuse*, recommends that drug services make contact with as many of the hidden population of drug users as possible. *Smack in the Eye* is being used as a tool to facilitate this contact along with outreach and detached work. Outreach and detached workers use the comic as a way of opening up a dialogue with drug users. They are then in a position to discuss some of the points made in the comic. Drug workers have reported that this is a particularly useful way of beginning discussions about sexual behaviour with a group whose primary concern relates to reducing the harm that can arise from drug use. Similarly, those working with groups whose primary concern relates to reducing the harm that can arise from sexual behaviour have been able to use *Smack in the Eye* to highlight drug issues. The distribution of subsequent issues is also a clear reason for maintained contact between detached worker and client.

Prior to the production of *Smack in the Eye* there was much talk about the need to develop radical and imaginative health education initiatives in response to the presence of the HIV virus. However, the parameters for such efforts were never defined. Everyone who attempts to do something radical and imaginative, therefore, must be prepared to take the criticism of those who feel they have 'gone too far'. *Smack in the Eye* was no exception. The reaction from other workers in the 'caring professions', and indeed in the drug field itself, was mixed. There were those who thought the comic exciting and innovative, and eagerly awaited the chance to distribute it. There were also those who viewed it as irresponsible and/or pornographic.

Our critics inform us that the boundaries that we have gone beyond are those of public decency. Many possible outlets were, and still are, denied to the comic because workers or their managers find the comic 'offensive'. Although we accept that some people find the comic offensive we have prioritized the reaction of drug users. This has been overwhelmingly positive. The comic has elucidated the 'boundaries' within which radical and imaginative initiatives can succeed. It has helped to identify those people who are prepared to go beyond conference rhetoric and actually be involved in the dissemination of radical material. This project is a serious departure from standard drugs and HIV education. It is proving to be a successful attempt to face the real challenge posed to us all by the presence of HIV and AIDS in contemporary society.

REFERENCES

Advisory Council on the Misuse of Drugs (1988) *AIDS and Drug Misuse, Part 1*, London: HMSO.

Gilman, M. (1989) *Comics as a Strategy in Reducing Drug Related Harm*, Manchester: Lifeline Project Ltd.

Klee, H., Faugier, J., Hayes, C., Boulton, T. and Morris, J. (1990) 'Sexual partners of injecting drug users: The risk of HIV infection', *British Journal of Addiction* 85: 413–18.

Lewis, R. (1985) 'Selling smack and chasing dragons', *Emergency* (3).

Newcombe, R. (1987) 'High time for harm reduction', *Druglink* 2 (10): 11.

—— (1988) 'Serious fun: Drug education through popular culture', *Druglink* 3 (6):10–13.

Stimson, G. V. (1990) 'AIDS and HIV: The challenge for British drug services', *British Journal of Addiction* 85: 329–39.

Chapter 15

A harm reduction educational strategy towards Ecstasy

Erik Fromberg

INTRODUCTION

The use of XTC (methylenedioxymethamphetamine, MDMA or Ecstasy) has been increasing in the Netherlands since 1985. First supplies came from the USA, but production of the drug in the Netherlands is presumed to have started in 1987. In general, the first producers sold their product only to friends and relations, so the nature of these relationships more or less guaranteed the quality of their product. The producer–consumer chain was short, the production local.

In 1988, XTC was brought under the Dutch Narcotic Law on list 1, alongside heroin, cocaine, etc. As a result, many small producers stopped their production. However, at the same time the popularity of XTC increased logarithmically. This discrepancy between supply and demand resulted in the provision of more dangerous 'impostors', such as LSD and MDA, but particularly amphetamine.

The increasing popularity of this 'new' drug and the widespread presence of impostor-drugs necessitated an educational strategy to reduce harm as well as prevent use.

GOALS AND METHODS

It is self-evident that the essence of our advice can be formulated as the reduction of the harmful effects of drug use, which is in accordance with the central purpose of the Dutch drug policy. Harm reduction is a preventive goal. When we, albeit reluctantly, acknowledge that the primary aim of the narcotic laws is prevention, we also have to acknowledge that these laws have failed completely – drugs are and will be used, notwithstanding laws. Since XTC has been placed under the narcotic law, the demand for it has increased enormously. One might state that the law has resulted in a reduction of the availability of the drug. However, this is not the whole story. The demand is met with the supply of more dangerous drugs. The crux of the problem lies in the fact that narcotic laws take away the responsibility for individual behaviour from the individual and place it in the hands of the government. The availability of all sorts of illegal drugs makes clear that governments are not able to bear this responsibility.

In our educational strategy we emphasize the individual's responsibility, in a way which can best be compared with 'safe use' AIDS campaigns. This implies that we neither want to moralize nor assume a missionary point of view. The starting point is the supposition that everybody is capable of acting responsibly with regard to themselves, as long as no impediments exist, such as a lack of information, etc. The existence of a small number of innately irresponsible people has never been an argument to prohibit car driving or other potentially dangerous activities.

In the Dutch drug policy the spreading of factual information has always been an important part of our prevention strategies. In contrast to some other countries, where information on drugs and their effects is often considered propaganda and punished as such, people in Holland can freely discuss and write about drugs. No one who acknowledges that drugs as such are neither good nor bad, and that drugs legally considered as entailing 'unacceptable' risks can (in certain circumstances) even have more positive than negative effects, has ever been prosecuted because of alleged drug propaganda. In the Dutch drug policy the relativity of 'unacceptable' is taken into account.

As a result, the Dutch public is relatively well informed about drugs compared with the public abroad. Thus, a second aspect of our educational strategy is that we make use of and rely on the already existing knowledge of the user.

However, information as such is not sufficient. Education is not the same as information. Education implies that the information is being placed in a normative frame of reference. Occasionally establishing norms is confused with moralizing. In such cases it is stated that the use of a drug is bad, with an implicit argumentation on ethical considerations. It has to be stated emphatically that ethical considerations have their own value, but are subjective.

In short, the goal of our education is harm reduction, by giving factual information offered in a normative frame, without moralizing, taking into account the responsibility of individuals and their existing knowledge on drugs.

THE TARGET GROUP

The target group for our educational intervention are those who use XTC, because there exists a lack of information among them. Furthermore, we also expect to reach those who are considering whether or not to use XTC. This expectation is based on considerations regarding:

1 the properties of XTC;
2 the structure of the market;
3 the local character of the market.

The properties of XTC

The most important property is that XTC is characterized as a 'drug for social occasions'. Next in importance is that XTC has a low 'entry threshold'. This threshold is determined by pharmacological and sociological factors. The pharmacological factors are:

- the soft action, when compared with 'real' hallucinogens like LSD;
- the 'practical' duration of action, not as short as cocaine, not as long as LSD;
- the drug is relatively easy to combine with other drugs;
- the drug is easily dosed, also with regard to its differential effects;
- the user can function socially;
- the drug does not cause physical dependence.

Relevant sociological factors are:

- the reinforcement of feelings of togetherness;
- the 'light' trend – XTC is being preferred above 'hard' drugs such as LSD, and more importantly amphetamine or cocaine; the old drugs are being rejected or being used more pragmatically;
- the 'varia' trend in consumption patterns of legal as well as illegal drugs;
- the revival of the 'sixties';
- the feeling of personal stardom: with your head in the clouds, but with your feet solid on the ground.

This low entry threshold is the main cause of the quickly growing popularity of this drug, but also causes a remarkable openness about the use of it. The properties of the drug and the form in which it is supplied also means that, at the consumer level, there are no means to check whether the product offered indeed contains the drug, something which is possible with a drug like cannabis.

THE STRUCTURE OF THE MARKET

New drugs are always introduced by a small group of people who have a relationship that had already been established. From this group, which usually belongs to the top layer of the community, the use spreads to the bottom. When this happens with an addictive drug, the relationship between users becomes more obscure as it spreads to the bottom. The spread of cocaine use is a good example.

The same process occurs with non-addictive drugs like cannabis and LSD, with the difference that the intrinsic criminal structure, which is so characteristic for the heroin and amphetamine trade, never developed, in spite of the illegality of these drugs. The differences between the cannabis market and the LSD market can be explained by the difference in entry thresholds, being low for cannabis and high for LSD. Due to the low threshold of cannabis this drug is attractive to many, while the high threshold of LSD limits its use to a small group. The cohesion within this group ensured that as soon as sufficient information on LSD was present within this group, its use gave no more problems. In this sense the self-correcting capacity of this market was and is large.

Until now, the market structure of XTC can best be compared with that of LSD and cannabis. The structure has certain characteristics:

- a quick spread among a relatively large number of people;
- the self-correcting capacity of the market is, in principle, strong enough to limit possible dangers of the use of the drug;
- there is only a weak coupling to specific group characteristics: XTC use persists, while, for example, the acid house musical trend passed its zenith and, while the use spreads to the bottom, it does not diminish in the top group.

The local character of the market

XTC is not a product that is traded by way of a worldwide network as is the case with cannabis and heroin. The production does not require a high degree of technical expertise or a large financial investment. It is a drug that can be produced relatively cheaply in a small laboratory from base materials that can be obtained legally. The entry threshold is not only low for the consumer but also for the producer. This resulted in a number of producers supplying a small local market. The chain between producer and consumer is short.

Within the local group of consumers, relations exist that go further than the use of the drug. As a result, the use is strongly determined by friendship-relations, in contrast with heroin, where commercial interests play a very important role, not only on the level of international smuggling but on the consumer level as well, trade to finance one's own use. This means, in the case of XTC, that information about the drug is spread in the buying and selling process.

Although the popularity of XTC has a number of aspects that can be compared with the emergence of cannabis and LSD in the 1960s and early 1970s, there exist remarkable differences too. The most important one is the 'pulverization of the scene'. While in the 1960s the binding forces between the scenes were stronger than the dividing forces, the reverse is now true: the youth culture is pulverized. In the 1960s the hippy subculture was characterized by a strong feeling of togetherness, the binding factor being a lifestyle, a value system, in which the use of cannabis was not only a binding factor, but a symbol of those binding values. In 1990 we see a multitude of different groups, having few mutual affinities, and which do not consider the use of XTC as a binding factor. Acid-house and jazz-pop fans, older and neo-hippies, New Age groups, motorclubs and yuppies: each group has its own goals, values and lifestyles. These groups seem to have little in common, though they do have some common characteristics:

- musical interest;
- outgoing personalities;
- looking out for something special;
- acceptance of drug use, i.e. of cannabis, and being relatively well informed about drugs;
- rejection of the pragmatization, the no-nonsense attitude of the 1980s, contiguous with the revival of the 1960s;
- a rather strong collectivity within the group, not being drug-oriented;
- strong indifference to the government and politics.

To illustrate this last point: most XTC users we talked to did not even know the drug had been brought under the narcotics law.

GOAL OF THE EDUCATIONAL INTERVENTION

The goals of the educational intervention are on three levels: primary, secondary and tertiary.

Primary prevention

- Emphasizing the considerable chance that what one uses may not be XTC but a more dangerous drug, because what is offered as XTC is

often adulterated or contains other drugs (i.e. amphetamine or LSD).
- Giving the aspirant consumer more tools for decision-making about whether or not to use the drug.
- Prevention of over-identification by avoiding scene-words.

Secondary prevention

- The building of knowledge and experience among user groups.
- Reinforcing the self-correcting capacity of user groups and the market. Even on the 'black market', standardization is possible as can be seen with LSD.

Tertiary prevention

- Stimulation of self-help, teaching people what to do when they are confronted with problems in others.

COMMUNICATING THE INFORMATION

The problem is how to reach different groups, especially while the differences between the groups are so large that media specifically directed at these groups do not exist, in contrast to the underground press in the 1960s. So two approaches are possible:

High key: a broad campaign directed at the general public, but having the risk that such a campaign evokes interest in the drug that did not exist beforehand.

Low key: communicating by many different channels, directed to all special groups.

We handled both approaches in the following way:

High key: a publicity campaign around a conference on XTC in which the drug XTC was not central, but the 'market pollution', i.e. the general risk of all black market products not being what they are supposed to be, due to lack of control of the products. This is information that is relevant to all people, consumers as well as potential consumers of nearly all illegal drugs, and is supposed to have a demand reduction effect.

Low key: aimed at the different groups of (potential) users with specific information on XTC, contiguous with the high key approach. The chosen media were a leaflet, an information pack and, as an experiment, a public service telephone number.

The most important consideration was that it was necessary to give a lot of factual information since, the media-hype on XTC notwithstanding, the main facts on XTC were not available. Both our information pack and the telephone message try to give these facts and can be used as the basis for further information. We had to fulfil two requirements:

1   The heterogeneity of the target groups made it difficult to find terms addressing all groups. We had to avoid words that are specific for some of these groups. For the same reason we omitted advice on condom use.
2   The status as a hard drug. Apart from upsetting the distinction between hard drugs (list I) and soft drugs (list II) which is cherished in Holland, the fact that XTC has been scheduled as a hard drug hampers the spread of information about it. One of the most important characteristics of the user group is their acceptance of soft drug use, i.e. cannabis use, so the most obvious places to spread the information are the coffee-shops where cannabis is sold. However, these shops are tolerated as long as they are not involved in any way with the hard drug scene. This makes most coffee-shops very reluctant to distribute the XTC information as this might be considered by the police as involvement with schedule 1 drugs. In fact, all coffee-shops we approached refused to distribute the pack, in two cases with a threat of violence. To involve the shops, we requested the cooperation of the local police forces, in some cases with success.

THE EDITING OF THE INFORMATION PACK

As mentioned before, we chose a very factual approach, due to the heterogeneity of the target group. The style of the pack insert was modelled on the insert enclosed with medical drugs. With regard to the contents, we used the following items:
- *The effects of the drug*, by which we hope to reduce the influence of *mala fide* suppliers.
- *The market pollution*: one never knows what one is buying. This makes an appeal to the responsibility of the potential user and connects to the high key campaign – the risks of the use, if one has proper XTC: acute poisoning and long-term effects.
- *Combinations with other drugs*. We answered the question whether specific combinations should be discussed by only mentioning them

in general terms. Combinations that are used only in small circles (e.g. XTC with poppers) were not mentioned, while we considered the risk involved in drawing attention to such combinations as heavier than the lack of information. We are considering making smaller leaflets on such topics to be spread among relevant circles.
– Contra-indications.

The question whether or not to give an indication of price was answered with a clear 'no'.

THE PUBLIC SERVICE PHONE NUMBER

We prepared a tape recording with the same information for use on a public service telephone. The number was advertised in several national newspapers and in the first month over 400 people dialled the number, for which they are charged 50 cents per minute by way of their telephone account. We consider this a success and are discussing how to extend the use of this medium in the future.

FINAL REMARKS

It is clear that this information is just one part of a prevention strategy. The prosecution policy also plays an important role, since the local market structure implies a self-correcting capacity which is absent in large-scale production and supplying. Therefore, prosecution should be directed at large-scale operations and leave local production and consumption more or less unhampered. We consider a balanced dismissal policy an important matter, which mainly serves the harm reduction policy by barring adulterated drugs and limiting the use to local markets. The judicial powers as well as the police have so far followed such a subtle policy. We have since noticed a clear reduction of impostor drugs on the XTC market, and consider this a first success for our policy.

Chapter 16

An empirical study of the relationship between heroin addiction, crime and medical treatment

C. S. J. Fazey

There is a wealth of evidence, both quantitative and qualitative, which demonstrates a clear relationship between crime and addiction, not only from the obvious perspective that possession of certain drugs is a crime, but that there is a necessity for the vast majority of addicted illicit drug users to commit crime in order to support their addiction. However, the effect that treatment has upon the criminal activities of the patients is less well researched. One reason for this, at least in the United Kingdom, is that many in the medical profession who treat addicts argue that this problem is no part of their professional concern. Their concern, they maintain, is to treat patients, which for them means to reduce and eliminate the legal drugs which they receive. So often there is not only a lack of concern for the criminal activity which may ensue from a decision not to prescribe certain drugs, but also there is a positive assertion that this should not even be the concern of the medical profession. Therefore, the number of studies which actually try to relate the effect of treatment to the criminal activity of the patients is very limited.

As part of a wider study into the working of a drug dependency clinic in Liverpool, the effect of the treatment on the criminal behaviour of the patients was studied. In looking at the relationship between heroin addiction, crime and medical treatment it is important to remember that they are variables and not constants, and this research has been conducted within clearly defined parameters for each of these variables.

It is worthwhile examing these parameters and definitions – not for any semantic ritual, but because the very results are dependent on the parameters and limit the applicability of the results.

First, the term 'illicit demand' is used simply because this research is concerned with drug taking which has an illegal status – not with whether it is use or abuse.

Second, this research was concerned with people who had sought medical help because they were, or thought they were, dependent on heroin. (This study did not include anyone who used amphetamine at the weekends, or smoked cannabis or used any other drugs.)

Third, and very important, the medical treatment available was of a different kind from that practised in many other countries. What is understood by treatment seems to vary not just from one culture and country to another, but, as we have seen in the UK, from one part of the country to another, as well as over time. The results outlined here are specific to the type of treatment regime on offer, for reasons which will be discussed later.

The manner in which drug treatments in the UK are delivered must also be noted. Someone who is prescribed a drug picks up the prescription from a pharmacy. Usually the prescription is sent directly to the pharmacy, and will cover a period of two weeks. Patients can pick up their daily dose each day for consumption at home, but the most common practice, certainly in Liverpool, was for the patient who was in receipt of a prescription for oral methadone to pick up one week's supply at a time. Those who received intravenous drugs usually picked up their prescription three times per week. No drugs were dispensed from the clinic, all were dispensed through various pharmacies.

Most of the patients who sought help at the clinic were put on a reducing amount of methadone over a period of one month. Not everyone succeeded in reducing completely, so their time on a reducing regime would be extended. Those who went through this reduction regime, at the end of one month, simply did not return to the clinic. There was no way of knowing whether the detoxification was successful, if the patient were now drug free and therefore did not need the services of the clinic, or whether the detoxification was not successful and the patient returned to buying drugs illegally on the black market. In the event of the latter case, there was, however, some feedback. If the latter case were, in reality, the fact, then the patient often returned to the clinic, perhaps several months later.

Immediate in-patient detoxification was available, as well as this out-patient detoxification, which, in effect, comprised the main means of treating heroin-dependent clients. Three-quarters of all patients were initially treated in this fashion. Those who could not be treated in this manner were stabilized or maintained on oral methadone or on intravenous methadone, and even more rarely on intravenous heroin. However, only 6 per cent of all patients started off with a prescription for intravenous drugs.

Fourth, some qualification needs to be given concerning the measurement of crime. The extent of criminal activities was measured on a self-report basis. The reason for this was simply that much of the criminal activity of the patients was in the area of unreported crime – mainly shoplifting. However, another study has shown that during the time concerned, the number of burglary offences and theft offences increased in a neighbouring area where no treatment facilities existed, above the national average and at a faster rate than where services were available (Parker and Newcombe, 1987).

Lastly, the other limitation is place. This study took place in Liverpool, a city in north-west England, which contains pockets of severe deprivation and an economy which has considerable problems. It may be that patterns of drug use vary from one economic climate to another, but it is certainly true, for these data at least, that the problems of illicit heroin use were strongly related to other social problems. Therefore, there are three elements in this analysis – crime, drugs and treatment.

THE ASSOCIATION BETWEEN DRUGS AND CRIME

The association between drugs and crime is both unequivocal and well documented (Mott, 1989; Anglin and MacGlothlin, 1985). In this particular study of 1,019 patients who attended the clinic, 90 per cent admitted to committing crime in order to pay for their drugs, and only one-fifth had no convictions. They came overwhelmingly from the poorest and most deprived parts of the city (as measured by census data) where crime most often preceded drug use. This finding generated another project which examined this relationship in more detail (Fazey et al., 1990). Of those with convictions, only a quarter claimed that it was their drug use which led to crime.

Taking out about one-fifth of patients who said that they had no criminal convictions, of those that remained, well over one-third (37 per cent) admitted to a conviction prior to any illegal drug use, and a further 11 per cent admitted to a conviction in the same year that they began their drug use. When examining age of first conviction and age of first heroin use, over 60 per cent had convictions before they used heroin and a further 12 per cent had convictions in the same year as their heroin use.

The number of patients who had a criminal conviction before they thought of themselves as dependent on heroin represented 67 per cent, but taking dependency and conviction in the same year the figure rose to 76 per cent. Therefore, 24 per cent of patients had had convictions after they became dependent on heroin.

THE COSTS OF BUYING ILLEGAL DRUGS

The average amount spent per patient was £40 per day or £280 per week. This figure may represent an overestimate because many addicts will not spend that much every day of the week. On the other hand, many addicts will spend more on drugs when they have the money. If, for example, they committed a robbery and obtained £280, it is extremely unlikely that this money would last for a week. They would reward themselves for their daring, luck or narrow escape, and therefore spend the money on drugs in only a few days, thus requiring more for the rest of the week.

The range of spending varied from nil, where the patient either obtained drugs legally or was given them by a partner or friend, to £210 a day. The mode – that is the category with the highest single number – was £20. Only 2 per cent claimed that they did not have to pay for their drugs.

TREATMENT AND CONVICTIONS

In order to look at the effect of treatment on the lives of patients, a sample of 127 patients who had been in continuous treatment for one year were compared with a group who had at one time been clinic patients, but had dropped out of treatment and later returned.

Re-attenders

The study wanted to look at what had happened to the patients in the meantime – that is, what had happened to the patients, what was their drug history, as well as their criminal, personal and social histories? Information was gained on 66 patients. ('Dropped out of treatment' was defined as not attending the clinic for six weeks or more. Most prescriptions ran for one month, although picked up on a weekly or more frequent basis, and so if no prescription had been issued for six weeks the patient was without legal drugs for at least two weeks.) The average age of the re-attenders was 23·5, and the average time that they had dropped out of treatment was almost one year.

The drug that they had been using while away from the clinic was predominantly heroin. Six claimed that they had not had to commit crime in order to maintain their drug consumption, but two of these said that they had had to sell their houses in order to keep their habit going. All the rest admitted to committing crime in order to pay for their drugs. Shoplifting was again the highest single category of offence mentioned when illegal activities in relation to drug use were recorded.

Only one-third of patients said that they had been drug free at some time during their absence from the clinic. The average length of time of those who claimed to be drug free was seventeen weeks. When looking at crimes committed while away from the clinic, 13 per cent had cases pending; when they returned to the clinic, 10 per cent had just finished a prison sentence, 6 per cent were on probation, 6 per cent were on community service or supervision order, and 3 per cent were on bail. Altogether, almost 40 per cent of those re-attending for treatment had had involvement with the criminal law while away from the clinic. This is considerably higher than that admitted to by the group who were in treatment during this time.

Annual review data

Data were obtained on 127 patients who had attended the clinic for a year or more. Some 25 per cent of this group were working, 5 per cent full time and 20 per cent part time, but 40 per cent had been working or in full-time education at some time during the previous year. However, these figures must be viewed in the context of an unemployment rate in the area exceeding 20 per cent, with pockets of unemployment rising to 40 per cent in some of the more deprived districts.

There had been very few prescription changes during the year, 97 per cent being on the same drug, but 6 per cent went from linctus to intravenous drugs, while others went from ampoules to linctus, and then back to ampoules. Of the changes in the amount of drug prescribed, twenty-eight had their prescriptions reduced, and forty-one increased; the rest remained the same.

These changes are important because although these patients were maintained for a year or more this does not mean that they had unchanging prescriptions. Maintenance does not mean uniformity.

Only 52 per cent claimed that they did not buy any drugs on the black market. Almost one-third, however (31 per cent), said that they still bought heroin. A closer examination of the data revealed that some of these patients had not been in continuous treatment, but had been in hospital, or in custody. Twenty-two patients said that, for whatever reason, they had been drug free for at least one week during the year, but there were still 36 per cent of these who said that they did not buy illegal drugs. The average amount spent by those who said that they bought drugs on the black market was £20 per week. Taking out those who said that they were drug free during the year, the amount rose to £22. This compares with £40 per day, or £280 per week, from the total population before they came into treatment, and £40 per day for this particular group before treatment.

Treatment certainly seems to cut down the amount spent on the purchase of illegal drugs. It does not eliminate it entirely, and also it could be argued that the figures are an underestimate since many patients would not like to admit that they are still using illegal drugs.

The average number of criminal convictions for the total population was four, and for this group 3.8. During the year almost three-quarters of the patients (74 per cent) claimed that they had no convictions, with 20 per cent admitting to one conviction and 6.3 per cent to two.

Table 16.1 Re-attenders v. those in treatment more than twelve months

	Re-attenders N=66 (%)	12 months attending N=127 (%)
Said not committed an offence	9	74
Cases pending/on bail	16	0
Some time in custody	10	3
Probation/CSO	12	NK
Any work/education	6	40
Any time drug free*	33	17
Any illicit drug use	100	48
Any illicit heroin use	100	31
Crime to pay for drugs	91	26
Weekly cost of illicit drugs	£280	£20

* Includes time in custody

Table 16.1 compares the re-attenders with those in treatment for more than twelve months. Comparing those who had dropped out of treatment and returned with those in continuous treatment, the former group committed more crime while away from the clinic and had more convictions and cases pending than those in treatment for a year or more. They also used more illegal drugs and spent more on drugs. This is not to say that treatment miraculously turned a highly criminal population into a band of angels. It didn't. It did, however, reduce the criminal activity of most of the patient population, comparing their pre-treatment convictions with their in-treatment convictions, and also comparing them with those who had dropped out and returned.

In essence this research demonstrated that medical treatment reduced the criminal activity of patients. However, this cannot simply be applied to any medical intervention which is called 'drug treatment'. The drug treatment regime in this study can best be described using the latest buzz word 'flexible'. But then drug treatment policy always used to be flexible, in the UK at least, until a group of medical practitioners decided to be inflexible.

The inflexible approach, which declares that only one option exists for all patients – usually a detoxification programme within a specific period of time – is one that is often enshrined by some medical practitioners. It is doubtful whether these results would be replicable within substantially different treatment regimes.

One apparently important factor distinguishes between the treatment regimes: the relationship between the medical practitioner and the patient. In the inflexible regimes the relationship can only be described as medical hegemony, or 'doctor knows best'. In the clinic where this research took place the patients were not given anything and everything they asked for – but at least most felt that they could ask, and that the type and quantity of drugs that they received would be a matter of discussion between doctor and patient, and not a regime imposed upon them against their will. The resulting prescription might not have been what ideally they would have liked, but it was usually near enough for them to put up with it. This meant that patients would stay in treatment, but would also feel confident enough, when their drug taking was stabilized, to try to reduce or come off, knowing that if they could not manage then their previous prescription would be restored. Some tried to reduce, others to change from injectables to linctus, but reverted back again if they could not cope with the new regime.

The difference between the flexible and inflexible medical approach has also been illustrated in another study conducted by the author (Fazey and Wibberley 1990). Here, a small number of patients who were receiving prescriptions for intravenous drugs were subjected to an enforced change to oral medication. Instead of ceasing to use intravenous drugs, they resorted to illegal rather than legal drugs. But their physical health deteriorated; some suffered severe social disruption and, for most, crime had to serve as the means of supplying the cash to replace the intravenous supplies they previously had on prescription.

CONCLUSION

As long as patients stay in treatment their criminal behaviour reduces, but whether they stay in treatment or not seems strongly related to the type of treatment they receive. If they do not see it as meeting their needs – even if the medical practitioner thinks that it does – then they vote with their feet, and go back to committing more crime to finance their street habit.

REFERENCES

Anglin, M. D. and McGlothlin, W. H. (1985) 'Methadone maintenance in California: A decade's experience', in L. Brill and C. Winick *The Yearbook of Substance Use and Abuse*, New York: Human Sciences Press.

Fazey, C. S. J. and Wibberley, L. (1990) 'Preventing the spread of HIV infection: A study of drug patients' syringe and condom use', *Studies of Drug Issues*, no. 4, University of Liverpool: Centre for Urban Studies.

Fazey, C. S. J., Brown, P., Batey, P., Wibberley, L. and Stevenson, R. (1990) 'A socio-demographic analysis of patients attending a drug dependency unit', *Studies of Drug Issues*, no. 5, University of Liverpool: Centre for Urban Studies.

Mott, J. (1989) 'Reducing heroin related crime', Home Office Research & Planning Unit, Bulletin No. 26: 30–3.

Parker, H. and Newcombe, R. (1987) 'Heroin use and acquisitive crime in an English community', *British Journal of Sociology* 38: 331–50.

Chapter 17

The role of the police in harm reduction

A. Fraser and M. George

The original aim of this study was to look at the drug-using careers of a group of heroin users in a fairly small south coast town. However, very early in the study it became obvious that the group's drug use was dependent on the supply or distribution systems of heroin operating in the town, and that these supply networks were themselves affected or changed through police action. The study therefore focused on the effects of police interventions into supply networks on the harmfulness of users' behaviour.

The Health District studied was a mixture of urban and rural communities, predominantly white and middle class, and had a population of just under a quarter of a million (of whom half live in the main town of the district: Worthing). As a result of its reputation as a retirement centre the population distribution shows a disproportionate number of elderly residents. However, in spite of this, or perhaps because of this, the district has had a significant heroin problem since the late 1960s, until recently largely ignored by authority and unnoticed by residents.

The heroin users in this study were not of course a homogeneous group, but some common characteristics could be identified: they were mostly male, in their late twenties to early forties (peaking around the mid-thirties), had worked their way through the spectrum of drugs, finishing up with heroin, were all injectors and had been using heroin for a number of years. They were a group that was born and bred in Worthing, went to school together, started using drugs together and finished up using opiates together. As a consequence of this there were, as one might suspect, strong social and friendship bonds between the cohort members.

The overlapping catchment areas of the two treatment agencies – DAIS and Options – has meant that the heroin users present to either

agency; the two agencies have developed long-term helping or
therapeutic relationships with the cohort members based on trust,
understanding and mutual respect. Pooling of data between the two
agencies and snowballing allowed the construction of comprehensive
accurate 'networks' of the heroin users and dealers. At the beginning of

Table 17.1 Interaction between heroin dealing structures and the police

Dealing structure	Police action	Market response
1980-4: Mixture of entrepreneurial action and mutual society action. Social Centre based	Very little from local police. No County Drug Unit	Market flourishes and evolves into a classic pyramid structure as a result of increased demand
1984-6: Pyramid structure. Social Centre based	(a) County Drug Unit targets the large wholesalers (b) Local police target the social centre NB: (a) and (b) are unrelated and do not indicate a coordinated police strategy	(a) New wholesalers quickly found to replace those removed by police ops (b) Cohort's attempts to establish a new social centre fail due to the persistent police pressure on pub landlords. 'Diehard' users form a street-based mutual society. However, since it is small with erratic supply most of the cohort move to displacement drug/activities
1986-8: Mutual society. Street based	County Drug Unit withdrawn from Worthing. Little drug actions by local police	In spite of low police presence no success in establishing a stable long-term Social Centre. Mutual society becomes house based and more 'commercial'. Increased supply leads to increased demand as the cohort drops displacements and returns to heroin use. New house dealers enter the market as 'business' booms
1988–90: House dealers	County Drugs Unit returns to town at request of local police after a series of publicized ODs. Arrest of a large house dealer puts pressures on the others	House dealers adopt a range of strategies to minimize the 'damage' from police pressures, e.g. customers must use on the premises; early a.m. doorstep deliveries; taxi couriers; carrying internally; house dealers keep only one day's stock in house

this study 101 heroin users were identified. In the following three and a half years only a further seventeen members were added to the original chart, of whom five were new to the area; nine were returning to the area, sometimes after a custodial sentence; while only three were 'missing' from the original head count or were not using heroin at that time. In Worthing it is almost as if someone had shut all the doors and allowed the natural course of evolution to take place, with relatively few individuals either leaving the system or entering from outside.

DRUG DISTRIBUTION NETWORKS AND THE POLICE

Using the nomenclature developed by Lewis *et al.* (1985) and Dorn and South (1987) the drug distribution networks for heroin have been identified and reported in detail elsewhere (Fraser and George, 1988; George and Fraser, 1989). Table 17.1 summarizes the types of heroin distribution networks operating in Worthing over a ten-year period, police action against the networks and the corresponding network response.

Focusing on the 'cops and robbers' aspects of heroin distribution in Worthing it was seen that police action against dealing networks usually led to a corresponding reaction. Dealing networks usually 'self-healed' minor damage, but where major damage was done to a dealing structure it mutated into a different form. For example, police action against the 'traditional' social centre for the pyramid structure of dealers and users successfully destroyed the pyramid; however it then, over time, reformed hydra-like as a house-dealing system, a more difficult challenge to policing.

It was seen in Worthing and has been reported from several other studies, that policing of heroin distribution networks can rarely eliminate heroin from an area on a long-term basis. While policing is ineffectual in this respect, it is however of interest to look at the effects of policing on the drug-using behaviour of the heroin cohort.

The street scene, as it presented in the heyday of heroin availability, had a stable and identified hierarchy of distribution with a universally recognized and accepted market place/social centre, a seafront pub widely frequented by the heroin-using cohort. Continuous monitoring of the cohort gave much detail about the way in which the street scene and problems encountered by users varied as a result of the disruption of this network and the costs and benefits of upsetting this particular apple cart (Table 17.2).

Neither of the treatment agencies existed during the first phase, but current clients still reminisce wistfully about the mid-1980s when 'the sun always shone' and the 'gear' was cheap and pure. Those who ran into difficulties were referred to the Brighton Drug Dependency Unit where medium-term methadone detoxification provided temporary relief from the complexities of the user/dealer network. Briefly the situation was stable and contained.

Table 17.2 The Worthing opiate scenes 1986-9

Phase	Cohort behaviour–displacement activities
Stable distribution network with communal base	Little data, high levels of primary opiate use. The 'scene' concentrated and contained. High levels of peer group cohesion and unified identity
Unstable mutual societies without permanent base	Increase in bad deals, rip-offs, alcohol and other drug consumption. Increase in drug thefts, manipulation of GPs, non-heroin-related overdoses, visible street drinking. More contact with GPs and treatment centres. Public order offences
Emerging multi-base house dealing network	Increasing stability. More in treatment extended treatment contact. More scoring out-of-town. Drug-related charges replace public order offences

Following the two police actions in 1986 (Operations Mauritius and Anthill) which disrupted both the dealing network and the central distribution/social centre, Worthing moved into a second and different street scene. As described in earlier papers (Fraser and George,1988; George and Fraser, 1989), a series of unstable mutual societies sprang up and withered as the drug-using and dealing network attempted to re-establish itself in a series of town centre public houses and cafés. Since by this time both the treatment agencies had thrived and achieved wide acceptance, it was possible to observe much more closely the displacement activities which grew up over the next three years. Initially there were many reports of bad deals, rip-offs and increasing numbers of identified primary opiate users who turned to benzodiazepines, alcohol and other problematic combinations in ill-fated attempts to satisfy their addiction.

Similarly there was a 22 per cent increase in thefts from pharmacies and general practitioner or veterinary surgeries from forty-five in 1986 to fifty-five in 1987. The figure for 1988 was identical at fifty-five.

These points can be further illustrated by analyzing the fatal overdoses which have occurred in the town over this time. Of eleven identified fatal overdoses for which there are Coroner's post-mortem details, a large variety of substances have been identified both in isolation and in combination, notably Diconal and alcohol, also tranquillizers and prescription opiates.

The most important outcome of this investigation is that heroin and its metabolites are conspicuous by their absence. It can therefore be justifiably argued that chaotic displacement-type drug use is significantly dangerous and has accounted for a number of deaths in the Worthing area.

However, the news has not been all bad.

The disruption of 1986 led to a steady increase in opiate users presenting for treatment. In autumn 1987 the Options project was treating thirty-six of the 101 identified cohort members (36 per cent); by autumn 1988, Options was seeing sixty-three of the cohort of 118, an increase of 58 per cent.

For many, the disruption of the stable network and the stepping up of police action provided the impetus which led them to present. The data, however, reflect pessimistically on the association between contact with treatment agencies and reduction in risk-laden drug use. The majority (eight out of eleven) of the overdoses and all of the natural cause deaths were among clients in contact with the treatment agency. The three overdose subjects who were not in contact with the treatment agency all met their deaths as a result of a Diconal overdose in isolation, although in one case small quantities of Dihydrocodeine were also identified.

The available data for 1989 point to a gradual re-emergence of stability. A house dealer network has evolved, which in combination with a larger number of users benefiting from a more liberal prescribing policy, appears to have stabilized the situation. Clients presenting or representing for treatment do so more as a planned, internally motivated action rather than as a crisis response. There have been no known overdoses for the last six months and the number of crimes involving the theft of drugs has reduced from fifty-five in 1988 to thirty in 1989.

Could all this be an indication that the clear waters muddied by police action in 1986 are gradually re-stabilizing? The tentative conclusion is that police action aimed at disrupting the distribution and social network of drug use has had a negative impact on the harmfulness of drug use. Increased harm may be associated with more chaotic drug use, increased theft of drugs and a dispersion of drug use and drug users which gives the (possibly erroneous) impression of an increase in prevalence, reflecting the observation of Power (1987) describing the 'Pool Hall' phenomenon in London's West End.

THE ATTITUDES OF LOCAL POLICE TO HARM REDUCTION

Measures taken by local police appear to have had major direct and indirect effects on the type and extent of drug use in the local population and this has had knock-on implications for levels of risk-laden behaviour. It is therefore worth investigating the extent of match or mismatch between police attitudes and actions, and effects thereof.

A questionnaire was completed by fourteen members of the local police force and fifteen members of the Sussex Drug Unit. The purpose was to explore any difference in attitude and impression between specialist and non-specialist officers (see Table 17.3). While this study cannot be regarded as anything more than a pilot study of the police force in general, it does in fact canvass a sizeable proportion of local police, giving it some authority as a local survey.

Table 17.3 summarizes the results of this survey and shows a remarkable similarity of response between specialist and non-specialist officers. In only one respect do they differ significantly: non-specialist police advocate an increase in counselling and treatment agencies as the most effective way of reducing illicit drug use, while specialist drug unit officers favour more arrests and convictions.

The survey reveals that all specialist and non-specialist local police feel that drug use has increased and become more visible over the last three years in and around Worthing. This may be partly a direct result of fragmenting and disturbing the stable hierarchical structure of the mid-1980s. Few officers feel that the strategy adopted over the last few years has been successful in suppressing or eradicating drug use from the town.

As regards attitudes to effective responses to first-time offenders in comparison with habitual drug-related offenders, few officers surveyed advocate treatment alone. There is a moderate preference for early punishment, presumably as a deterrent strategy. When this has failed (i.e. in the case of a habitual offender) a combination of treatment and punishment, (for example, community service, probation or a fine in combination with counselling and/or detoxification) is more likely to be indicated as the preferred strategy. The low proportion of police officers advocating treatment alone for drug-related offenders is hardly surprising. As one Detective Inspector put it: 'When you start arresting them we'll start counselling them!'

Table 17.3 Police attitudes and impressions

	Drug unit (N=15)		Local Police (N=14)		Total (N=29)	
Amount of drug use						
Increased	12	(80%)	12	(86%)	24	(83%)
Decreased	0	(0%)	0	(0%)	0	(0%)
Remained the same	3	(20%)	2	(14%)	5	(17%)
Type of drug use						
More visible	11	(73%)	11	(78%)	22	(76%)
Less visible	1	(7%)	0	(0%)	1	(3%)
Neither more nor less	3	(20%)	3	(22%)	6	(21%)
Effective response: first-time offenders						
Punishment	6	(40%)	6	(43%)	12	(41%)
Treatment	3	(20%)	3	(22%)	6	(21%)
Both	6	(40%)	5	(35%)	11	(38%)
Effective response: habitual offenders						
Punishment	5	(33%)	2	(14%)	7	(24%)
Treatment	0	(0%)	2	(14%)	2	(7%)
Both	10	(66%)	10	(72%)	20	(69%)
Would give information about:						
Needle/syringe	11	(73%)	8	(57%)	19	(65%)
Safe disposal of works	12	(80%)	11	(78%)	23	(79%)
Treatment agencies	14	(93%)	13	(93%)	27	(93%)
Most effective ways of reducing illicit drug use:						
More arrests/ convictions	6	(40%)	1	(7%)	7	(24%)
Stiffer penalties	5	(33%)	5	(35%)	10	(34%)
More counselling	1	(7%)	8	(57%)	9	(31%)
More prescribing	2	(14%)	0	(0%)	2	(7%)
None of the above	1	(7%)	0	(0%)	1	(3%)

The survey also suggests that a majority of local police officers would be prepared to give information to drug users to encourage treatment and harm reduction strategies. Nineteen respondents (65 per cent) were prepared to give information about local needle and syringe availability.

A larger proportion (79 per cent) were prepared to give information about safe disposal of needles and syringes and virtually all those questioned (93 per cent) were prepared to give information about local advice and treatment centres.

The largely positive attitude towards harm reduction is to be welcomed since the police, by virtue of their type of work and hours of duty, are most likely to be the agency present at the moment, or just after, a crisis occurs which may provide a valuable choice point in the decision-making process of a drug user.

Furthermore, an interesting discrepancy arises between the drug unit officers' preference for arrests and convictions as compared with the local police preference for counselling. Various explanations may be posited, including a personal knowledge (almost camaraderie at times) which develops between well-known local faces and police officers. It might also be suggested that the closer the liaison between local drug agencies and the police, the greater the likelihood of counselling being judged an effective intervention by the police.

Finally, it is both interesting and significant that virtually none of the respondents felt that a liberal long-term prescribing policy was an effective way of reducing illicit drug use. This important mismatch between treatment and enforcement agency attitudes deserves further study and indicates a need for ongoing combined educational input to update working philosophy at a local level.

POSSIBLE FUTURE DIRECTIONS

The Sussex Police have joined other forces throughout the country in employing a pilot scheme to put young people who get into trouble with drugs, and their parents, in touch with local advice and treatment agencies.

In the Sussex area the telephone number of a local self-help organization is given on a card, offering help and advice. The scheme is called 'The Families Referral Scheme' and was piloted by the Institute for the Study of Drug Dependence (ISDD). A further component of this pilot scheme is to caution first-time offenders as well as encouraging them to present to treatment agencies. The guidelines to caution rather than to prosecute extend to all drugs and not just, as might be expected, cannabis.

Further possibilities for the police and the courts to become involved in harm reduction arise from the White Paper *Crime, Justice and Protecting the Public* (February 1990). This influential paper makes no bones about the practical futility of incarceration: 'Nobody now regards imprisonment, in itself, as an effective means of reform for most prisoners' (Paragraph 2.7).

Furthermore, imprisonment is costly at a minimum of £320 weekly. The report gives an example, on the other hand, of a young offender, addicted to heroin, who was put on probation for shoplifting and received treatment at a local drug clinic. He obtained stable accommodation, got married and applied for a job. He completed his two-year probation order without re-offending. The implication of the White Paper is to make such therapeutic intervention a condition of the court; effectively the offender is sentenced to treatment. This may provide many possibilities as long as the treatment outlined by the court is not too specific (and therefore liable to being breached), nor is it necessarily abstinence orientated. Either of these measures (Haynes, 1990) would inevitably lead to higher rates of breaching and subsequent imprisonment. Not only are prisons ineffective and expensive but they are also very dangerous by virtue of the high-risk sexual and drug-taking activity which several studies have found to take place within these institutions.

Courts could make better use of residential therapeutic assessment programmes as an alternative to remand in custody where the offence or offences are obviously drug-related in origin. Initial experiments are already being undertaken. Conditions of treatment or attendance at a counselling centre could also be associated with deferred or suspended sentencing. These measures would enable offenders to demonstrate to the courts a sustained level of stability and cessation of offending.

Finally, and more controversially, the role of harm reduction within the prison system should be urgently reviewed. Since it is unlikely that the use of illicit drugs would ever be condoned by the provision of sterile injecting equipment, the role of an oral opiate substitute such as methadone during periods of imprisonment might be considered. The present system often involves either the use of chlorpromazine hydrochloride or an unmodified withdrawal in the prison hospital. Many clients report illicit drug use within prison at some point during their sentence and the risks involved cannot be underestimated.

ACKNOWLEDGEMENTS

To colleagues at Options and DAIS for their encouragement and assistance throughout this study. To members of the Sussex Police Drug Unit and Worthing Police who took part in the questionnaire. To

South East Thames Regional Health Authority and the Pompidou Group Fellowship scheme for their funding of this study.

REFERENCES

Dorn, N. and South, N. (1987) *Some Issues in the Development of Drug Markets and Law Enforcements*. 'Workshop, Drugs: Side Effects of Policy Controls', Commission of the European Communities, Luxembourg. London: Institute for the Study of Drug Dependence.

Fraser, A. and George, M. (1988) 'Changing trends in drug use: An initial follow-up of a local heroin using community', *British Journal of Addiction* 83: 655–63.

George, M. and Fraser, A. (1989) 'Changing trends in drug use: The second follow-up of a local heroin using community', *British Journal of Addiction* 84: 1461–6.

Haynes, P. (1990) 'Sentenced to get better', *Druglink* 5 (1): 8–10.

Lewis, R., Hartnoll, R., Bryers, S., Daviaud, E. and Mitcheson, M. (1985) 'Scoring smack: The illicit heroin market in London 1980–83', *British Journal of Addiction* 80: 281–90.

Power, R. (1987) 'After the Pool Hall – pressure on the streets', *Druglink* 2 (3): 21–2.

White Paper (1990) *Crime, Justice and Protecting the Public*, London: HMSO.

Chapter 18

Reaching the unreached
An outreach model for 'on the spot' AIDS prevention among active, out-of-treatment drug addicts

*J-P. C. Grund, P. Blanken, N. F. P. Adriaans,
C. D. Kaplan, C. Barendregt and M. Meeuwsen*

INTRODUCTION

Around 1985 the spread of HIV among drug addicts in the Netherlands became a serious concern to policy makers, drug service agencies and users themselves, organized in so-called Junkie Unions. The first AIDS prevention initiatives, aimed at Injecting Drug Users (IDUs) were established by these pressure or interest groups of drug addicts. In Amsterdam the AIDS-inspired syringe exchange was initiated by the MDHG, a user-based organization, in 1984. The earliest AIDS prevention leaflet for drug users in the Netherlands was produced by the Rotterdam Junkie Union. In 1981 this union was already distributing clean syringes at places in the drug scene where IDUs gathered to prevent the spread of hepatitis. When it became apparent that HIV would also mean a menace to Dutch IDUs, the Rotterdam Junkie Union immediately started a syringe exchange. This was long before the municipal syringe exchanges opened. At first, these activities were exposed to firm opposition from the police, the treatment agencies and the municipal authorities. Insight into the magnitude of the AIDS epidemic was yet to come about at these levels. In Rotterdam, where this research was conducted, the municipal syringe exchange system was established in the first half of 1987. This rather late start was due to resistance in some parts of the treatment system. Among other arguments, it was felt that syringe exchange would encourage injecting and undermine drug-free treatment (van Heiningen, 1988). Nowadays, these arguments are generally seen as obsolete and, more important, it has been proved that they have no scientific basis (Buning, 1988). At the end of 1986 HADON, at that time a small and experimental outreach and drug information programme, took the initiative and set up a syringe exchange. Soon the rest of the city was to follow.

In Rotterdam, as in many other Dutch cities, syringe exchanges are predominantly tied to the methadone programmes, mainly methadone maintenance programmes. The advantage of this Rotterdam approach is that these programmes are in contact with approximately 1,000 heroin addicts (both smokers and IDUs) on a daily basis. However, estimates of the number of heroin addicts in Rotterdam vary between 2,500 and 3,500 (INTRAVAL, 1989), not counting those drug users from the suburbs, that are also oriented on Rotterdam, both for drugs and help. The proportion of IDUs is approximately 25 per cent for both in and out of treatment groups (Grund et al., 1991b). Although the syringe exchanges at the methadone programmes are open to non-clients, few actually use them. This means that on a daily basis at least 60 to 70 per cent of the target group is not reached by the municipal syringe exchange system. Additionally, the composition of the 'in treatment' cohort is often subject to rapid changes (Toet 1989). Furthermore, many addicts have switched from heroin to cocaine as their drug of preference (Grund et al., 1991a), and for this reason methadone presumably has become less valuable for them. For these reasons, the outreach and information project HADON, which in 1989 fused with the Odyssee foundation, made reaching the active out-of-treatment drug addicts, generally the 'unreached', into its main AIDS prevention priority. This chapter will give a brief description of the working methods of this project and present some results of the pilot evaluation study we conducted.

METHODS

In this pilot evaluation study, syringe exchange contacts of the HADON programme were registered. For each exchange contact the programme staff registered date, minimal demographics, the number of syringes and containers dispensed, and the number of syringes returned. When syringes were returned in a container, the actual number of syringes was estimated by a weighing procedure (Blanken, 1990). Quantitative data analysis was conducted at the level of (1) the individual exchanger, and (2) the exchange contacts. Staff of the program were questioned on the contents of their work and their knowledge on the attendants and programme routines were observed. Data on how the programme's goals were addressed in the networks of contacted drug users were collected through ethnographic field work in an ongoing research project in the Addiction Research Institute (Grund et al., 1991b).

PROGRAMME DESCRIPTION

HADON is a neighbourhood-based information programme providing outreach, prevention and referral services to active out-of-treatment DUs in the north of Rotterdam. The programme started in 1985, before the health implications of the AIDS epidemic among the IDU population was generally acknowledged in Rotterdam. Due to this evolving epidemic, the priority of the programme has been shifted towards the prevention of HIV transmission. Besides the contacts in the project's storefront premises, the outreach workers visit on a regular basis many places in the scene called 'user collectives'. The outreach workers supply clean syringes, condoms and up-to-date information on HIV/AIDS to people who visit these places. The uniqueness of the programme lies in its two-tiered organization of syringe exchange. In addition to supplying these prevention materials in the storefront and while doing outreach, the workers stimulate key people to exchange syringes at their user collectives. The user collectives are frequently visited by other addicts from the same or related networks. Thus, visitors can exchange individual syringes (individual exchange) or, upon special agreement, exchange containers of used syringes for boxes of 100 new syringes (collective exchange). The containers are plastic and can hold approximately 200 used syringes. The HADON collective exchange tier has been experimentally initiated in order to determine if the outreach component of the programme could be extended and improved.

Second, the experiment examined if the motivation of visitors could be reinforced through stimulating a willingness both to exchange and collect used syringes and take more responsibility, not only for their own individual health, but also for the health of their injecting drug-user peers. This second aspect is based on the observation that social support is a common phenomenon in addict networks. The stereotype of addicts is that of ripping each other off as predatory individuals. While this behaviour does indeed occur, a more prevalent pattern seems to be sharing. Addicts share many, for them, important things like housing, food, clothing, etc., and often they help one another with daily problems associated with addict life (Grund et al., 1991b). These sharing behaviours have been documented in many studies in different places and seem universal (Preble and Casey, 1969; Feldman and Biernacki, 1988; Mata and Jorquez, 1988; Des Jarlais et al., 1988). They fit the broader context of addict life and find their function in coping with craving, human contact and needs, and life in the margins of society. Drug use is not the only factor that brings and keeps drug users together. Drug users engage in many common activities and they spend considerable time on social activities (Kaplan *et al.*, 1991).

RESULTS

From May 1988 to June 1989 the HADON syringe exchange project involved 104 regularly registered exchangers, and 1,255 syringe exchange contacts were registered. The collective exchange has been defined as 'making available large amounts of sterile syringes and sharpsafe containers at strategic places in the drug scene in order that there are always clean syringes available at those places where drugs are being used'. Individual exchange has been defined as 'those exchanges and supply transactions concerning small quantities of syringes' (Barendregt, 1989). According to these programme definitions we have defined a collective exchanger as 'an exchanger who has at least once taken out a box with syringes and a container and has at least once returned a container'. Based on this, twenty-five clients (24 per cent) were classified as collective and seventy-nine clients (76 per cent) as individual exchangers. The mean number of supplied syringes over the 595 individual syringe exchange contacts is almost nine. For the 660 collective syringe exchange contacts this number is seventy-nine. Given the above definitions, it is no surprise that this difference is statistically significant (Table 18.1). During the research period a total number of 57,328 syringes were supplied, of which 91 per cent went out through the collective exchange. In total, 46,610 syringes were returned, which gives an exchange rate of 81.3 per cent. Profound differences in exchange rates were found between the two groups: 46.4 per cent for individual and 84.8 per cent for collective exchangers (Table 18.2).

Table 18.1 Number of dispensed syringes per exchange contact for all HADON clients and divided into the collective and individual exchangers

	All exchangers	Collective exchangers	Individual exchangers
Mean	45.7	79.1	8.6
Median	10	100	4
Mode	100	100	2
Minimum	0	0	0
Maximum	400	400	100
Standard dev.	57.3	59.9	18.2
N	1,255	660	595

The programme's holding power was remarkable in retaining especially the collective exchangers. The mean number of contacts of individual exchangers is 7.5; for the collective exchangers this is 26.4 – a clear and statistically significant difference. Fifty-two per cent of the collective exchangers visited the programme twenty-five or more times. Moreover, the collective exchangers (only 24 per cent of the clients) accounted for 52.6 per cent of the total number of syringe exchange contacts. The mean number of days between each syringe exchange contact is 15.8. A breakdown for the days of the week does not show big differences in contact rate. Individual exchangers have their 'top day' on Thursday and collective exchangers on Friday.

Table 18.2 Number of syringes dispensed and returned and 'return rate' on a monthly basis for all HADON clients and divided into the collective and individual exchangers

Month	All exchangers			Collective exchangers			Individual exchangers		
	Syringes		Return rate	Syringes		Return rate	Syringes		Return rate
	Out	In	%	Out	In	%	Out	In	%
06-88	4,941	2,624	53.11	4,753	2,517	**52.96**	188	107	56.91
07-88	4,119	3,635	88.25	3,642	3,452	94.78	477	183	38.36
08-88	3,947	3,112	78.84	3,633	2,924	80.48	314	188	59.87
09-88	3,309	3,566	107.77	3,035	3,398	111.96	274	168	61.31
10-88	3,753	2,621	69.84	3,213	2,370	73.76	540	251	46.48
11-88	4,104	3,856	93.96	3,575	3,623	101.34	529	233	44.04
12-88	5,240	4,261	81.32	4,949	3,860	77.99	291	401	**137.80**
01-89	6,871	6,361	92.58	*6,781*	6,329	93.33	*90*	32	35.55
02-89	6,135	4,754	77.49	5,982	4,685	78.32	153	69	45.09
03-89	4,641	3,684	79.38	4,040	3,601	89.13	601	83	**13.81**
04-89	3,600	2,306	64.06	*2,731*	2,138	78.29	*869*	168	19.33
05-89	3,763	3,675	97.66	3,490	3,338	95.64	273	337	123.44
06-89	2,905	2,155	74.18	2,358	1,990	84.39	547	165	30.16
Total	57,328	46,610	81.30	52,182	44,225	84.75	5,146	2,385	46.35

Italic numbers refer to lowest/highest number of dispensed syringes; bold numbers refer to lowest/highest return rates.

To complement these results, the ethnographic fieldwork data provide insight into how the programme's goals are addressed in the networks of IDUs contacted by the programme. Although during the fieldwork places were visited where hygiene regarding injecting was poor, the impression is that users who are engaged in the collective exchange are more aware of risk behaviours and put more energy in health and hygiene, as can be seen in the following excerpts from fieldnotes:

1   R. is still cleaning up the room: 'It is always possible someone might call and I don't like this stuff laying around.' The syringes, swabs and other papers go into the plastic bag that's already filled with other used spikes, bloody swabs, etc. 'This is for Sak' (= worker of the neighbourhood exchange programme). For extra security C. takes off the needle from the syringe. Then he takes out the piston totally and puts the needle inside the syringe. Then he puts back the piston and presses it so the needle inside crumbles together. C. – 'Now nobody can hurt himself on it. You have to be aware, I think.'

2   When Freek had finished injecting he rubbed some Hyrudoid balsam on the needle wound. 'One of you guys want some too?' He asked Ronald and Frits. Frits took some of the ointment and rubbed it on his arm. 'It's good stuff for your veins,' said Frits. 'Yes, it also disinfects the wound,' Freek replied.

As at many dealing addresses injecting the purchased drugs on the premises is not allowed, IDUs often go to a friend's place to inject. Karel is participating in the collective exchange and lets his friends 'get off' at his place:

3   Karel agrees to Jerry taking a shot at his place. Jerry wants to shoot up pure cocaine. He puts his spike on the table and asks Karel for a spoon. Karel asks: 'Is that an old spike you want to use ?' J. – 'Well, old, I've used it one time before, so it's still good for usage.' K. –'I've got some new ones left from HADON,' he hands one over to J., 'you want some more for tonight or the weekend ?' J. – 'If you can spare them I'll take some with me.' K. gives him four in total.

The syringes distributed through the collective exchange evidently are distributed beyond the user collectives. As well as for use on the spot they are distributed among other users to take home. There is even an exchange of new syringes between user collectives.

4   Harry left with a bunch of new syringes to go to the dealing place where Ronald and Frits had bought their dope. 'They have a shortage of shooters there,' he said before leaving.

CONCLUSION

When considering the programme's goals (extending the outreach component of the programme, stimulating the users to take an interest in their own health and that of other users) we feel that the programme is making an important contribution. In the evaluation study of the British syringe exchange schemes, a return rate of 62 per cent was found (Stimson *et al.*, 1988). Often it is felt that a high return rate is due to strict rules regarding a one-for-one transaction. Our findings do not support this thesis. The high return rate of the collective exchange is not accomplished by strict rules but through trust, respect and a shared responsibility in combination with supplying the necessary tools for safe injecting practices. The retention rate of the collective exchangers can be regarded as very high compared to the results of the British evaluation study – 33 per cent over five visits (Stimson *et al.*, 1991). An interesting difference is that between the busiest days of individual and collective exchange. On Thursday most addicts receive their social benefit and the individual exchange rises markedly. Friday, the day before the weekend, when the programme is closed, is the busiest day for the collective exchange. It seems that individual exchangers are driven more by situational determinants (the availability of money) and the collective exchangers have included getting clean syringes in their daily life as a planned activity. The ethnographic data show that the goals of the programme are positively anticipated in the injecting community. Clean syringes are at hand at high-risk places when needed, distributed through IDU networks and even exchanged among user collectives.

A disturbing factor: police raids on dealing addresses

A closer look at Table 18.2 shows that after a steady growth of the issued syringes from June 1988 to January/February 1989, in March/April an immense downfall occurs. This collapse can be attributed to increased police raids on dealing/using addresses in that period. While the collective exchange goes down 60 per cent from January to April, the individual exchange rises by almost 1,000 per cent (see italic numbers). This may be called a short-term effect as in the following months the individually issued syringes join the downward trend of the collective exchange. This is, however, due to the space reallocation of many of the regular visitors of the closed-down addresses towards the west and other parts of Rotterdam. And in this west part of Rotterdam recently history again repeated itself (Grund *et al.*, 1991a). These findings not only support the assumption that many active IDUs are actually reached by the collective exchange; they also show that this kind of repressive police activity has a negative effect on AIDS prevention efforts (Des Jarlais and Friedman, 1990; Chitwood et al., 1990). In the spirit of the theme of the First International Conference on the Reduction of Drug-Related Harm, one might even speak of 'drug enforcement-related harm'. A fine tuning of public health and judicial policy in favour of an effective AIDS prevention policy is urgently needed.

In conclusion, our findings suggest that the exchanging of syringes can be made more effective by employing collective social means in contrast to individualistic psychological strategies. The use of 'naturalistic settings' (e.g., the placing of the plastic container at 'user collectives' and dealing addresses), existing drug user networks and appeals to injecting drug users' responsibility may be more powerful determinants of variations in syringe exchange rates than psychological characteristics of individuals. In any case, engaging drug users themselves as an integral part and partner of the outreach work provides an interesting topic for further investigation and development. In Rotterdam, it will be interesting to see in the future whether this human resource and social manner of exchanging will be more effective than more technologically inspired approaches (e.g. syringe exchanging machines) that are also planned for the city's AIDS prevention efforts.

ACKNOWLEDGEMENTS

This research was supported by a grant from the Nederlandse Organisatie voor Wetenschappelijk Onderzoek (Dutch Organization for Scientific Research), MEDIGON, Social Psychiatry Working Group (grant n. 900-556-046). Opinions expressed in the paper do not necessarily reflect the policy of the supporting organization. We thank the drug users who participated in this study for their cooperation.

REFERENCES

Barendregt, C. (1989) *Toen was er AIDS, of de ontwikkeling van de collectieve spuitenomruil* (Then there was AIDS, or the development of the collective syringe exchange), Rotterdam: HADON/Odyssee.

Blanken, P. (1990) *Spuiten ruilen bij HADON: Een evaluatie van de individuele en collectieve omruil*, Rotterdam.

Buning, E. C. (1988) *De GG & GD en het drugprobleem in cijfers, III*, Amsterdam: GG&GD.

Chitwood, D. D., McCoy C. B., Inciardi J. A. et al. (1990) 'HIV seropositivity of needles from shooting galleries in South Florida', *American Journal of Public Health* 80: 150–2.

Des Jarlais, D. C. and Friedman, S. R. (1990) Shooting galleries and AIDS:

Infection probabilities and "tough" policies', *American Journal of Public Health* 80: 142–4.

Des Jarlais, D. C., Friedman, S. R., Sotheran, J. L. and Stoneburger, R. (1988) 'The sharing of drug injecting equipment and the AIDS epidemic in New York City: The first decade', in R. J. Battjes and R. W. Pickins (eds) *Needle Sharing Among Intravenous Drug Abusers: National and International Perspectives*, Rockville: NIDA, pp 160-75.

Feldman, H. W. and Biernacki P. (1988) 'The ethnography of needle sharing among intravenous drug users and implications for public policies and intervention strategies', in R. J. Battjes and R. W. Pickins (eds) *Needle Sharing Among Intravenous Drug Abusers: National and International Perspectives*, Rockville: NIDA, pp. 28–39.

Grund, J.-P. C., Kaplan, C. D., Adriaans, N. F. P., Blanken, P. and Huisman J. (1990) 'The limitations of the concept of needle sharing: The practice of frontloading', *AIDS* 4: 819–21.

——, Adriaans, N. F. P. and Kaplan, C. D. (1991a) 'Changing cocaine smoking rituals in the Dutch heroin addict population', *British Journal of Addiction* 86: 439–48.

——, Kaplan, C. D., Adriaans, N. F. P. and Blanken, P. (1991b) 'Drug sharing and HIV transmission risks: The practice of 'frontloading' in the Dutch injecting drug user population', *Journal of Psychoactive Drugs*.

INTRAVAL (1989) *Harddrugs & criminaliteit in Rotterdam*, Groningen: Stichting Intraval.

Kaplan, C. D., Vries, M. de, Grund, J.-P. C. and Adriaans N. F. P. (1991) 'Protective factors: Dutch intervention, health determinants and the reorganization of addict life', in H. Ghodse, C. D. Kaplan and R. D. Mann (eds) *Drug Misuse and Dependence*, London: Parthenon Press.

Mata, A. G. and Jorquez, J. S. (1988) 'Mexican-American intravenous drug users' needle-sharing practices: Implications for AIDS prevention', in R.J. Battjes and R. W. Pickins (eds) *Needle Sharing Among Intravenous Drug Abusers: National and International Perspectives*, Rockville: NIDA, pp 40-58.

Preble, E. and Casey, J. J. (1969) 'Taking care of business – the heroin user's life on the street', *International Journal of the Addictions* 1: 1–24.

Stimson, G. V., Alldritt, L. J., Dolan, K. A., Donaghoe, M. C. and Lart, R. A. (1988) *Injecting Equipment Exchange Schemes: Final Report*, London: Monitoring Research Group.

Toet, J. (1989) *Het RODIS uit de steigers. Resultaten 1988 Rotterdam*, Rapport 65, Rotterdam: GGD Afdeling Epidemiologie.

van Heiningen, R.M. (1988) *Spuitomruilfaciliteiten: Voorstellen tot uitbreiding van de spuitomruilfaciliteiten binnen Rotterdam*, Rotterdam: Odyssee.

Chapter 19

The streetcorner agency with shooting room ('Fixerstuebli')

Robert B. Haemmig

For many years drug users in Bern were not allowed to use public facilities such as restaurants and cafés and, therefore, had nowhere to rest and meet friends. This led to an open 'street drug scene' developing, which drew many complaints from local people. Consequently, in 1983, a group of employees of the Contact Foundation in Bern decided to establish a project for drug users, where they could rest, get a hot meal and a drink. Apart from simply providing a meeting place, the workers' aim was to also establish a cultural centre to provide alternative activities and stimulate other interests in drug users. It was planned to have video-projects, guided theatre visits, promote self-help initiatives, and so on.

A suitable venue was found near the drug scene, but there was no money for the necessary constructional alterations. However, after long negotiations, the construction work began in 1985. For this work the group engaged unemployed junkies. This experience proved so encouraging that the project still exists today, as an independent programme. The café finally opened in the summer of 1986 but, by this time, the drug scene had moved because their meeting place had been closed temporarily due to the construction work.

Looking back, we have learnt a lot from the experience of establishing such a revolutionary concept and we can also learn that in the development of such an idea there are crucial points. Responsibility for developing the concept on a day-to-day basis was an unexpected event which, although perceived as an occasionally unthinkable demand from the clients at the time, was not stopped. So, the concept of the centre was developed to provide:

- a room for junkies where they can meet without being forced to buy or consume anything, as is expected in a regular restaurant;

- a café bar which has sandwiches, cookies, yoghurts, fruits and hot and cold drinks available, but no alcohol;
- clean needles, syringes and condoms, free of charge, for everybody. Information on safer drug use, safer sex and proper use of condoms is also on display.
- A café, run by social workers who are willing to talk and to counsel the clients.
- A second room where the consumption of intravenous drugs is allowed. One of the main aims is that the consumption of drugs should be possible in a hygienic and stress-free manner, which means that there should be enough time for everyone to test the drug through injecting a small amount first. Clients are encouraged to exchange information about the purity of the drugs.
- Safer drug use techniques, like 'chasing the dragon', should be promoted and unsafe methods like sharing injecting equipment eradicated.

Later we added to this a health service operated by nurses, who provide counselling, deal with physical problems such as abcesses, change dressings and so on.

The news about this place quickly spread through the drug scene. The uptake of this project was tremendous; despite the fact that most drug users gathered at another location, they moved during the opening hours to our place.

OBSTACLES

However, from the beginning we encountered a lot of difficulties – drug-related, environmental and legal. For example, we had to deal with overdose cases, so all the workers are trained in First Aid and resuscitation, but we use Ambubags to avoid direct contact. Respiratory failure was most common on days when the quality of the drugs was high. We do not use Naloxone as we believe this is only manageable in a hospital and overdosing on opiates alone is rare. We have to take into account that people are using a variety of drugs – heroin, cocaine, Flunitrazepam (Rohypnol), alcohol and other substances – in an unknown mixture.

We also had problems with the neighbourhood. The shopkeeper next door claimed to be losing sales, so we changed the opening hours of the café to between 7 and 10 p.m. on Monday to Wednesday and Friday.

On top of these problems the legal situation was still unclear. Two employees who talked about the project in public were accused of letting people know where they could consume illicit drugs, and were charged with 'assisting others to commit an offence' which is forbidden by drug law. The charges were later dropped, because consumption of illicit drugs is not a major offence and for minor offences the accusation of 'assisting others' does not stand in Swiss law in general.

However, Swiss law works on the principle of legality and not of opportunity. This means that if the police know where illicit drugs are regularly being used they have to react, i.e. to chase the drug users until they no longer know where to go to take drugs. At this crucial point, we got help from the legal system. From personal contacts the authorities had always been informed about our work and, even though they did not totally agree with our concepts, they had some respect for it. A working group of judges and prosecutors met to find a way for the project to operate that was still consistent with the law. They found an article in the drug law which states that if someone is receiving medical treatment it is possible to drop criminal proceedings for consumption of illicit drugs. So they agreed that we were running this project under the basic premise of providing medical treatment. We agreed to ensure that no dealing took place on the premises and that minors were sent away. Under these conditions the police were advised to drop any further action against the centre and its clients, which they have respected so far.

Our local authorities came under pressure from the administrations of other cantons, mainly Zurich, but they stood firm. One of the most famous professors of penal law came to the same conclusions, so it is generally no longer considered as unlawful. This has encouraged several other Swiss cities to establish 'Fixerstueblis' (Basle, Lucerne, St Gallen).

Meanwhile, news about the project had spread all over the world. We were soon inundated with TV teams, journalists and professionals wanting to study the project and interview the clients. We had to be very unfriendly to many of them to protect our clients and to prevent them from becoming exhibits in a human zoo. Also, it was not desirable to have too much publicity as we had enough problems to deal with.

As the project became more successful in attracting clients, it also attracted the dealers, who hung round outside the agency during opening hours. This made the project even more attractive for drug users as they knew that they could score near our agency during opening hours. The place slowly became overcrowded. More people meant more problems with the neighbours. We told the authorities that in order to disperse the problem we badly needed a second similar place, but there was no money and there were no other suitable premises.

Meanwhile, our landlord had had enough and terminated the contract of tenancy. The only thing we could do was stall until we could open another place. The project that had opened in summer 1986 finally closed on 12 January 1990.

A NEW BEGINNING

After some time we found a suitable location – a cellar ('Nageligasse') that belonged to the city. However, we were unable to begin operating from the new location straight away because of long negotiations with the authorities, and also because there was an election during which no one wanted to make a decision. During these discussions, it was mainly the director of police who opposed the project.

It was obvious that, with only one room, we would soon encounter all the same problems that we had with the first premises. So we decided to set up temporary premises near the open drug scene, on a place called 'Kleine Schanze' or 'Schanzli'. This opened on 15 January 1990 as the successor to the first project, but had to close a few days later because of operational difficulties: it was much smaller than we had wanted, there was no room for counselling, there was enormous stress on both clients and workers and, to top it all, the police photographed everyone coming in and out. So we covered the entry with a tent, broke through a wall to enlarge the space and demanded an additional unit. This addition was promised for the end of April and the place reopened. The second location, the cellar, was supposed to open in June 1990.

On 2 April the authorities closed the public toilet where the open drug scene was centred and the scene moved to our temporary premises at Schanzli. The place quickly became overcrowded each night and it was almost impossible to pass or enter our building. Inside, you could not go one step without colliding with someone. Providing care, which is what we set out to do, was virtually impossible. We were just about able to give out clean needles, syringes and condoms and were ready for emergencies, like resuscitation. Consequently, we need to re-think our aims to adapt to the circumstances.

EFFECTS OF THE PROJECT

In setting up a street-level drugs agency with shooting room, the Contact Foundation of Bern established a service for drug users that was, from the very beginning, at the heart of the drug scene. With this project it was possible to reach drug users who had had no previous contact with any helping agency. The close proximity and easy access to the project meant that workers were much closer to the daily reality of their clients and, consequently, relationships became more genuine. With this growth of trust came many examples of the positive impact the project has had on clients' lifestyles. By providing information, advice and education, the project has enhanced the self-awareness of the drug user. Therefore, the drug scene is more visible today and the junkies do not hide which, in our opinion, is very important for the political process. More importantly, since the project started there have been no deaths due to overdose in the neighbourhood of the agency.

A recent Swiss study of former alcoholics and drug addicts demonstrated that giving up the habit of taking alcohol or drugs was typically related to situations where negatively experienced stress was lowered. We are convinced that our service helps the user to plan new steps towards an improvement in their lives. But, as all our energy has been devoted to establishing the service during the past four years, there has been no time (or money) for scientific evaluation. However, as we are frequently asked for results, mainly from politicians, we have established a research programme, which is about to start. At last, the project may serve as a model for other cities.

Chapter 20

AIDS prevention with injecting drug users in the former West Germany
A user-friendly approach on a municipal level

Heino Stöver and Klaus Schuller

There are between 50,000 and 100,000 injecting drug users (IDUs) in the former West Germany. HIV infection first occurred in 1982 (Bornemann *et al.*,1988) and by August 1990, IDUs made up 13 per cent of infected people. By 1990, 18.4 per cent of people with AIDS were IDUs.

The HIV prevalence rate among IDUs is about 20 per cent (Kleiber, 1990). The link between HIV and needle sharing is, by now, well known. Such sharing is caused, not by ritual practices, but by restricted availability (Schuller and Stöver, 1989).

In the FRG, syringes and needles are freely on sale in pharmacies and medical equipment shops; nevertheless, in practice restrictions exist which hinder easy accessibility: too costly, sale of large packets only, incorrect needle sizes, restricted opening times of the pharmacies, etc. On top of that, in the mid-1980s, pharmacists became uncertain whether the sale of needles was legal, or whether they were liable to prosecution ('Creation of the opportunity to use an illegal drug'). In 1987 the national association of German pharmacists published a recommendation to sell needles to IDUs.

In north Germany (Bremen, Hamburg, Berlin, Hanover and some towns and cities in North-Rhine Westphalia) sterile injection equipment was available through syringe-exchange schemes by the middle of the 1980s. This was not the case for the cities and towns in south Germany, where it took place later, if at all. Professional and ethical considerations against needle dispensing play a decisive role in this.

One can say, however, that the supply of needles is no longer perceived as contradictory to abstinence-orientated goals. More and more needle supply and exchange programmes have been integrated and are considered an important part; the services should contribute to the drug user surviving the phase of drug dependence without irreversible damage to health.

In West Germany and Berlin, different models for needle supply have developed, each with advantages and disadvantages. The pharmacies, as before, fulfil the most important task of supplying. They have longer opening hours than the drug counselling centres or exchange projects run by the regional AIDS agencies, and offer decentralized availability. Many grassroots initiatives, AIDS-Hilfe groups, or drug counselling centres which offer needle exchange programmes in West Germany are in the initial phase of bringing about a sustained improvement in the provision of sterile needles. Seen from a quantitative viewpoint, some of these programmes can be considered to have only symbolic meaning as, in most cities, in the evening, at night and also at weekends, a severe shortage still exists.

For the police, possession of a syringe is an indication of drug use. This initial suspicion serves as a legitimate reason for further investigation and searches as the needles are examined for traces of illicit drugs. So, drug-dependent people will try to get rid of the incriminating piece of evidence as soon as possible after use. The consequence of that is a shortage of needles which, quite often in stressful situations, leads to needle sharing. Meanwhile, in some big cities, arrangements with the police exist whereby used needles are no longer seized, but this still offers the IDU no legal security.

Contrary to pessimistic assumptions that IDUs would not respond to education and would not be ready for a change in behaviour through increased knowledge, the opposite development has become clear – more and more IDUs have become conscious of the health risks of sharing needles.

This, nevertheless, does not mean that all IDUs have given up their risky behaviour. The messages of 'safer use' and 'safer sex' (here only insignificant changes of behaviour can be reported) must be reinforced. Various studies have shown that an essential precondition for behaviour change is a significant improvement in the provision of sterile syringes (Kleiber, 1990).

In Bremen, there are approximately 1,000–1,500 injecting drug users. Bremen has a relatively large and open drug scene in the centre of the city, in an attractive residential, shopping and entertainment area. In this redevelopment area, there was a marked influx of well-to-do residents and business people who, among other things, manage flourishing coffee-houses and fashionable boutiques. These citizens form a strong pressure group against the presence of drug users, who stamp their mark on the image of the main shopping street. Through their crimes, committed to buy drugs, and prostitution, the inhabitants of the area perceive them as a plague and a menace.

The health-impoverishment and social deprivation in the drug scene is apparent; it is connected with very risky poly-drug use, including opiates, barbiturates, benzodiazepines, alcohol and other psychotropic substances, as well as a growing resignation among long-term IDUs. A drastic expression of this development is the steadily increasing mortality rate. The ideological barriers and failings of the past are now presenting themselves as the pressure of circumstances and weakness of provision, most of all in the areas of health and housing.

THE ASSOCIATION 'KOMMUNALE DROGENPOLITIK/ VEREIN FÜR AKZEPTIERENDE DROGENARBEIT'

In 1982, a project at the University of Bremen looked at drug policy and drug work in various European countries. In comparing countries, it became clear that the policy of the Federal Republic was marked by tough sentencing of users, as well as by a one-sidedness in treatment. Drug counselling had an abstinence-orientated philosophy, and had come to terms with the criminal justice system. The drug user was forced, through suffering, into in-patient treatment institutions.

Together with drug users, who had organized themselves along the lines of the Dutch 'Junkie Bunden' (Junky Unions), participants in the University Drug Project came out against developments in the drug policy in Bremen, which could be seen leading to a further deterioration of the living conditions of IDUs and saw the necessity of practical help and treatment alternatives, to mitigate against increasing health and social impoverishment.

The working group which emanated from this project became a registered association with the aim of increasing low threshold treatment. In April 1987 a drop-in centre close to the drug scene was opened. By the beginning of 1990 this had become a focal point for drug users, where they could get advice on HIV prevention as well as legal and welfare advice.

During this time the link between drug work and drug policy became evident. Drug workers were confronted with the consequences of prohibition. Pragmatic drug policy, necessary for HIV prevention, requires the will to engage in the political process.

THE BEGINNINGS OF A PRAGMATIC AIDS PREVENTION POLICY

In December 1984 the association, together with the 'Bremen Junky Bund', distributed sterile needles and leaflets around the drug scene, in order to communicate the risks of HIV infection; at that time this was a very unusual thing to do. In the leaflets and in a press statement, it was made clear that the living conditions of the users – criminalization and black-market supplies – would contribute to a rapid spread of AIDS, if the relevant departments were unable to react quickly to the new development and to take new measures, or at least facilitate introduction.

The following demands were made: distribution of sterile syringes at affordable prices and in small packages (not in bulk, as for clinics); no seizure of syringes by the police, and no prosecution for the possession of syringes; controllable prescription of methadone, accompanied by other supporting measures designed to de-escalate and stabilize the living conditions of IDUs.

The association, together with the Junky Union, also tried, through letters and visits, to persuade pharmacists in the area of the drug scene, of the necessity of selling syringes. Moreover, the members of the Junky Union informed the local users of the pharmacies which were prepared to do so. However, the supply remained unsatisfactory at weekends and after hours because only two pharmacies were willing to sell needles and syringes in small quantities. The attempt to encourage other pharmacists to supply syringes was made more difficult when the Welfare Department advised pharmacies against such supply. In the autumn of 1985, after the Welfare Department had changed its position, the General Prosecutor of Bremen declared that the sale of syringes to drug users constituted an offence against Section 29 of the Illegal Drugs Act ('Creation of an opportunity'), and accordingly would lead to prosecutions.

Meanwhile, members of the association had learnt about AIDS preventive measures in the Netherlands and Denmark. After ten months of effort to improve the supply situation without tangible success, the Working Group resolved, in September 1986, to carry out the exchange of needles at a meeting-place of the drug scene. This was along the lines of a Dutch programme. The intention in Bremen was to procure concrete help and education for the drug users and, at the same time, to confront the thoughtless disposal of used needles on the streets and in public places. The members of the association, after conversations with experts in Denmark and the Netherlands, came to the conclusion that the time-factor played a decisive role in AIDS prevention, and that to delay action any longer would be a mistake.

NEEDLE EXCHANGE

The opening of the needle exchange on 10 September 1986 was observed by more than ten members of the police force. After representatives of the press had left the square, the police moved in and seized the needles. On the second day, many more drug users came to the exchange point. The police finally took possession of the rubbish bins placed there for the collection of used syringes. The traces inside these syringes would constitute an offence against the Illegal Drugs Act.

Among the drug users, the activities of the Working Group were met with much acclaim. In addition, most passers-by showed an interest and understanding of the action. Through mediation with the police, talks with the relevant senior prosecutor took place on the second day. At these talks the experience of other countries, and the urgency of pragmatic AIDS prevention, were highlighted. On the following days, it was possible to continue the exchange undisturbed. Because the IDUs had reported that at night and on Sundays and public holidays it was almost impossible to obtain clean needles, volunteer members of the association continued the exchanges during the following months, throughout Sundays, public holidays and religious festivals. These took place near the drug scene in newly acquired premises. Each Sunday about 200 needles and syringes were handed out to 40–50 IDUs, along with information material concerning 'safer use' and 'safer sex'. The costs were covered by donations from the drug users. Moreover, people attempted, through letters and visits, to win pharmacies round to the distribution concept. Further talks with the police were held, in order to convince them that seizure of needles had a negative effect on the AIDS prevention moves.

Table 20.1 Exchange 1989 (syringes and needles which were returned)

	Syringes	Needles
January	2,783	6,310
February	1,681	6,228
March	2,550	5,269
April	1,913	5,492
May	2,732	6,791
June	2,751	10,612
July	5,576	11,436
August	5,944	16,633
September	6,248	18,467
October	884	21,695
November	9,457	24,426

The opening of the advice centre made syringe supply available during the week. This was coupled with advice and was provided with no preconditions. Subsequently, a new-for-old policy was made obligatory. Funding from the Health Authority, in June 1989, and increased use of volunteers, enabled the opening hours to be extended with a consequent marked increase in client contact (Table 20.1).

SYRINGE DISPENSING MACHINES

In June 1987, having seen needle dispensing machines in operation in Copenhagen which had been installed to eradicate lack of supply outside pharmacy opening hours, the Association decided to install machines in Bremen. The first one, a second-hand converted cigarette machine, was installed in the doorway of the drop-in centre. The machine dispensed syringes upon introduction of a German Mark coin. The package also contained messages asking drug users not to throw away used syringes thoughtlessly. Leaflets and posters were used in campaigns to encourage the use of the syringe exchange scheme and responsible disposal.

Later in the year a second machine was installed at the centre of the drug scene and a third one has been situated near the main railway station (see Table 20.2).

Table 20.2 Supply through the dispensing machines: 1989

	Syringes	Needles
January	4,373	8,131
February	3,509	6,691
March	3,938	8,358
April	4,791	9,395
May	7,548	14,058
June	7,237	13,833
July	6,853	13,042
August	5,327	10,297
September	4,270	7,657
October	4,737	9,047

The automats are filled almost every day and there are regular maintenance checks, paid for by the revenue from the machines along with the syringes and packaging. The surplus is used to provide a breakfast once a week, in the drop-in centre, free of charge, for drug users. The IDUs have come to identify with the scheme and work on the project packing the boxes (at least 1,000 per week), for example. The number of dispensed works is still increasing. In the middle of

1990, approximately 17,000 syringes and 38,000 needles have been exchanged monthly, and approximately 9,000 syringes and 19,000 needles have been distributed by the three machines.

ASSESSMENT

The advantage of the drop-in centre over sale through pharmacies and through the dispensing machines, is that proper disposal of the used injecting equipment can take place. The problem of the careless disposal of syringes and needles can be brought to the attention of the drug users. Therefore, the association has successfully tried to increase the exchange, rather than supply through machines. The free-of-charge exchange has continually outpaced the dispensing machine.

Experience shows that the IDUs adjust themselves to the exchange, and that any formalities present no serious barrier. It is important that a relationship of personal trust develops between employees and clients, and that through the talks with the police, conditions can be created which allow the smooth operation of the scheme.

Exchanges in drug counselling agencies give an opportunity for personal counselling, and thereby for integrating syringe supply with counselling and support. From an AIDS prevention viewpoint, a relationship of personal trust between the centre worker and the client assumes increasing importance. This is because the greatest risk of infection occurs in areas which are taboo and can only be discussed with trusted people.

In order to ensure that, during the evening and night hours as well as at weekends and national holidays, there is a continual supply of syringes, dispensing machines are recommended. Since the implementation of this service in Bremen, approximately fifty machines have been set up in about thirty-five cities and towns, most of them in north Germany.

EFFECTIVE AIDS PREVENTION REQUIRES A REORIENTATION OF DRUG WORK AND DRUG POLICY

The unrestricted and user-friendly availability of sterile injection equipment is an important part of an AIDS-prevention strategy. Although an adequate availability of injection equipment is a central precondition for behaviour change, it is not the only one. Other preconditions, like personal communication and information, are essential for attitude change in relation to risk behaviour (Buning,

1989). Change in behaviour can be supported by technical and therapeutic means like condom distribution and low-threshold methadone programmes, but adequate detoxification and drug-free programmes are also required.

A comprehensive AIDS prevention strategy, however, has to encompass the social dimension. An improvement in the living conditions of IDUs, housing, employment, social acceptance, and a reduction of the threat of criminalization may lead to lasting avoidance of risk situations.

Social support and the establishment of a group identity seem to have an important influence on the infection risk (Kleiber, 1988). Therefore, social integration emphasizing the self-help abilities of drug users should be a central objective of AIDS prevention measures. Social integration often precedes abstinence from illicit drugs, it does not necessarily have to be considered as the outcome of a long counselling and treatment programme (Raschke et al., 1985). The leading concept which sees increasing social and judicial pressure as a necessary precondition for an abstinence-motivation, can damage the process of social integration.

A reorientation of the practice and policy of traditional drug work along the lines of acceptance and integration is required. Acceptance-orientated drug work and drug policy means first of all the recognition of the reality, that the goal of abstinence from drugs is not equally valid for all drug users, and not realistic for all at every juncture. Help should be given non-judgementally. Survival help should be oriented to reduce risks to health, social isolation and judicial harassment.

REFERENCES

Buning, E. C. (1989) 'The role of methadone in Amsterdam's AIDS policy', presentation at First Scottish National Symposium on Caring for AIDS.

Bornemann, R., Kalinna, V. and Bschor, F. (1988) 'AIDS- und HIV-Progression 1982-1987 bei i.v. Drogengebrauchern und -abhängigen in Europa', in AIDS-Forum, Bd 1, Deutsche AIDS-Hilfe e.V.: AIDS und Drogen, Berlin.

Kleiber, D. (1988) 'AIDS und Drogen: Erste Ergebnisse einer differentiell-epidemiologischen Untersuchung', Suchtgefahren 4: 317–22.

—— (1990) 'HIV-positiv und drogenabhängig', Sozialmagazin 15 (1): 41–5.

Lesting, W. (1990) 'Die Abgabe von Einwegspritzen im Strafvollzug zur AIDS-Prävention–strafbar oder notwendig', in Strafverteidiger 5/1990, S. 225ff.

Raschke, P. and Schliche, F. (1985) 'Therapie und Rehabilitation bei Drogenkonsumenten', Ministerium für Arbeit, Gesundheit und Soziales NRW (Hrsg.), Düsseldorf.

Schuller, K. and Stöver, H. (1989) 'Die Zugänglichkeit zu sterilem Spritzbesteck', in *AIDS-Forum D.A.H, Band III.*

Chapter 21

Representations of drug users
Facts, myths and their role in harm reduction strategy

Peter McDermott

INTRODUCTION

Before one begins to think about drug use and drug users, one needs to be aware of the connotations of the words employed. When we come across terms such as 'drugs' or 'addiction', we all bring to it a limited 'common-sense' view of these concepts that are shaped by our culture, the media, our own prejudices and other factors. In order to understand the phenomenon, we must begin to sort out fact from myth. Which aspects of our understanding of these matters are socially constructed, and which have a material basis in the pharmacology of the drug and the psychology and biochemistry of us as human beings?

The social meaning of drug use differs across time and geographical space. The non-medical use of drugs, the desire for intoxication, is an ubiquitous phenomenon. Virtually all human cultures (perhaps barring the Eskimos) have made use of some consciousness-altering substance on a regular basis. Tobacco, alcohol, tea, coffee, khat, kava-kava, mush-rooms, coca, opium. The list is endless. Where such behaviour is an integrated part of social life, use of that drug may not be regarded as particularly problematic. In the nineteenth century, both in the UK and in the USA, opium use was both unregulated and widespread. Purely hedonistic drug use was mainly associated with the middle and upper classes, becoming a fashionable pastime among the literary classes who saw its use as an aid to the imagination. A letter to William Wilberforce, from his friend, Dean Isaac Milner, demonstrates the way people thought of opiates during this period.

> Be not afraid of the habit of such medicine, the habit of growling guts is infinitely worse. There is nothing injurious to the constitution in the medicines, and if you use them all your life there is no great harm.

This statement implies the common man knew more about the properties of opiates in the nineteenth century than we do today. Milner correctly identifies the major side-effect of opiate use – addiction – but is also aware that continued use produces no other organic or psychological damage. Many noted individuals have lived long, productive lives while continuing to use opiates, yet the dominant ideology tells us that to use such drugs is inevitably a step towards despair, degradation and death.

PROHIBITION

Accompanying the various changes in the laws that prohibited the use of certain psychoactive drugs for non-medical purposes, there was also a change in the way drug users were perceived in the public arena. Duster, in his study of nineteenth-century opiate users (1970), claims many middle-class pillars of bourgeois morality were addicted and noted that, while addiction might have been regarded as a weakness, there was no psychiatric or moral judgement involved. Brecher's report for the Consumers Union remarks:

> Opiates taken daily in large doses were not a social menace under 19th century conditions, and were not perceived as a menace... there was little demand for opiate prohibition. But there was one exception to this. In 1875, the City of San Francisco adopted an ordinance prohibiting the smoking of opium in smoking houses or dens. The roots of the ordinance were racist rather than health oriented.
>
> (Brecher, 1972)

Other racist legislation was soon to follow. In 1887, the importation of opium by Chinese was banned. In 1909, the smoking of opium was prohibited. Smoking was a predominantly Chinese practice, yet 'white' forms of opiate consumption such as morphine or laudanum use were still acceptable. Cocaine and marijuana came under prohibitionist pressure due to a belief that they so excited the Black men who used them they then went on to entice and rape White women, or even after being shot six times were still strong enough to kill White men. Such stereotypes were widely reported by the US precursors to the modern Murdoch tabloids, the so-called 'yellow press' of William Randolph Hearst. One possible motive for promulgating such stereotypes was the current attempt by US business interests to break into Far Eastern markets.

During this period, Britain retained a virtual monopoly over trade with China, as a result of British control over the Indian opium market. At the same time, doctors and pharmacists were defining themselves as a profession through establishing a monopoly control over the legitimate supply of the instruments of the healing trade – drugs. During this period, opiates were the most useful drugs in the pharmacopoeia, and were widely used in self-medication. Doctors and pharmacists then, had much to gain by regulating the supply of such drugs, and lent their backing to the various international diplomatic agreements, pressed for by the USA. As a consequence of these agreements, most of the Western world passed laws prohibiting the non-medical use of drugs. Then, as today, this occurred regardless of whether those countries had a drug problem and as developing countries sought aid, it was often dependent upon the introduction of such drug laws.

CONTROL SYSTEMS AND REPRESENTATIONS

Following these changes in the law, a number of control systems emerged in order to enforce them. These differed in the UK and the USA, yet both still play a role in defining the dominant view of the essential nature of drug addiction. In the USA, the imposition of criminal sanctions produced a shift in the visible drug-using population from predominantly middle-class women, to an overrepresentation of young, lower-class ethnic males. This distinction was noted by one judicial commentator at the time, who sought to discriminate between 'good citizens who had become innocently addicted' and 'physical, mental and moral defectives. Tramps, hobos, idlers and criminals, for whom narcotics poisoning is a vice as well as a disorder produced by narcotic poisoning' (Szasz, 1975).

What we see here is the emergence of a bifurcation in how we think about drug use and users, between 'respectable' therapeutic addicts and hedonistic or recreational drug use. These definitions have an explicit class basis; it was acceptable behaviour for the well-to-do, but there was always a concern to regulate the pleasures of the 'dangerous classes'. The same distinctions were also operative in the UK, but because the majority of drug use here had a therapeutic basis, a rationing system of providing addicts with a legal supply of the drug was allowed to emerge. As this ration was allocated by doctors, the UK developed a model of control that laid its emphasis upon the medical aspects of addiction, albeit with the backup of criminal sanctions. However, the criminal law was rarely used until the late 1950s when a new, young, often Black crowd of drug users who hung out in nightclubs, listening to jazz, began to engage in drug use as a public pastime rather than a private vice.

THE MEDIA

One of the ways in which our thinking about drug use has been determined is through the process of 'moral panic' (Cohen, 1972). This process can be broken down into several phases. The first phase he terms 'inventory', which refers to the initial warning or threat. The media uses exaggeration and distortion to portray a phenomenon. This phase is able to imbue neutral objects with a symbolic power and shape popular moral indignation. The second phase of a moral panic is the 'societal reaction' and has two effects: First, it reorients the public's emotional and intellectual response through the construction of 'scapegoats'; second, it attempts to remedy the situation through changes in the 'control culture', legal change, medical responses, new policing strategies, etc. An illustration of this process has recently been available in the way that the British media, the state, and drug treatment services have responded to stories about crack cocaine (McDermott and O'Hare, 1990).

In order to achieve this, the media adopts a systematic world view based upon an imaginary consensus that governs all reporting. This portrays the world as bifurcated into certain binary oppositions, e.g. Normal/Deviant, Sick/Wicked, Corrupt/Innocent. A further device used is the myth of the 'in-built justice mechanism' invoked to resolve the contradiction between the attraction of illicit pleasure and this consensualist ideology (Young, 1973). One way in which this is achieved is by portraying drug use as a psychiatric or psychological illness, by portraying drug use not as an existential or lifestyle choice based upon certain human values, but as a compulsion.

Young has made the point that the portrayal of drug users by the media is so consistently ill-informed and inaccurate one might suppose journalists lack access to the facts or bear an irredeemable prejudice. However, the systematic nature of this type of coverage implies that the origins of this portrayal has its place in the social structure and reflects the tensions and fears that the dominant classes feel about the underclass.

Lindesmith (1940) identified a number of fundamental myths that continue to inform representations of drug users. In particular, the drug addict is a violent criminal; the drug addict is a moral degenerate; the drug addict wishes to convert non-users; the drug addict uses drugs because of an inferiority complex. As long ago as 1940, he found no evidence to support any of these proposals, yet the images persist. The article concluded, 'the dope-fiend mythologies serve a rationalization of the status quo. It is a body of superstition, half truths and misinformation which bolsters up an indefensible and repressive law, the victims of which are in no position to protest'.

Superstition, half truths and misinformation are still prevalent. During the British 'heroin epidemic' of the early 1980s the *Liverpool Echo* published stories, repeated in the national press, that typify Lindesmith's thesis. One story told of rumours that pushers had been waiting outside a Wirral school, offering 'free samples' to children as young as eleven, in order to secure customers. Another story mentioned school dinners 'spiked' with heroin. Such stories can only be circulated by people with no knowledge whatsoever of the drug scene. Neither the drug treatment agency, nor the schools involved, nor the newspapers stopped to wonder what type of criminal would seek a relationship with customers so unlikely to have much money and so likely to inform should minimal pressure be applied. In the words of a Liverpool addict asked about such stories in a Liverpool youth club in 1985:

> It's a load of bullshit isn't it? I've never had smack given to me off any dealer. If they said that, you'd be able to go around to every dealer and say 'Look, I'm just starting out. You'll have to sort me out' and get into it.

> (Matthews, 1985)

CREATION OF THE HIDDEN SECTOR

The major consequence of this criminalization/stigmatization has the effect of causing addicts to conceal the fact that they use drugs. Therefore we have a large number of people, engaging in a very dangerous form of behaviour, and with a high potential for inflicting unnecessary damage on themselves and others. The most obvious example here is HIV infection. Those who do not attend agencies are more likely to share injection equipment, and less likely to have a good knowledge of how HIV is transmitted and thus can be avoided (Lart and Stimson, 1989).

Another consequence of this situation is that even the best informed view of what drug users 'are like' is typical of a certain type of illegal drug user, the subgroup whose drug use has become a problem for them, with adverse legal or medical consequences. Thus, while a recent study can describe the typical heroin user as an unemployed White male in his mid-twenties who lives with his parents, that is not because they are the only people who engage in it, but because they are least successful at 'managing the effects' of their drug consumption (Parker *et al.*, 1988). Most people of my generation and younger will have some voluntary involvement with illegal drugs during their lives. That involvement will not be limited to one particular social class. I have a number of friends who are addicted to opiate drugs. None of them fits the picture of the 'typical addict' that *living with heroin* finds on the Wirral. One is a company director who built a business of fourteen employees. One has a PhD and teaches at a northern university. One is a subeditor on a notorious national newspaper. One is a training manager with the YTS. One is a computer programmer. All have been using opiates for ten years or more. All own their own homes, are married, with children, pay taxes and live, more or less, like any other good citizens. Some, though not all, receive a legal supply of drugs from the state.

CONCLUSION

The adverse consequences of this relationship between drug user and society is not one-directional. For as long as our society comprises individuals who discriminate against drug addicts, who stigmatize them, addicts will continue to be an ever-increasing body of people who exist outside society and their lack of ties to the social fabric increases the sense of alienation of those who use drugs, increases the likelihood that they will act in an anti-social manner to fund their drug use, and decreases the likelihood that they will come forward for treatment or education, all of which contribute to a situation wherein drug use is a greater social problem than it need be and the adverse effects that it has on us as a society continue to increase. While drug use is criminalized, and drug users are marginalized, it is very difficult for the informal sanctions to develop that will regulate drug use in the same way as alcohol use, very difficult to work towards the emergence of a safer drug-using culture.

In order for this to occur, it is necessary to adopt a progressive policy towards drug users – a policy that is assimilative, rather than coercive, that seeks to integrate drug users into society rather than marginalize them. Furthermore, such efforts must be genuine. At the end of the day, drug addicts are just people who happen to use drugs. They know as well as anyone when they're being humoured or patronized. As citizens, I believe that they have certain entitlements, one of which is an entitlement to services that meet their needs. Drug workers, social workers, counsellors and the like are being paid to provide a service. If users do not like, or wish to use the service that is offered, if it has little or no relevance to their needs, then drug workers are not doing their jobs. Drug workers who are not active in seeking to integrate drug users into the wider community, are not only not helping to solve the drug problem, they are actively making it worse.

REFERENCES

Brecher, E. (1972) *Licit and Illicit Drugs*, Boston: Little, Brown & Co.

Cohen, S. (1972) *Folk Devils and Moral Panics*, London: McGibbon & Key.

Duster, T. (1970) *The Legislation of Morality*, New York: Free Press.

Lart, R. and Stimson, G. (1989) 'National Survey of Syringe Exchange Schemes in England', Monitoring Research Group, London: Goldsmiths College.

Lindesmith, A. (1940) 'Dope fiend mythology', *Journal of Criminology and Police Science*, No. 31.

Matthews, A. (1985) 'Drug abuse: Research on Merseyside' (unpublished paper from author).

McDermott, P. and O'Hare, P. (1991) 'Crack in Thatcher's Britain: A harm reduction approach', in C. Reinarmann and H. Levine, *Crack in Context* (forthcoming).

Parker, H., Newcombe, R. and Bakx, K. (1988) *Living with Heroin*, Milton Keynes: Open University Press.

Szasz, T. (1975) *Ceremonial Chemistry*, London: Routledge & Kegan Paul.

Young, J. (1973) 'The myth of the drugtaker in the mass media', in S.Cohen and J. Young, *The Manufacture of News*, London: Constable.

Name index

Subject index